Human Stupidity

The Search for Terrestrial Intelligence

"No one is hated more than he who speaks the truth" - Plato

Frank Scurio

Published by Frank J Scurio
Chicago, IL

Book website: www.franscur.com

ISBN 978-0-9977059-0-4

Table of Contents

Table of Contents

Forward

This book is entirely about the subject of intelligence, what it is, how it gets produced and some suggestions for how humans could synthesize and improve on the human trait of being smart. Since I consider stupidity to be the reciprocal of intelligence, providing a solid framework and understanding of intelligence will shed light on the phenomenon of stupidity. While it may appear that I delve into lots of political turmoil, I believe this is necessary in order to accurately describe the human condition. We cannot talk about intelligence, and omit the most important indicator of intelligence: The socioeconomic history of the human race. So while some of this book may be construed as political, I can assure the reader that this is done only because it is strictly required. In case the reader is not aware; the world is literally awash in stupidity. Many of the hypotheses I present in this book can only be proven with what could be called "circumstantial evidence". The evidence I speak of is the historical record of the world. When human behavior such as, the forces responsible for two world wars, is viewed through the lens of my hypothesis, then that behavior begins to make sense. The world order has been shaped by human behavior there is no doubt. My ideas present a plausible explanation for that behavior.

The above claim applies to micro-behavior as well as macro-behavior. My ideas apply to human social groups, small and large. They apply to families and work place groups as well as governmental groups at all levels. Current governmental affairs provide me with excellent proofs of the ideas I am attempting to promote here. One of the ideas I promote here is that stupidity is the cause of all of humanity's problems and to ensure intelligence will prevail, the freedom of humans is imperative. In that regard, I am very alarmed with the current state of affairs in my country, The United States of America.

I am presenting the ideas in this book in what may end up being a feeble attempt at mitigating some of the damage that has been done by the two stupid political parties who are in essence; running things here. I seriously doubt if this writing will have any effect in swaying the minds of electorate who in the last 100 or so years have been methodically brainwashed to the extent of being non-thinkers. The voting public acts on the emotional whims of politicians and follows along in lock-step to anything dished out to them. This is a dangerous situation for freedom loving people and it bodes ominously for the propagation of intelligence. Ronald Reagan said that the loss of freedom was never more than two generations from extinction. He was right; one hundred percent.

Having made this dire prediction, I nonetheless must try. I feel it is my duty to do the things that I am capable of doing, because to sit back and only observe in the face of adversity, is to aid that adversity in doing its job. Therefore I have decided that my ideas on human stupidity fit in nicely with the current situation in the United States and they also accurately describe the underlying cause of how we got into the mess we are currently in. The underlying cause is of course: Human stupidity.

Forward

I want to forewarn the reader that some of the human descriptors made here may apply to you. So if you are not a coward and are willing to take the chance of knowing your own intellectual capabilities, then read on. Everything I present here, I believe to be true. Many of the ideas in this book happen to be my own, but are based on pure logic and years of observations of other humans. Anyone reading this could have done the same thing and if you are honest, you will also come to the conclusion that what I present here is fact, not fiction.

This book is written in two threads of thought. One thread is the socio-political impact of the lack of intelligence as well as some philosophical definitions of the underpinnings of intelligence. The other thread is a technical explanation of how intelligence is produced and how it could be artificially produced. I believe the technical explanations bolster the hypothesis that intelligence is mostly a choice which has impact on the socio-political aspect. So while the mixing of the technical with the socio-political may seem paradoxical, it is definitively done with a purpose.

Frank Scurio, June, 2016

Abstract

The sheer quantity of human stupidity present in today's world is astonishing and astounding. Because of his fact, I felt the need to clarify and define what humans label as stupidity. This book is a philosophical and logical view of what comprises stupidity as well as how it has shaped humankind's past and the effect it will have on our future. It could be easily argued and proven that stupidity is the cause of all of humankind's problems, past and present. I cannot imagine why anyone would argue that point because this statement qualifies for the level of axiom.

It follows and could be argued and proven that the cure for all of humanity's problems could be as simple as eliminating stupidity. This begs the question: Is it possible to completely eliminate stupidity? I believe some stupidity can be cured but I doubt if all can. Even a small percentage of cured stupidity would be an enormous improvement over no improvement at all. I believe the only caveat for a cure in the *curable population* are that a few basic simple rules are followed which I cover extensively here. Also, there is a very real and highly probable chance that strong artificial intelligence will be developed at some point and that will lead to a complete understanding of everything, including our own stupidity. Curing any problem requires a complete understanding of that problem first. In that regard; I believe it is possible.

Throughout this book, I present my theories for what comprises human intelligence and how stupidity is usually the result of humans not adhering to a few basic rules. If we really do have "free will", then everything I am suggesting here is possible. If we really don't have free will, then things will probably never improve. I believe we do have free will (we would not have survived without it) but underlying forces are great and they are very difficult if not impossible to conquer. Brainwashing works and we are all brainwashed to some extent throughout our lives.

There are three basic hypotheses that I intend to argue for in this book and I elaborate on each of these following my list:

1. The current definition of what intelligence is; is categorically wrong
2. Intelligence is the driving force and impetus behind all human actions
3. The brain produces intelligence with a specific architecture of memory access
   (Intelligence is storage enabled and dependent)

Current definitions of intelligence are wrong

Intelligence and it follows the reciprocal of intelligence; stupidity, is something much different from the currently held paradigm. Many self-proclaimed experts in the field of human intelligence seem to believe that intelligence can be identified by using a set of metrics, such as the so called "IQ test". My belief is that notion is naïve and an oversimplification of a super complex subject. Some of the currently used metrics in IQ testing include knowledge acquired

Abstract

pertaining to sets of subjects which specific individuals have been exposed to and this does not identify intelligence.

Other currently believed metrics are being able to spell and the proper use of grammar in any one particular language, the ability to master different languages and last but certainly not least; math skills. Ability to acquire mathematics prowess is universally accepted as being a sort of Holy Grail of intelligence. I argue that intelligence is a much more complex process than the current metrics are capable of defining.

Intelligence is the main driver of human action

Intelligence is the single most important driving force behind human psychology. In other words, it is *not* sex, money, power, status, etc. that drives the human condition. It is intelligence, because without intelligence none of the previously mentioned supposed driving forces are possible. I believe intelligence is the ultimate survival tool and survival is the key to understanding why intelligence trumps all the currently accepted drivers. Humans are programed to place a very high value on intelligence, and I believe this is due to survival causing that appreciation. Smart people had much higher probabilities for survival in the early stages of human development. Intelligence is the reason people will congregate together in clubs and other social activities. We either want to demonstrate or compare our own intelligence to others or we want to learn from others so we may become smarter.

Intelligence is possible only because of storage

The brain produces intelligence by means of a very specific architecture of storage utilization. In other words, the uniform processing of information, which enables intelligence, is only possible due to the systematic storage and retrieval of that information. Humans know how memory systems work in the machines we create which requires a "table of contents", "a directory", "a registry" or some method of logging the identity and location at storage time and then referring to that "log" at retrieval time to locate stored information for present use.

We will see that nature in its unending simplicity does things in a different manner than the machines humans have designed. There are no such things as directories or tables of content in the brain so there has to be another way to locate stored information. The method the brain uses to locate information is the key to understanding how intelligence is produced and how thinking is enabled. Intelligence is made possible by storage and that storage in composed of two important parts. One part is the structure or architecture (information pathways) and the other part is the vast amount of storage available in the human brain.

Chapter summaries

Chapter 1 – Intelligence and Stupidity defined

I shall demonstrate that the commonly held belief systems of intelligence (and it's reciprocal; stupidity) are not necessarily true. In fact, I will argue that none of the commonly accepted metrics really mean anything when it comes to true intelligence. If during the course of interaction with the educational system, you were deemed to be "below average"; you just may be in for a big surprise. You may be way smarter than you think! Conversely this means that some people may not be as smart as they think they are. There are also many people who "get the idea" that they are smart simply because they have completed some educational program. This is wishful thinking because just learning what is already known does not demonstrate high intelligence. I present a hypothesis of what intelligence actually is. This is necessary, if we are to understand stupidity.

I break intelligence down into what I think are its fundamental parts as experienced by humanity from its very beginning. The methodology we used as a species to survive in our early times is just as important in understanding our present level of intelligence as is learning European history in an American history class. We need to get a full picture of the evolution of intelligence, because in order to understand the present, we need a full picture of the past.

This is by no means, a testimonial to the theory of evolution. Whatever evolving of the brain architecture that took place was already completed by the time humans began the evolution of our intelligence. To the best of my knowledge, we are not much different brain hardware wise than we were fifty thousand years ago. This is what anthropologists tell us anyway. To find out what makes intelligence the important survival tool and that in turn gives rise to the human appreciation of intelligence (covered in Chapter 5), read this chapter.

Chapter 2 – Spiritual and Intellectual Enlightenment

This chapter posits the importance of morality in the processing of intelligence and how this keeps stupidity at bay. Want to be smarter? Just be honest! Find out why this is so important as well as many other morality based concepts. These concepts prove that being stupid is a sometimes definite choice and it can be entirely up to you whether you are stupid or smart! Additional topics include: Is there really such a thing as "good" or "evil"? Can truly "evil" people ever be truly "smart"? This chapter is all about making the most of the brain architecture that you were born with. Stated another way, no matter how your brain is wired, save for individuals who have had brain trauma or were born with defects of some type, the vast majority of humans can be smart just by changing the attitude they have. Perhaps Albert Einstein's brain was different from 99% of all other humans but he could have very easily wasted that power with a bad attitude. Read this chapter and find out why.

Chapter 3 – The Brain

This chapter attempts to explain how the brain possibly produces intelligence through the structure or architecture that we should all be born with. I start off with some classic neuroscience explanations of cognitive processes and detail the operation of several human capabilities such as vision and hearing. Then I submit my idea of the human memory structure and posit that it is this structure that enables all of the factors of intelligence. I also present some comparisons to the human computer (the brain) and human-made computers. This comparison should shed light on the capabilities of the brain. I also attempt to explain the various theories of consciousness as well as what it really is, along with its many possible purposes.

Abstract

Chapter 4 – The Mystery of thought

In this chapter, I present what I believe is an understandable and logical hypothesis for how the brain produces thought. I have been disappointed by many claims for doing this in many other writings because the explanation presented in those writings was in fact; no explanation at all. So far in every book I have read on how the brain produces thought, the authors claim to explain this key feature of intelligence but fall agonizingly short to the point where all of these so-called explanations could be categorized as pure nonsense. I hope to change that here. My explanation of thought will simultaneously provide an explanation of how the brain produces intelligence.

I continue my presentation with what I believe are the fundamental modes of thought and I attempt to provide the reader with a basic understanding of the historical uses for these modes as well as how modern humans combine the primitive with the advanced. The advanced mode is language thought and I hope my explanation is adequate to establish at least a perfunctory understanding. In any case, the reader should be enlightened to begin pondering these topics and if I accomplish that I will have done my job. The difficult aspect of understanding language thought is the part about understanding. This may be further clarified in the next chapter when I apply the principals established here to an artificial version which should possess the attribution of understanding.

Chapter 5 – Computer Science and Artificial Intelligence

This chapter covers some of the main concentrations of computer science and how they relate to artificial intelligence (a concentration by itself). I present a view of this science major in terms of how the different concentrations could possibly contribute to the development of strong AI (Human level Artificial Intelligence). I call this RAI for Real Artificial Intelligence. RAI does not need to be the "darling" of computer science as most academics believe without question. It could have just as easily been adopted by computer engineers and my belief is that that particular group would be better suited to actually produce strong AI. This belief is based on my assertion that intelligence is solely enabled by the hardware architecture of the brain as I discuss in chapter 3.

I also believe that a revolution in computer architecture is bound to occur at some future date and that will most likely come about due to researchers in AI dabbling in architectures much different from the currently accepted paradigm which is the Von Neumann architecture used in all PCs, Macs and super computers. I believe they will do that in an attempt to mimic the human brain and the center of that new architecture will be optical based memory systems, replacing the RAM currently used along with an entirely different supporting architecture. I will present my belief on how AI will proceed to develop in the near future and what the possibilities are for RAI in the not so distant future. Will machines ever possess the ability to think? Will machines eventually consider us non-essential and decide that they don't need us? Read chapter 5 to find out these and many other topics.

Abstract

Chapter 6 – Social implications of stupidity

One of the three main hypotheses that I present in this writing is that intelligence is the main driving impetus for all of humanities' actions. I should clarify at this point that it is not intelligence itself that is the main impetus for all human action but the desire to be deemed intelligent by one's peers and contemporaries. Questions like, "why have millions of people died in the name of a political system known as communism?" beg to be answered.

I believe that in order to find that answer, we only need to look at the root cause, the main impetus for all human action: The desire to be recognized as being intelligent. I believe survival is the key element in understanding why intelligence is deemed as the most important of all human attributes. I believe the smartest people were considered the most valuable in the group for survival in early human development and that instinct is present in modern humans and has been present since the beginning of human existence. There are two aspects of the human desire to place a high value on high intelligence. One is the desire of all humans to be deemed as highly intelligent. The other is the human trait of comparing your intelligence to all other members in the group, which is an attempt to identify the hierarchy of intelligence levels within that group. Thus, I have coined the acronyms IRD, for *Intelligence Recognition Desire* and ICP for *Intelligence Comparison Phenomenon*.

Of course it follows that in order for one to be deemed intelligent there must be some "track record", some "accomplishment" if you will; that will identify the human who desires to be known as being very smart. I attempt to make a point that intelligence is the single most important factor in how we relate to and interact with other humans. Many of the beliefs and actions of people in all areas of the world and in all walks of life make no sense unless those beliefs and actions are viewed through the lens of IRD and ICP. I will supply the reader with numerous examples to prove this hypothesis.

It is a well-known fact that the bastions of liberalism are contained in Hollywood, academics and at least 3/4 of the media in the United States. I have no doubt that there are similar statistics in other parts of the developed "free world" but I limit my discussion to my country. One does not need to be considered to be a member of the "genius club" to recognize what these three groups have in common. I will "let the cat out of the bag" just in case you're not following me here. *They all have positions in which they are watched and are judged by many other humans on a regular basis.* In fact, they all chose those positions for some reason and so it follows it is not much of a stretch of the imagination to believe that IRD was a big factor in their career choice. Liberals, socialists and communists all have one thing in common. They see themselves as "creators" of some grand utopia, a heaven on earth, where there is no crime, no hunger, and no wants of any kind. Everything is just "nicey, nicey" all the time, about everything.

The common misconception about communism was that it was invented by Karl Marx in the 1860s. Nothing could be further from the truth because the idea of promoting one's own intelligence through IRD probably goes back to when people were first able to think about promoting themselves as smart. This is common thought with communists; "See this wonderful idea I have? Everyone will be happy and everything will be just wonderful!! And the best part is: I will be deemed as being very smart because of my ideas!"

Abstract

Chapter 7 – The medical profession

In this chapter I expose the medical profession who are in reality controlled by medical academics. I believe this profession is partly responsible for epidemic proportion disease in the world today. The reason this is so is because medical doctors suffer from the same intelligence related drives as the rest of us. It appears that the one group who is responsible for the health and well-being of us all has basically dropped the ball. I explain the reason why the main methodology used to diagnose disease is flawed.

Chapter 8 – UFOs

This chapter describes how what may be the most important issue for humankind has turned into a three ring circus complete with a bunch of clowns getting stuffed into a car the size of a roller skate. What should be a serious topic for scientific investigation, has morphed into the modern day adult boogie man. I personally have had four UFO sightings and I describe each in detail here. I also explain my views about the so called government cover-up and the phenomenon known as "Alien Abduction". I explain why the subject of UFOs is a glaring example of human stupidity, expressed in two basic paradigms, science and the "tin foil hat crowd". The UFO topic is probably the largest single glaring example of a human capacity for stupidity and that is the big reason why it is here. I also list a denial of the existence of UFOs as a big stupidity indicator. Find out why and read chapter 8.

Chapter 9 - How to identify stupid people

In Chapter 2, I describe how anyone can be smarter simply by changing a few personality traits. In Chapter 3, I describe the role of the brain in producing intelligence. So, perhaps we are not all born with a brain like Albert Einstein (I am certainly not), but we certainly can change our personality, if we really want to and that will help us become smarter. The thing is; what about all the stupid people who have not read this book? We need a few basic guidelines to assist us in determining who or what we are dealing with. I present some basic ideas on how to spot stupid people. This is a survival guidebook for the smart floating in a sea of stupidity. Consider chapter 9 as a "guide through stupid land".

Chapter 10 – The Future

This chapter predicts what the future may hold for humankind. If we stay on our present course things don't look that great. We don't have an unlimited amount of time to figure the big problems out. We must invent RAI. This is my argument for the attempt at developing human level intelligence and beyond. What will the future hold for mankind if we stay on the present course to stupidity and what can be done to change our course to high intelligence? For a prediction of the real future, read chapter 10.

Chapter 1 - Intelligence and Stupidity Defined

This chapter describes what intelligence actually is. There are many misconceptions about what intelligence actually is and I believe this ignorance promotes stupidity. In that regard, I attempt to prove that the currently held beliefs on what constitutes intelligence are wrong. This is good news for the vast majority of people walking the earth today, as they are victims of the academic and social elite establishment. I supply many philosophic and scientific reasons given as proof for this new rational view of intelligence throughout this book.

Quite simply, intelligence can be thought of as some level of *performance*. The word "performance" can be used to describe the qualities of many things. Most of the time, it is used to describe a measure of work and the level of achievement that work has produced. For automotive enthusiasts, performance means how fast a car accelerates, the top speed and perhaps how far the car is able to travel on a gallon of fuel. We say the car "performs" at some level and usually the higher the level, the more advantageous the performance is deemed to be.

So, performance is always the result of some amount of work being done. In the case of gas mileage that is expressed in terms of efficiency. If car one has the same zero to sixty acceleration as car two but burns less fuel than car two, we say car one has better fuel efficiency *performance* than car two. In other words performance means how well something does its intended job and actually expresses how much work (with a given input amount of energy) was done for any given task.

When the word performance is applied to intelligence, it is a measure of how much work was done in a complex series of tasks that must be done correctly (incorrectly for stupidity) and in the correct order (incorrect order for stupidity). Performance is used in part to describe how well humans assess and analyze any information that is presented to them. After the assessment and analysis phase humans attempt to make a decision based on how they interpret the given facts. Part of that interpretation might be attempting to ascertain whether or not the data that is presented to them are indeed facts and not some contrived anomaly.

The decision they make may be to physically act on an external subject or it may be a decision that merely leads to a conclusion that is to be kept in storage for use at a future date. Whether the decision results in some physical activity or is a knowledge base fortifier, the correctness of the decision is of paramount importance. Correctness at this point means success, incorrectness means failure. High performance relates to correct decisions and vice versa. This is the basis for the theory that the purpose of intelligence was originally a survival tool.

We can surmise, without any reservation, that we as a species must have made enough correct decisions in the past for us to be here at this moment. If humanity's assessments, analyses and corresponding decisions were mostly incorrect, we would not have continued as a species. If our ancestors were not smart enough to learn that running up to a woolly mammoth with a small rock in

Chapter 1 - Intelligence and Stupidity Defined

hand as the only weapon, was not a good idea; we would not be here now. Our ancestor's intelligence performance level was high enough for humans to continue as a species.

So, it is *performance* that counts when it comes to intelligence and it follows that correct decisions translates to higher performance and that in turn translates to higher intelligence. Only the very stupid could argue with that statement. This is just common sense and I believe it qualifies for the status of an axiom. It most definitely qualifies as an empirical phenomenon. It has happened throughout recorded history, it happens now and there is no reason to believe it will not happen in the future. If we make the right decisions, we succeed, if we don't we fail. That's it! No frills, no complicated algorithms to decipher, just common sense and a very simple algorithm. Intelligence may indeed be controlled by a complex algorithm(s) at micro level brain operations, but we don't need to have a degree in computer science to understand what it's supposed to do on a macro level. It's supposed to produce the most correct result (a decision) given the situation at hand. That's all.

If it is high performance that counts, and high performance is defined as making correct decisions, then is it important to be able to spell and be grammatically correct when writing in our natural language of birth (English, Spanish, etc.)? What for? We have things called computer programs that handle that stuff for us. In the past, those qualities would have been a distinct advantage, but machines are now assisting us in mundane tasks such as spelling and grammar, which are both of limited usefulness in actually transmitting ideas from one person to the other. If you have been unfortunate enough to attend any class an "institution of higher learning" then you have been hard pressed to locate a professor who speaks English well enough to be clearly understood by all. But in spite of the confusion caused by broken English speaking professors, students seem to understand enough of what is being said to get the points of the subject matter. Get the point?

It is important to point out that stupidly is not merely the absence of intelligence, but it is the result of the incorrect processing of information leading to incorrect assessments, incorrect analyzing and incorrect decision making. It is possible that that same amount of effort (work) is expelled in the processing of stupidity as it would have been in the processing of intelligence. The difference is the intelligent brain is processing available information properly whereas the stupid brain is not.

An 8 cylinder engine that has 2 cylinders working against the other 6 will be working very hard indeed, but the net result of power output will be less than a 6 cylinder running on all 6 cylinders. This analogy relates to the use of effort or energy expelled during the processes necessary for high performance of intelligence. It is not the amount of effort or energy expelled, but it is the correctness of the usage of the effort put forth. In other words, it's not how hard the brain works, but how correctly the brain works. There are many factors to consider when attempting to identify what constitutes the "correct processing of information".

Learning how to process information correctly is a big factor. This suggests that our formative years are important. The many ways in which we are brainwashed is yet another. Our genes may play a role in the way our brain is wired. The point is: If we have learned to assess and analyze correctly, and make decisions correctly, that is intelligence at a high performance level and we have a much higher probability of succeeding at anything and that is the goal of intelligence as a survival tool. It is important to define intelligence as survival related as it is this angle that shapes human interaction today. Keep that in mind for the rest of this book.

Chapter 1 - Intelligence and Stupidity Defined

We believe that we are smart if we pass a number of criteria set forth by our educators. The educators believe this because that is what their current belief system tells them. We are taught what is smart, based on some incorrect assumptions that the people that are teaching us have been taught and it is passed down to us and so it goes. The old adage, "to assume makes an ass out of you and me" holds true. This starts in elementary school and continues all the way through any higher education we are "smart enough" to get through. We are brought up with these false notions pounded into our developing brains and that becomes part of us and our personality.

So, what exactly is "smart" and how do we perceive "smartness" and is what we perceive a reality? In elementary school children are told they are smart if they can remember things like multiplication tables, how to spell words correctly and remembering the fundamentals of grammar. The ability to write in cursive and draw nice pictures is also used as an indicator. Are these ideas correct? I can tentatively answer this by saying no. Our beliefs are not necessarily truths. We were all brainwashed to believe in these concepts, and as we shall see brainwashing works but the things we are lead to believe as gospel truth may not be.

Rote memorization ability is not in itself an indicator of intelligence. The ability to memorize sure helps intelligent processes but is not a guarantee that what we do with the information we recall is analyzed correctly by the brain. Computers don't have any problem remembering things. As I write this in installments, what I have written is remembered by the computer. Does this make the computer smart? No.

In recent years there have been a number of books written that claim mathematics and language skills are large determinates of intelligence. I believe this is categorically untrue. My reasoning is due to my core belief in what constitutes intelligence in essence which is dependent on the suggestion of some advancement and not adherence to the status quo. I explain this in more detail shortly. I will admit that people who are able to learn other languages and mathematics most definitely do have terrific attitudes towards learning and that in itself is a positive asset for the production of intelligence.

Learning math may be easier for some and learning a new language may be easier for others and yet a third group may learn both subjects at a faster rate. This means nothing when it comes to intelligence. This is because intelligence is a product. It is the result of a computation (the application of an algorithm). Learning is just a small part of the entire process and it is the results (high or low performance decision making, mainly) of the process that count. In other words, how accurate, beneficial and useful is the final product?

Remember, it is performance that counts. Many people are good at math and are able to master several languages but have never invented anything new or formulated a new and useful concept. I have personally known many people who could be labeled as math wizzes, who could not apply those principles to daily life or even the physical world around them, if their own lives depended on it. Remember the purpose of intelligence is survival, and if there is no advancement, then the ability to survive is suspect. There must be new ideas and new useful concepts or survival is not guaranteed.

Chapter 1 - Intelligence and Stupidity Defined

In order to define intelligence and it's reciprocal; stupidity, we need to observe the human methodology of the production of intelligence. I believe that intelligent behavior is programmed into humans as an algorithm. In other words intelligence is driven or guided or controlled by a pre-conceived set of steps that humans should all be born with. The intelligence algorithm is inborn in most of us as hardware in the brain. An algorithm is a set of steps or procedures that when "played" or "executed" produce some useful function.

There are many different established and well known algorithms in the area of science known as computer science. Some of the common well-known algorithms do things such as compress data so that a file containing the ones and zeros that computers use will be more compact and more easily storable. Once an algorithm has been written (coded as in computer programming) it can be saved and later called upon to perform its mission on any file assigned to it. The one algorithm that just about everyone is familiar with is the MP3 algorithm that compresses an audio file into less than 10 % of the original size. When you "RIP" an audio file from an audio CD to your computer's MP3 collection you are invoking the MP3 algorithm.

The intelligence algorithm has a very different purpose but the idea is nevertheless the same. It is a set of pre-defined, pre-conceived, actions or steps if you will, that perform a useful function. The useful function is not to compress an audio file but it is to allow humans to act intelligently by acting out the steps necessary to ensure the original intent of the algorithm is adhered to. There are several important aspects of the intelligence algorithm that make it a survival tool and this is the reason most of us inherit a minimal level of intelligence; it has become part of our genetic structure. I have taken the liberty of coining my own terminology for the main objectives of the intelligence algorithm. I call it:

The Three Foundation Stones of Intelligence

Stone one

The first stone and in my opinion the most important foundation stone, is assessing and then analyzing information we have learned and then using that information to come to a conclusion about the current situation we are in. After we arrive at a conclusion we make a decision.

Anyone who has been in a survival situation can appreciate the intelligence related evolutionary processes that were at work to give mankind advanced intelligence. I'm not talking about Darwinian evolution; I'm talking about the evolution of intelligence, brought about through usage, application, storage and the transfer of information to the prodigy of the species. If you suddenly find yourself in an unfamiliar place with no food, shelter or protection, you become instantly aware our how our ancestors had to make hundreds of decisions everyday just to survive. Of course, knowledge of what to do and how to do it will increase your chances but you will still need to make life dependent decisions. "Do I make a shelter first or try to look for food first or do I try to walk out of here"? This decision may ultimately determine whether the decider survives.

Being correct about a new set of circumstances that possibly could save a life or two is a very good feeling, indeed. However this ability does not come free, it has to be worked on. Prior information is absolutely essential and the more the better. The more information points there are for any subject or object, the greater the probability of a correct assessment being made. There is a difference between "assessment" and "analysis". During the assessment process we observe the difference in what was to what now is. Have things changed? If so, how have they changed? Is there something completely new to be observed? If so, what is it or what do you think it is?

Native Americans were faced with this kind of observation as they watched the white man move into and through their land. The white man was something entirely different than what they normally observed. They were accustomed to other tribes and were frequently at war with other tribes but this was entirely different. This is the assessment phase. Native Americans knew that the new intruders were not other Native Americans. The Indians came to the conclusion (made the decision) that the new men were just men, like them but had different skin color, clothes and weapons. They also had horses which the Indians called "big dogs", not having anything else to reference to.

The next step is to analyze what we have just assessed. From observing these men further, they observed that the weapons they carried were much more advanced in some respects to the native weapons. The analysis part comes into play as they tried to decide on whether or not it was a good idea to confront them. Part of the analysis could have been; "Their weapons are more powerful than ours but it takes them time to reload their fire sticks. We may have a chance in defeating them because we can shoot more arrows in the same time as it takes them to load one shot. If we defeat them we can take possession of the big dogs they ride."

After a time of "deliberation" they decided they had a good chance of defeating the intruders and they went on to planning an attack. Planning an attack falls under the category of stone 2 of the 3 foundation stones which is covered next.

For the pioneers moving through the uncharted wilderness in the early 1800s with hostile Native Americans all around them, these skills meant the difference between life and death. If they made correct assessments, analysis and decisions, they evaded or repelled any attacks. If they did it incorrectly, the pioneers did not survive. An important point here is intelligence is *not* automatic. Since the whole process relies on decisions there is always an element of effort needed in the decision process itself. If it were automatic, with no decisions required, the number of mistakes we would make *should* be far outnumbered by correct assessments, analyses and decisions to a point where we could claim a minimal number of wrong decisions, but it would not.

The notion of automatic decision making would basically take away what we call "free will" and is also basically impossible for anything other than a system that fails consistently at complex decision making. Once free will is removed from the repertoire of human control agents the only available tools would be primitive ones such as more primitive animals use when deciding to attack. If humans just relied on "gut feelings" for the actions they took, the probability of making more correct decisions than not would be nearly zero. The reason for this is because "gut feelings" are emotions based and emotions omit large logical parameters from any complex informational problem. Fortunately, humans are not programed in an automatic decision making system, and if we were, we probably would not have survived. Human survival is different than survival in other animal species. We survive with smarts, not because of how fast we can run, how powerful our bite is, or the sharpness of our claws. We should also be cognizant that there is always the possibility of

Chapter 1 - Intelligence and Stupidity Defined

bad things happening even if correct decisions are made. The point is to make the most correct decision most of the time, and that is usually not easy.

In summary, high performance intelligence would not be possible without the advanced inborn skills of assessing, analyzing and decision making. We have always used those and do to this day.

Stone two

The second stone is the ability to transcend what is known to that which is unknown. This is how we invent things like tools. The human ability to daydream or, a fancy way of putting the same thing; to do mind experiments, was the enabling factor for the tools we used from the very first stone axe to the most powerful supercomputer of today.

It is said that Albert Einstein's general theory of relativity began with him daydreaming about how space was like a piece of bendable and stretchable fabric and celestial bodies warped the shape of this fabric and so the shape of the fabric of space influenced the body's movement through the fabric. This is what our intelligence can do if we only have the courage to apply our dreams to the things we already know. If you noticed, it would have been impossible for Einstein to daydream the way he did, with no prior knowledge of things like "fabric". Prior knowledge is essential in any kind of daydreaming effort. We always use what we know to conjure up dreams about what we don't know but might create. Try to think about something (anything) that is *not* related in some way to something you already know. You can't. It is impossible.

In a more down to earth example of stone 2, I go back to my Native American friends and what mechanisms might have come into play with the attack plan they were formulating against the white invaders. This was an attack plan that must have taken a fair amount of thought. The first Native Americans confronted with the white man were confounded in several ways. The white man looked different, had different weapons and had horses which must have seemed horrifying to a people that had never seen such an animal. The process of "dreaming up" a plan of attack against such an adversary must have been a daunting task to say the least.

Native Americans had never fought an adversary on horseback, but they had hunted large powerful animals such as moose and elk with the weapons they possessed in conjunction with some maneuvering tactics they had developed over centuries. Through the thought processes of the second stone, they were able to transcend what they knew to what they didn't know by using some of the same hunting tactics on the white invaders. Lie in wait, ambush and disperse and run if not successful are guerilla tactics still used today and were originally developed by Native American warriors by the process of transcending what you know to what you don't know.

In summary, the process of looking into the unknown as in daydreaming is one of the most useful, performance measurable aspects of human intelligence. This is the facet of intelligence that drives humanity's advancement. It could also end up being the most important aspect of intelligence because if humanity does not advance, it may not survive. It is this part of intelligence that is not taken into account in the "IQ tests" currently used. The reason this is so is that testing someone in this aspect is difficult because what usually drives advances in science and all fields is the situation at hand and the number of possible situations approaches infinity. That said, it could be done with a little ingenuity and would be well worth the effort because we could actually identify the people who can solve problems. This would be a boon to industry and the economy.

Stone three

The third stone is actually an element of the first stone. People's lacking of this ability, is the reason the world has so many unsolved problems today. In the first part we do an analysis of what we already know through some learning experience (what we have assessed). The third part is the same thing only performed at a much higher processing level. This requires a high level of processing, to "keep in mind" every known piece of relative information and glean relative information pertaining to whatever the topic at hand may be.

People that have ADD (attention deficit disorder) are said to be processing nearly everything they are aware of and sometimes things they have recently been exposed to. This creates problems for them in a traditional school setting. The instructor, lecture, classroom environment proves to be a big distraction for some of these people. Their active mind never stops proposing multiple possible scenarios and, that prevents them from paying attention when it is prudent to do so (like when the instructor is giving important information).

It is the very people that don't do well in a classical educational system because they can't pay attention (when someone else says they are supposed to pay attention) are usually the very people who are able to "see the forest through the trees". These are the people that "notice" things that other people don't notice. It is unfortunate that the learning disabilities of these people usually interfere with them becoming knowledgeable in useful professions. Having some measure of these abilities of the third stone has led to some of the most important discoveries in science. These discoveries were made by the researchers that "noticed" things during the normal course of tasks during experiments.

It is one thing to use the given facts to arrive at a conclusion. It is quite another matter to see unrelated elements that pertain to some other problem that has been analyzed in the past or is currently being analyzed. That is in essence the third stone; gleaning apparently unrelated (which in reality is related, if only in a minute way) information from a mine of related or seemingly unrelated information that we have looked at some prior time. The reasons we have previously looked at this information are varied. It could be it was of some interest because of a hobby. It could be it came up as part of another profession you had. The possibilities are infinite.

"Not being able to see the forest through the trees" is an apt description of man's inability is this regard. Many of the solutions for the problems we now face are probably right in front our noses but they have gone by unnoticed. The highly intelligent usually notice things in current data that everyone else misses. In my opinion, people who are gifted with this ability, have super positive and unstoppable inquisitive personalities. They are driven for the love of their interests whatever those interests might be. This is proof that attitude is important in the production of intelligence. As the reader can readily see, this has little to do with how many languages one can master, or how good one is at math.

Chapter 1 - Intelligence and Stupidity Defined

Researchers such as Louis Pasture are a good example of how noticing things can lead to scientific breakthroughs. He noticed how some molds inhibited bacterial growth in his laboratory. He then did experiments to prove his hypothesis correct. The point here is he was not initially looking for anti-bacterial substances. He could have very easily missed this important clue entirely. These discoveries lead to drugs such as Penicillin; which saved thousands of lives in later years.

When Enrico Fermi was engrossed in thinking up a way to improve a particle accelerator, he happened to be swinging his daughter at arm's length in a circle out in his back yard. He had an epiphany which turned into the circular accelerator, still used to this day at places like Fermilab in Illinois and the Super Hadron Collider at Cern, Switzerland.

In summary, stone 3 allows mankind to solve problems by surveying numbers of things that are already known. This does not require a lot of "out of the box" thinking as in stone 2. It only requires that we pay attention to what is going on around us. The inquisitive are usually ahead of the game with stone 3 as they *want* to know something about everything.

Summary - The 3 foundation Stones

In summary, I have distilled all the stupidity and intelligence "mash" down to three distillates:

- Access, analyze and decide
- Transcend
- Observe (Notice)

At this point, the reader may ask why this seems so simple. It surely must be more complex than this? I don't believe it is any more complex than what I have laid out in my three foundation stone hypothesis. Think about it. Any intellectual product we produce as humans can be produced using the main points outlined above. It is just that simple. It also follows that being as simple as it is, humans who were not familiar with what actually comprises stupidity and intelligence, now have a simple set of guidelines to work from. In Chapter 3 – The brain, I provide an illustration of this important algorithm which may serve to clarify the whole picture.

It should be observed that in using the three foundation stones, they could be further defined as a set of rules. For example, making a decision with no prior knowledge of the topic at hand is not a good idea. The rule here would be: "Don't try to make a decision with incomplete knowledge." The decider could get lucky and inadvertently make a correct decision but the odds are very much against that scenario. Probability is always a factor when decisions are made since a decision is never really more than an educated guess. Humans can only "guess" that the decision they make will be the most correct one. This is why I say intelligence is like a game.

"Intelligence is a game?" Yes Virginia, That's exactly what it is: a game and nothing more. Let me explain. In any game there are always rules. Ditto for intelligence but I would classify the essential guidelines for intelligence to be more like laws. In the game of intelligence, the rules are much more important than in any game and could spell disaster if not adhered to. I would say that constitutes a law. A law is a rule that cannot be broken without severe repercussions.

Chapter 1 - Intelligence and Stupidity Defined

So, as games have rules the game of intelligence has laws. These are laws that if broken will usually result in failure. The winners in the game of intelligence are the people who have used their inherent intelligence (whatever that level might be) to the utmost. To accomplish that goal, playing by the rules was instrumental in their success. Play by the rules and you win, ignore the rules, you lose. The reader may say, "OK Frank so what are the rules?" Here are the 3 main rules but for a complete description see the next chapter.

1. Be honest.
2. Be honest.
3. Be honest.

Of course there's much more to the rules besides being honest but if you strive to be honest with everything you do and say, you will be on top in the game. Since I brought up the topic of inherent intelligence this leads to this subject: Are we are born with intelligence or is it learned?

Is stupidity a choice?

It stands to reason that we are all born with some level of inherent intelligence. I believe that when it comes to intelligence, people are *NOT* all born equal. This has to with the way our brains are wired as we are being "assembled" in the womb. However I do not believe that there is a significant enough difference in the majority of humans to warrant any concern that the individual cannot learn a subject if that subject is presented correctly. I say this because of my experience teaching young people electronics. I found that regardless of the backgrounds of my students, if the subject material was presented in terms they could relate to AND they had interest, they could be taught anything. In other words, if the impetus to learn is deemed worthy by the student, learning can take place. It's all a matter of attitudes and perception of the benefits of learning, and not any differences in brain hardware.

Learning is always the first step prior to any assess/analyze phase. We cannot assess something that is not related in some way to something we already know. We cannot analyze something we know nothing about. We also cannot transcend ideas that are not there to begin with. Seeing the forest through the trees requires prior knowledge; that point should be obvious.

An adult cannot be expected to understand linear equations if never exposed to some learning process, either done by simply reading mathematics books or taking a course or having a friend explain them. If presented with written equations, they would be meaningless without the background stored in memory to draw on. The same would be true for anyone who was never taught the alphabet, and how words make up sounds and how words can be put into sentences. There has to be some background training before being shown a written language and making sense of it.

The point I am attempting to make here is that stupidity may be a choice and anyone who really wants to can change from a stupid to a highly intelligent person just by following a few rules. One reason I believe this is because of my theories of how the brain actually works. This is explained in chapter 3 but I will just briefly say that the vast majority of people have the necessary hardware. It all has to do with how the hardware is used. There is a little more to all of this than just adhering to

Chapter 1 - Intelligence and Stupidity Defined

the 3 foundation stone hypothesis. This has to do with morality, honesty and perseverance. As I just alluded to, I cover this in greater detail in Chapter 2; Spiritual and intellectual enlightenment.

Is stupidity forever?

Can anyone be smart, or are the stupid condemned to a life of missteps, incorrect decisions and failures in every aspect of life? My belief is that most humans can be very intelligent. I say that because of my view about what stupidity actually is rather than the status quo version of the commonly accepted version. I can prove that view point and I can do it relatively easily. The explanation is simple but somewhat lengthy, so don't despair and read on.

I believe that people unknowingly choose if they are smart or stupid. This is due in part because of the brainwashing we all undergo from the educational system. It is also due to beliefs, prejudges and more brainwashing we are brought up with through parental and community sources. These are usually totally beyond our control; we have no choice in the attitudes of our teachers, parents and our peers in the neighborhood. Once the currently accepted criteria for intelligence become part of our own personality, the brainwashing is complete.

We are taught in elementary school that if we can't memorize multiplication tables and the spelling of words, we are not so smart. Rote memorization is a highly valued tool for the evaluation of intelligence. This is all wrong. I don't know what the educational system is doing now, but I suspect they haven't changed much in this respect. I'm not saying that memorizing some things is *not* advantageous. I *am* saying that kids should not be told they are stupid if they can't do it!

In the early days of computing, it was common to hear the phrase, garbage in; garbage out. What this meant was that if you input faulty data into a system and the sole purpose of that system was to do calculations on that data, than don't expect the output data to be of any use. This is what we are doing to people. We are filling their brains with garbage and then we expect the brains we have corrupted to act in a logical fashion. People are not taught how to think, they are taught how to conform to a screwed up educational system. Because of this, many people who have a lot of potential intelligence are relegated to a life of mediocrity because they have been convinced they are stupid.

There are two possibilities for self-assessment of one's own intelligence: One possibility is that you believe you are stupid, but that is not true. The second is that you believe you are smart but that is not true.

You believe you are stupid but you are not!

Here, I present the people, who through life's experience and a bad educational system has been brainwashed into believing they are stupid. The good news is: Just because the educational system has tried its best to prove that you are stupid; you may actually be very smart! In fact, your inherent intelligence may be vastly superior to the other people who did better in school than you did. If you really believe you are stupid, the odds are it was the educational system you were put through that has brainwashed you into believing that.

Chapter 1 - Intelligence and Stupidity Defined

The above statement is not an exaggeration. The big problem with our educational systems as a whole is they do not have an understanding of what intelligence is because they themselves have been brainwashed into believing a false narrative of the constituents of intelligence. Many of them are still operating on the antiquated "Intelligence Quota" guidelines. As I have pointed out those guidelines are at best false and at worse destructive to what could be otherwise, smart people. In the past many kids from low income housing projects were thought to have "low IQs" but when the test subject matter was looked into in depth, problems with the questions were found. Many questions were written with an assumption that things such as "garbage disposers" would be common knowledge of the test taker. The problem was that the kids from low income housing had no idea what these devices were and so any questions pertaining to them made no sense. The so-called IQ test is more a measure of some level of exposure to specific information and not necessarily a measure of how any information will or can be utilized. We are shortchanging many smart people and sentencing them to a life of mediocrity.

I believe that what I have just described is way more common than one would surmise. What I mean by this is there are probably more people than not who have been shortchanged by the education system into a false sense of stupidity. This is, in essence; the main problem humanity has in dealing with our own intelligence: We don't understand intelligence well enough to be able to proclaim one way or the other if we are big dummies or little Einstein's. I hope this book changes that even if it only minutely.

You believe you are smart but in reality; not so much!

Again, I believe the educational system is responsible for much of this type of misunderstanding. There are many people who are gainfully employed and from all visible indicators would have to be thought of as being both smart and successful. Many of these people are not only successful but advance to positions of authority such as managers, professors, CEOs and even The President of The United States. A large percentage of these people are demonstrably incompetent. I have personally witnessed this phenomenon more times than you can shake a stick at, and that's a lot!

There is one example that I want to share with the reader. This person was my boss at a company I worked for several years ago. He was a graduate of one of the highest rated engineering schools in the country. He held a BSEE in electrical engineering with a concentration in electronics design. I had the unfortunate duty of working with him closely on several ongoing technical problems the company was having at the time. What I noticed about him almost immediately was that he had no solid understanding of electronics in the fundamental sense. When it came to electronics, he was a big dumb ass!

That didn't stop him from being promoted time and time again, and eventually he became the vice president of the department I worked in. He was single handedly responsible for the loss of over 2 million dollars for the company because he refused to acknowledge facts I was telling him about flaws in the products. He basically rejected everything I said because I had not graduated from what he considered to be a legitimate school. He was for all practical purposes; an idiot. The policies of the company promoted that sort of thing because the big wigs were all brainwashed into believing that education from a certain school somehow makes you smart.

Chapter 1 - Intelligence and Stupidity Defined

One last point I want to make here is that really smart people don't usually think of themselves as being smart. If they did, it would act detrimentally to their overall performance. The reason this is so, is that if anyone truly wants to perform at the best of their ability it is a waste of energy to be thinking about smart they are, compared to the rest of the world. This would be like a major league baseball player who was constantly thinking about what a great hitter he was. Just the process of thinking about the self-love he was feeling for himself would preclude his batting average from going up. This is just common sense. There is also the algorithm of intelligent behavior. I have alluded to the production of intelligence possibly being the result of complex algorithm(s) at the micro levels. I believe that part of that algorithm keeps our arrogance in check by reminding us constantly that we have a possibility of being wrong. The very smart have the ability to constantly monitor their assessments, analyses and decisions to increase the probability of making a correct decision. They don't allow arrogance to control them.

Brainwashing

Just in case you weren't aware: Brainwashing works! An explanation of brainwashing is: It is the process of implanting a concept or idea or sets of concepts or ideas into a human brain so that when the implantation is complete, the implanted human brain actually believes the concepts or ideas and accepts them to be fact. The implanted concepts or ideas become, in essence, factual beliefs.

Brainwashing works best when it is applied over very long periods of time; preferably starting during the developmental stages in the human brain when we begin the process of learning. We might say that brainwashing is just a very specialized type of learning. If we are taught or even casually lead to believe, that things are a certain way, from the beginning of our ability to remember what is presented to us; these ideologies will usually remain as facts to us for the rest of our existence. It doesn't matter that if the things implanted have no logical or scientific basis of fact or if they have never been proven. In fact, it really doesn't matter if the "facts" are actually a bunch of bold face lies! To the brainwashed; they are facts, and indisputable facts, at that.

Of all the belief systems we may have; the ones we are concerned with here, are the belief systems we hold about our own intelligence. If the reader is to come away from reading this with some sense of understanding about his or her own intelligence, it will be absolutely necessary to keep an open mind and consider that just because you have believed in a concept your entire life; that in itself does not make that concept true. This is what is known as logic; the most essential component of intelligence.

Here are some educational titles that don't prove or guarantee intelligence:

Having a high School Diploma
Having a Bachelor's Degree
Having a Master's Degree
Having a PhD Degree
Having an MD Degree

Going to school or just becoming educated is just learning and does not make you smart. It does give you a larger knowledge base to work with in the assessment, analysis, transcending and survey

Chapter 1 - Intelligence and Stupidity Defined

of information. Just being able to learn is not enough. To be considered smart you must be able to transcend what you have learned to create. You must also have the ability to notice things sufficiently to identify threats as they appear on the horizon and to connect things that may only have a seemingly perfunctory relationship.

Here are some job titles that don't prove or guarantee intelligence:

Being the president of The United States
Being a president or CEO of a company
Being a county, state or federal judge – this includes Supreme Court Justices
Being a state or federal representative or senator
Being an attorney or prosecutor
Being the mayor of a city
Being a governor of a state
Being a elementary school teacher
Being a high school teacher
Being a college professor
Being any kind of professional

While it is true that many people who hold these titles are in fact very, highly intelligent people, the point here is: The title is no guarantee of intelligence. There are many people in every profession listed above that have just risen to their own level of incompetence. People get promoted and receive prestigious college degrees for many reasons other than being smart. This is partly what is wrong with the world; we do not reward intelligence as much as we do conformity. This leads us to the next chapter in which I will prove in pure logic that it is impossible to be smart without a large amount of honesty and other moral attributes.

Summary

The currently held beliefs of what comprises intelligence are wrong. This is because the original purpose of intelligence is as a survival tool. In survival, if you are not advancing you are probably not surviving. The ability to learn math and other languages does not prove intelligence because that is merely learning what is already known. Intelligence needs to be proven by creating new things and solving problems. The current IQ tests are useless for identifying intelligence.

Human intelligence can be broken down into three major areas I call the three foundation stones of intelligence.

1. Assessment, analysis, decide
2. Transcend
3. Survey

Intelligence can be measured by the ratio of correct versus incorrect decisions people make. High performance in intelligence means correct decision making. It is also possible to measure intelligence by testing people's problem solving skills. This would be difficult but not impossible and well worth the effort. I should also point out that during the transcend and survey problem solving strategies, any solution arrived at is always a decision.

Chapter 2 –
Intellectual and Spiritual Enlightenment

The importance of morality in intelligence

I am not an overly religious person but I do believe in a God. I am not in any way a bible scholar nor do I really know anything about the two versions of The Bible (new and old testament). What I present next are some concepts I believe are contained in one or perhaps both versions but I am not absolutely positive of this. In reality it does not matter if these things are actually written somewhere in the scriptures because it's the ideas that count. They are nice ideas and I don't care where they came from and I don't think God cares if we know where they came from, as long as we make use of them.

The first idea I want to share with the reader I believe to be in the New Testament. Jesus Christ is referred to as the "Chief Cornerstone" in many places. The term, Chief Cornerstone refers to the capstone of a pyramid. The pyramid in general has always been symbolic to intellectual and spiritual enlightenment, with the top or "capstone" being the apex. There are other passages in the bible that say that the great pyramid in Egypt is a monument to the son of God. Whether or not the reader believes this last claim is of no consequence for our purpose. I also ask the reader to put aside any religious bias they may have. This course of ideas has no preference to any one particular religion or even a belief in God.

The point is: This paradigm says that Jesus Christ is symbolic of the apex of Intellectual and Spiritual Enlightenment as expressed through the Apex of the great pyramid's chief cornerstone. The back of the U.S. Dollar bill shows this along with the all seeing eye of God. The original use of this was done by the founding fathers of this country. In addition, it is said that Jesus died between two thieves, who are supposed to be symbols of regretting the past and fear of the future. Again, for the purpose of the point presently being made, it doesn't matter what your religious beliefs are. This last point means attainment of the peak of spiritual and intellectual enlightenment, always dies between two thieves; regretting the past and fear of the future. I believe this is a big problem with all humans in general. They can't get over the past and that holds them back and they are afraid of the future, possibly because of what has happened to them in the past. It is a no win situation.

This is a story with words of wisdom to guide our lives by, whether you are a Christian or not or even a believer in a God. This is solid advice that you cannot go wrong in trying to follow that may be literally thousands of years old. If you noticed the words, "spiritual" and "intellectual" are bound together and they are combined to form a concept that cannot be separated. You can't have one without the other. It's impossible. One cannot be truly smart and at the same time be truly evil, since evil is only a name tag we have given to stupid people. I explain my reasoning for this at the end of this chapter and in chapter 6. To summarize, the concept of spiritual and intellectual enlightenment, I interpret this as:

"We cannot expect to advance our intelligence, if we do not advance spiritually, and both will be stifled if we regret the past or fear the future."

How spirituality promotes intelligence and when lacking breeds stupidity

There are several human emotional traits that promote stupidity and stifle intelligence. I list them here in no order of importance, but in alphabetical order for convenience. This is not by any means an inclusive list. The reader is invited to add their own terms which define negative behavior that would be detrimental to intelligence. Below the list I have included my philosophical view of each and how these human emotions present problems for intellectual enlightenment. Many of these traits can be stupidity indicators as well as stupidity enablers. I elaborate more on how to identify stupid people in Chapter 9.

Definitions provided by: http://wordnetweb.princeton.edu/perl/webwn

1. Apathy – (an absence of emotion or enthusiasm) (the trait of lacking enthusiasm for or interest in things generally)
2. Arrogance - (overbearing pride evidenced by a superior manner toward inferiors)
3. Deceitfulness - (the quality of being crafty)
4. Dishonesty – Knavery (lack of honesty, acts of lying or cheating or stealing)
5. Egotism - (an exaggerated opinion of your own importance), (an inflated feeling of pride in your superiority to others)
6. Envy, enviousness - (a feeling of grudging admiration and desire to have something that is possessed by another), "Invidia" (spite and resentment at seeing the success of another (personified as one of the deadly sins))
7. Glibness – (a kind of fluent easy superficiality), Slickness - (verbal misrepresentation intended to take advantage of you in some way)
8. Hubris – (overbearing pride or presumption)
9. Immaturity - (not having reached maturity)
10. Jealousy - (a feeling of jealous envy (especially of a rival))
11. Narcissism – self-love (an exceptional interest in and admiration for yourself) "self-love that shuts out everyone else"
12. Skepticism – (the disbelief in any claims of ultimate knowledge)
13. Stubbornness - (resolute adherence to your own ideas or desires)

1. Apathy

One of the biggest destroyers of intelligence is apathy. The question is; what promotes apathy? Even very smart people can become depressed and depression can make anyone forget that they have interests in life. Interests can be anything that keeps humans occupied. It is tough to be smart if there is nothing to apply that smartness to. We need problems to solve; that's what intelligence is. In fact, my hypothesis of the 3 foundation stones of intelligence are merely a do it yourself problem solving strategy which I believe we are all born with.

Chapter 2-Intellectual and Spiritual Enlightenment

We need to be challenged in order to use any inherent intelligence we have, to its full potential. Apathy kills any intellectual spark before the fire of ingenuity can be lit. Apathetic people are usually people with emotional related problems. This is not a work on psychology and I am not a psychologist so I cannot be expected to posit why apathy affects so many people.

However, my opinion is that emotional related problems are for the most part a result of incorrect processing in the brain. This is not saying much as this could be from such mundane things as consuming too much alcohol or maybe even eating too much chocolate cake! It could also be a combination of factors such as an abusive environment in developmental years and many other things.

I feel very bad for and sympathize with anyone experiencing apathy towards life in general. I myself have had problems with not caring about anything and I know how that feels. I know I got out of it and I know of many others that beat it also. If you call on the logic you were born with, you can rationalize your way out of anything. Seeking help from a professional may also be an option.

I am lucky in that I have several interests that I have had continually since I was a teenager. One of my passions is cars. I love cars and anything connected to them. This enthusiasm has helped me out of dark points in my life on more than one occasion. It is something to dream about. It is a means to utilize the imagination on a number of levels. The key here is love and passion. We all can find something to be passionate about; it is just a matter of personal preference.

This is why so many "self-help" experts advise people to find something they love. If you find something that you are passionate about you will automatically be good at doing it. The love transcends any doubt or negativity and acts like your "guiding light" towards your fulfillment of life and happiness. This is what this chapter is all about.

There is another impetus to apathy and that is the socialistic view that is being promoted by progressives. This idea is that "you can't make it by yourself; the odds are stacked against you". Anti-capitalistic rhetoric about the rich stealing all the wealth and leaving the poor with nothing does little to curb apathy. I cover all of this in detail in Chapter 6.

It could be postulated that doing nothing in the face of adversity amounts to a surrender to stupidity. So if you want to advance your intelligence, change your attitude, or get left behind.

2. Arrogance

We are biological entities and as such our brains are imperfect computers and are always subject to some degree of error in the processing of information. We come to the wrong conclusions, given a set of conditions, and as a consequence, we make the wrong decisions based on those incorrect conclusions. If that weren't bad enough, some of us are arrogant to the point that we will stick to our decisions, even if we know deep down inside that they may be wrong.

Arrogant people are easy to spot. You know these people; they are the ones who always are correct about everything they say or do and they cannot possibly be wrong, about anything.

Chapter 2-Intellectual and Spiritual Enlightenment

Being arrogant has nothing whatsoever to do with being confident. Confidence is a good thing. A part of being smart is; knowing that you are smart, and that is confidence. It is when we become less than honest about ourselves that arrogance becomes a problem. But, there is an exception to this:

In some cases the arrogant are so involved with themselves that dishonesty never enters into the picture. They really believe they know everything about everything. These are the truly stupid and I doubt if anything can be done for them. The brainwashing they have received or even self-inflicted upon them themselves is sadly irreversible. It is in these cases where one could posit that the inherent intelligence that would allow them to understand themselves (know that they are not perfect) is just not there. In this sense, we were not really all created equal.

For the savable-arrogant, the only criterion for salvation is honesty. What this means is that if you are an honest person with the required level of inherent intelligence, you will never believe that you know everything. That belief may not be what you want to admit but if you concede that it is there (somewhere), there is hope. You will be better at whatever it is that you do if you are not arrogant. It is just that simple.

3. Deceitfulness

If you are truly smart, you will have no need to be deceitful. It is only the stupid that find a need to re-shape reality into something more likeable to their needs. As I have alluded to, there may be some people who are incurably stupid and these people will continue to be deceitful as this is necessary in their interactions with the rest of society. In other words, if they told the truth, everyone they interacted with would know that they are totally incompetent and dysfunctional.

However this book is an optimistic view of what people can become, as opposed to what they are sentenced to for their entire life. In that regard, anyone who has the ability to do what is right, rather than use deceit as a band aid for actions they should have correctly done, has a chance of actually being smart. I also believe there are people, who through some learning process, have been taught to believe that a prudent way to go about life *is* by using deceit as a social tool to their benefit. These people are totally wrong and I hope they see their error of their ways. You cannot truly be smart unless you are honest.

The biggest problem deceitfulness causes is when we use it on ourselves. Many people lie to themselves about their own intellectual capabilities. This phenomenon usually appears in conjunction with several of the other negative human traits. Dishonesty, egotism, arrogance and narcissism are a few commonly found together. The worst thing people can do from an intelligence standpoint is lie about what they know and talk about things they really have no firsthand knowledge of.

One outcome of this type of misconduct is that the deception will usually have the exact opposite effect of what the perpetrator intended it to do. If you lie to yourself about how much knowledge you possess and you act without the benefit of that knowledge, the result is almost always failure. If on the other hand you were honest, and you took the usually more difficult path to learn about the subject before acting, you have a much better chance of success.

Chapter 2-Intellectual and Spiritual Enlightenment

4. Dishonesty

If you have to lie, cheat or steal in order to accomplish your goals, then I will bet the ideas you believe in and are attempting to promote are not sound ideas based in truth. It has been said that, "the truth shall set you free!" and I believe in that statement. The need to lie, cheat or steal is an indicator of a faulty premise. If the ideology that you live by requires nefarious acts to succeed, then there is something fundamentally wrong with that system from the beginning.

5. Egotism

This negative trait could have been covered in chapter 6, Social Implications of Stupidity, because it concerns a *comparison* of one's intelligence to the rest of the population. The belief that you are somehow superior and more important than your peers; can only cause problems in relating to and working with the other people that you need to deal with. Just to be clear, I want to stress that feelings of importance and the feeling of being superior is 100% intelligence directed. There is no doubt in my belief system. Egotistical people feel that way because of an overinflated self-view they have of their own intelligence.

Just imagine a world in which everyone believed that *they* were the most important and smartest person. Nothing would ever get done! Everyone would believe they were too important and too smart to do the task they were being asked to do. In fact, even the bosses might believe that *they* were too smart to be giving out orders! It would be a world of gridlock and chaos where little work was done. It is very fortunate that the number of highly egotistical people is low enough to prevent the above catastrophe.

There are also people who are so egotistical that they even admit that it is fun playing God. One of those people is a multi-billionaire and he believes he is *SO* smart and the poor common people of the world are *SO* stupid that *he* knows best when it comes to the way they live their lives. He even admitted that he believes it is fun playing God. This is egotism on a biblical scale.

6. Envy

I have heard people in religious circles say that money is the root of all evil. If people were not envious of others then there would be no problems. Since this book is about intelligence I want to convey the envy of money to the envy of intelligence, because that's what envy really is.

When someone is envious of you, they are actually feeling remorse of your ability to either succeed at something or acquire something. This envy could be because of the car you drive, the spouse you have, how well your kids are doing in school, the job you have, the house you have, the refrigerator you own, your do-it-yourself skills or basically anything. This is categorically true. Envious people are usually not selective in the things they are envious of. It is usually about *everything*.

This tells me that the envious don't envy the micro, they envy the macro. This means they wish they possessed the ability to obtain the things or abilities you do. In other words, they are envious of your intelligence and *that* makes them stupid! This originates in a naïve and false belief that the envied were able to obtain the things or the skills they possess automatically with practically no effort exerted. The knowledge you have to perform the job you have just came down from the sky and was somehow "bestowed" upon you from God. It is the same for your skills on the projects you work on around the house and just about any skill you are perceived as possessing. Of course, anyone who is successful in anything will tell you that they got that way through a bunch of hard work.

I have been working on cars since I was 15 and I can't remember how many times I've had neighbors come up to me and comment, "You know how to do that?" I usually say, "Well yes, I read lots of books." With that, I get the look of envy that I never could understand, until I realized this is what people are programmed to do. This is one of the many common human behavioral traits that were instrumental in formulating the hypotheses I have laid down here and outlined in the abstract for Chapter 6. This is the IRD and ICP traits I will explain in detail there.

I now know that the reason they are envious is not because I took the time to learn something about cars. They are envious because they have a somewhat low opinion of their own intelligence and they incorrectly access my intelligence as being greater than theirs because of a number of false premises. Don't be envious of other people. The skills and knowledge they have collected only came to them with hard work, diligence and a good attitude and were never just given to them as a gift. Read a book, take a class, you can learn stuff if you really want to. Perhaps you don't really want to learn? Perhaps you are just lazy? Come to grips with that. Be honest!

7. Glibness

Glibness is a tactic that stupid people use against their intelligent counterparts in an attempt to gain the upper hand in the workplace, in social settings, in courting, friendly relationships, etc. If you have ever been the victim of this type of "backstabbing" then you will have an easier task of understanding what this is. This usually but not always occurs between two people who have something to compete over. It could be a job, a love interest or just competition for someone who is deemed to be a desirable as a friend. There are other possibilities where this can happen; but the idea behind this behavior is always the same.

The perpetrator of this behavior is most likely a very stupid person. Anyone who needs to resort to this type of dishonorable conduct has very little in the way of smarts working for them. This is the type of interaction in which the stupid person will use their superficial charm and skill in selection of words to make subtle comments and suggestions. The comments purpose is to discredit or degrade the reputation, worth and in some cases the intelligence level of, the "mark". The idea is to attempt to label the mark as stupid while simultaneously labeling the glib as being smart. The purposes of doing this vary but the best example would be a situation in which discrediting of the mark brings about some advantage for the perpetrator. For example, telling a love interest that their other significant interest is a slob because of something you know about them which is probably not true.

Chapter 2-Intellectual and Spiritual Enlightenment

Unfortunately, it could be that glibness is a solid attribute of being sociopathic. Sociopaths are usually glib because they believe it is necessary to manipulate and control others in subversive ways.

8. Hubris

It is a good thing to have pride in you. However the pride you feel in yourself should be earned and be related to some goal you have accomplished. To have an overbearing pride in one's country of ancestry, ethnic background, political affiliation, military branch of service, occupation, race, sexual prowess, alcohol tolerance, etc. is a glaring indicator of stupidity. I have even met many people who were proud of the fact that they could tolerate hot spicy food such as "sport peppers". This is ridiculous and I am always amazed at the willingness and casual manner in which they flaunt this perceived "attribute". This demonstrates how stupidity can be easily displayed by the stupid and easily recognized by smart people.

If you openly display your pride in any of the above mentioned things, smart people will judge you as being stupid, and they are probably right. Really smart people do not presume anything, including a perceived value of eating hot peppers. The reason for that is intelligence forces you to be aware of many concurrent things and the intelligence algorithm is pushing them to constantly question their actions and decisions. Relating this to hubris, you cannot be smart and at the same time believe that your smartness is due to your ethnic background or any other superficial attribute (last of which is eating hot peppers). If you are truly smart, you are aware that you became smart by working hard to get there.

9. Immaturity

First of all what is immaturity? Webster's dictionary defines it as: 1. not mature or ripe. 2. Not finished or perfected, incomplete. Of all the negative traits, I consider immaturity to be the most important and as such deserve the lengthiest explanation. Immature people can exhibit all of the 12 other traits listed here. It is a self-destructive behavior that nearly always indicates as well as promotes stupidity.

Most of us associate immaturity with childishness and that is in complete agreement with the above definitions and is the appropriate attribute for this discussion. The point is: if we act like children but we are not children than I think it is safe to say that we are acting immaturely. What age is a child? For the sake of argument let us say that 7 is the age of reason, or whatever you wish to call it. That said; any 18 year old who acts like a 6 year old is acting childishly for our purpose here. What are the important social-interaction traits commonly associated with childishness? In other words, what are the things that children do, that should never be carried over to adult life? If you have experienced the gradual transformation of a child from birth to adulthood than you are already familiar with what I am about to tell you.

From the very beginning the child will cry for various reasons. Feeling uncomfortable, being hungry, being tired are all triggers for what seems to be a genetically implanted in the brain response to certain stimulus. These crying responses may have roots in the Darwinian evolutionary process that got us a foot-hold as a species (if evolution is truly responsible). This is one factor that allowed for a lengthy development phase which is necessary for the complex human brain. Crying notifies the parents that something needs to be attended to.

As the child progresses in age these crying responses become more and more connected to how the parent responds to the crying and the child quickly learns that attention can be had for any reason simply by crying. As the child gets older the ratio of crying episodes per day to age slowly decreases until the crying ends completely. We may still cry as adults but usually the causes are not to get the attention of others as it is with a child (most of the time). The causes of crying in adults *should* be traumatic and emotional such as the loss of a loved one, the breakup of a marriage, etc.

The problem is many adults never shake the baby crying response and continue to use it through their adult lives. The crying may be not the same crying we associate with a baby but it is crying never the less. I am talking about the phenomenon of complaining. Complaining about everything is just crying in a different mode. Many adults complain constantly about many things that are not really in their control but that doesn't stop them from doing it. The nature of the weather, it's too hot or too cold. The level of education they achieved, they never got the breaks other people received. The way they were treated by their parents, a sibling was given preferential treatment. The way their spouse is, he or she is lazy and sloppy. It goes on and on. These people go through their whole lives never realizing a simple fact. They never grew up! I believe that it is the complaining itself that makes some of these people happy. In fact, they wouldn't be happy if they didn't have things to complain about! This is immaturity at its best and a definite cause and indicator of stupidity.

Another thing children do is; they develop defense mechanisms to deal with problems they are confronted with. This may be because the developing brains of children simply do not have all the wiring in place that enables a sufficient amount of information processing to handle complicated situations. One of the defense mechanisms children use is that when faced with criticism they will accuse the parent of picking on them or being unfair in some way. "There is nothing wrong with me; you are just picking on me and putting me down!"

In addition, children do not have a collection of life experiences to draw information from. This causes children to react to situational stimulus differently than adults who should have completely wired brains and enough stored situational experience to draw conclusions about whatever it is they are faced with. A child is afraid of things that adults should not be afraid of; like being in the dark. This is due to the child not having any life experience to tell them that just because you can't see does not mean there are dangerous things lurking about. On the other hand, children are not afraid of things they should be afraid of; like getting hit with a car. An adult who is afraid of things like being in the dark or just being in unfamiliar places like the woods just might be immature.

Children also have a problem with honesty. It becomes much easier for a child to lie about things that happened, than it is to admit that they were the cause and possibly face retribution from the parent. They learn this very early in life and the unfortunate fact is many parents who were never able to shake this undesirable habit as they grew up, don't see it as much of a problem if their kids do it. Lying can be a bad habit. It is my personal belief that the amount of lying and intelligence are inversely proportional. That is: the more a person lies; the more likely it is that person is stupid. If you are really smart, you will not allow yourself to be put in situations where you are forced to lie. Lying is a band aid or a crutch for a lack of intelligence. Smart people don't need to tell lies because they have the situation in hand to begin with. Smart people also know that lying in order to repair a situation that has gone bad, just compounds the badness. There are also people who enjoy lying and will deceive other people intentionally just for the thrill; that is totally illogical and that means that those people are probably irrevocably stupid. In addition this behavior may fall under the category of sociopathic behavior.

There is no doubt that the causes of immaturity can be twofold. There is a physical component and a psychological component. It can be a brain problem or it can be a learned response to external stimulus or a combination of both. My personal belief is that some immaturity is caused from an incompletely developed brain. In other words the brain never fully developed.

If you are immature you might be stupid for one of two reasons:

Reason one: High inherent intelligence combined with immaturity

If you are immature and potentially intelligent that means that your brain is fully developed. Then you are already aware that you are childish and so you became stupid by not rejecting the childishness. Why would anyone want to act like a child purposely, unless they are not using their inherent intelligence to tell them that it is a bad idea? Calling this person stupid would not be a disrespectful putdown. It is not like telling them they are ugly or bald (two conditions for which the person cannot do much about), it is more of a criticism of that person's decision to act in a way that doesn't make logical sense.

The existence of the inherently smart and immature individual may suggest that there are other factors at work here. There is the possibility that some immaturity is a learned behavior and does not depend on any level of brain development at all. I believe there are probably many people who have learned to be childish from their parents and it is these people who are most likely candidates for improvement. They just have to be honest with themselves. Admitting to yourself that you sometimes act like a little kid is a tough thing to do for someone who has done it all their life and we even might say they were brainwashed into thinking that they are acting correctly because after all, this was how mom and dad acted!

Although the last statement may be true, I want to point out again that if the level of inherent intelligence is high; these people are already aware that they act like little kids, so they should want to stop it and just grow up! If they don't want to stop; then they just might have mental problems which I believe is just an extreme form of stupidity.

Reason two: Low inherent intelligence combined with immaturity

The second reason is, if you are immature and you do not even recognize this fact; then you are de-facto stupid for the simple reason that you failed to come to the correct conclusion about yourself. In this case the possibility of possessing a high inherent intelligence is very low. This should, but it won't become self-evident when other people like a psychologist point this out to you and you reject the idea wholesale. I seriously doubt if anything can be done for people in this category. They are the truly stupid but luckily they are very easy to spot.

Immaturity – summary

I think it is safe to say that immaturity plays a huge role in human intelligence. This is really not surprising since childish behavior is expected in children because they are still in the developmental stages. The brain has not fully developed and their knowledge base is only beginning to have information placed in it. We cannot expect an incompletely constructed machine to meet the design specifications of a completely constructed one.

If people remain immature and the immaturity is not the learned type when they are in their early twenties, (which is supposedly the age when the brain becomes fully developed); than the brain's developmental process has not completed! An individual with an immature brain cannot possibly be operating at whatever intended inherent level of intelligence they were supposed to be born with, simply because the processing architecture that is responsible for the production of that intelligence has not completely developed.

For the learned type, humans cannot possibly utilize whatever level of potential intelligence they were born with if they continue to act like kids. It is exactly like a half-baked cake, a car with an 8 cylinder engine running on 4, a computer with a keyboard in which only 2/3 of the keys work. I think you get the picture.

The reader might have questions on the absence of medical sciences' weigh in on the brain's incomplete development role for immaturity in adults. I answer those questions by simply stating: How would they know? What kind of tests could possibly be developed to ascertain the maturity of adults? I don't know and I also don't know why this has not been a subject of research in the medical community, especially in psychology. No one has ever thought of this before? I believe it's about time someone did.

10. Jealousy

Jealousy is one of the most destructive of all the negative traits and I believe is an indicator and a cause of stupidity. The worst possible manifestation of jealousy it is with a rival, usually someone you are forced to work with. There are also many problems created with jealous lovers and admirers of the opposite sex, etc. This second class is a whole main category of problems by itself and I pity people who are victimized by jealous people such as this.

While the second class of jealously may be dealt with through things like orders of protection and law enforcement, the first class necessarily must be handled by the victim. You are on your own when faced with someone who sees you as a threat to their own existence. They want to be promoted instead of you. They go out of their way to try to make you appear stupid while simultaneously making them look smart. This often manifests in conjunction with glibness. People like this resort to this kind of behavior because they have a low opinion of their own intelligence level. They are afraid.

Chapter 2-Intellectual and Spiritual Enlightenment

Regardless of the true capability of their own intelligence, this behavior makes them appear stupid. My opinion is that they probably are truly stupid. My reasoning is simple. Smart people have done the required studying and maturations to prepare them for the task at hand. They know what they can do and what they can't do. If they are not dishonest, as I alluded to previously, they at least do not have that indicator of stupidity hanging around their neck. So, the smart will not be jealous of someone just because that someone is alive and in the same room and perhaps has the same background and responsibilities.

In fact, smart people instinctively know that being jealous of someone is a tremendous waste of time and energy. All the manipulations that the jealous may try really serve no purpose other than make the perpetrator look stupid. Jealously is a strictly childish emotion and as such makes the jealous immature. That says it all.

11. Narcissism

It is quite natural to like yourself. You need to like yourself if you want to do good things for you and on your behalf. It is another matter altogether to be in love with yourself. If you have convinced yourself that you are the smartest, greatest, best looking, most charming, most desired by the opposite sex, etc. then you have a big problem. The main reason you have a problem is that it is pretty much impossible for you to be all those things, except in your own mind. If, you cannot accept that fact; then you cannot be all that smart. It is pretty much that simple. Narcissism is a cause as well as an indicator of stupidity. This is another trait found in sociopaths and is also a possible indicator of that condition.

12. Skepticism

I do not mean healthy skepticism here, I mean unfounded skepticism. There is a big difference. I am talking about people who make decisions about whether something is possible or not simply because, "it doesn't seem possible". This is about having an open mind. I don't see how anyone with a closed mind can be capable of "critical thinking" or "out of the box" thinking. If Albert Einstein summarily shot down every one of his concepts before ever doing the math on them, we would not have his theories to work with today.

I cover the UFO phenomenon in chapter 8. Mainstream science has summarily labeled the whole subject as not possible without as much as one serious investigation. This is a glaring example of unfounded skepticism being a cause as well as an indicator of stupidity. The so-called scientists who are skeptical of the UFO phenomenon are stating very publicly and openly that they are too narcissistic, arrogant and egotistical to ever be of any use to the advancement of the human species. In this case skepticism is an indicator of many negative traits.

Skepticism confounds science. There are numerous instances of medical doctors being "poo-pooed" by their peers and as a result, thousands of people died because they were treated under the same practices that were being protested by the doctor with the new theories. The doctor who first postulated the existence of germs had worked in a maternity ward where he saw hundreds of patients die of infection. None of his associates bought into the concept of germs, because it just, "sounded too far-fetched." He ended up dying without the recognition he deserved but years after his death there was a statue erected in his honor for his work. I don't think it mattered to him at that point, he was already dead.

13. Stubbornness

Some of the peers of the above mentioned doctor were not only skeptical, they were also stubborn. They could not get past the concept that their own ideas were not the center of the universe. This is a big problem in today's world as people refuse to be honest about what they really know. Stubbornness kills intelligence and cooperation between people in social interactions which take place at home, in business, in science, everywhere. If we can't cooperate as a species, we are done for. It is just that simple.

Summary

The probability is fairly high that the reader has known someone with one or more of the above traits. I could even argue that the present most powerful man in the free world; Barack Obama, possesses more than a few of the listed traits. I will talk more about him in the chapter 6.

I can honestly say that there have been times in my life where I did indeed act in some way that was detrimental to the process of being smart. The whole idea here is that we all can do something about the way we are. People *can* actually be smarter if they choose to! The only requirement is for *you* to be honest with *you*. None of us are perfect, and if we were all honest about that fact, the world would be a much smarter place to live in.

The reader may have noticed that many of the listed traits simply describe the *personalities* of many individuals. Since our personality is dependent of a collection of stored information we have collected since our first development stages, it is just an outward representation presentation of that stored information. Our personality may also be the result of a corrupted, bastardized emotional set as is the case in people with sociopathic attributes.

It has been postulated in other writings, of the possibility of "downloading" all of what we have stored in our brain to a computer, would it be possible to "wake up" in that machine? The surprising answer is yes. The big caveat is the word "possible". If in fact we could access every storage location in a human brain and somehow transfer that information to a computer, and then somehow access that information by the computer (this would involve a transfer of our "consciousness" along with our memories) then we would indeed "wake up" inside that computer. This is a horrifying prospect and would make the subject of a good horror movie. It would be a situation in which there was no escape and if the manipulators of the project knew how to stimulate pain receptors they could torture the victim as well.

While the above scenario has a zero probability (because some things are just not; nor will they ever be, possible) it demonstrates that our personality is just a stored collection of emotions, attitudes, perceptions, learned reactions, etc. So, many of the negative traits listed here become part of peoples' personality and personality is very hard to change.

Chapter 2-Intellectual and Spiritual Enlightenment

I have alluded to and it is interesting to note that many of the negative traits I have listed here could be considered to be the result of a bastardized version of the in-born human emotions we should all have. When we consider anything of a control nature in the hardware aspect of the brain we always need to place survival as the main reason why the control is there in the first place. Some of the survival purposed in-born emotions are: Love, hate, fear, courage, sadness, happiness, jealously, pride, loneliness and for lack of a better word; comradery which is the pleasure we get when we are in the presence of other people (especially when those people are the ones we like). All of these emotions have roots in the survival of people in a group and serve to hold the group together and deal with interpersonal relationships.

Unfortunately, nature makes mistakes and some people get flawed versions of the complete design. For example, the sociopath is shortchanged in the emotions department and instead of receiving a full-on version of the love emotion, gets a corrupted version in which the love is not outward based but only resides internally. This causes many problems because of faulty interactions between the corrupted version and the other emotions. It should also be easy to make a connection between immaturity and many of the negative traits and that is always a possibility. My opinion is that the people who were "left behind" in emotional hardware are the irrevocably stupid which should be obvious for many reasons. It is impossible to be smart when you cannot admit that you are ever wrong.

I close this chapter with the point that anyone who possesses enough of these traits could very well be considered evil. How many would it take? Would one, two, or possibly three of the mentioned traits cause an individual to be really evil? This is a matter of how severe the offender's traits are and how well engrained they become in their personality. This is a very important point and one of the main hypotheses in this book: There is no such thing as evil; it is only a label humans have given to ultimate stupidity. I talk about this in chapter 6 on how this has plagued mankind since the beginning of time with the stupid constantly attempting to gain control over the smart. They always do this in an attempt to prove that they are not really stupid, but really smart.

This has been depicted as the battle of good against evil but I contend that this is *not* the case. I contend that it is actually: A battle of the smart against the stupid. What is more, this has been going on since the beginning of human existence. I don't like to admit this because it is not a very comforting thought but, it appears that the stupid side is winning right now. This is some scary stuff but take heart; there is a solution to being ruled by a bunch of stupid people. I cover all of this and more in chapter 6. But first we need to understand how the brain works in chapter 3 and possible human intervention for increasing the intelligence of humanity through the use of RAI in chapter 5.

Reader's Notes

Chapter 3 - The Brain

In this chapter, I present a plausible explanation for how the brain produces intelligence and in the next chapter the subsequent requisite process known as "thought". In order to accomplish this goal, I present the brain in a systematic approach, starting with the hardware humans currently are aware of along with some of the methods currently used to explain brain function. Then I make an attempt at an explanation of my hypothesis of brain storage architecture and theories of the phenomenon of consciousness. I continue the discussion in chapter 4 by presenting an understandable explanation of how the brain produces thought and understanding. By the end of chapter 4, the reader should have a grasp of the principals behind the production of intelligence and thinking. I will demonstrate that the key to understanding thought is attempting to understand the purposes of consciousness. There are no provable theories of the mechanism of consciousness, nor are there even available methods suggested for doing that. We will need to accept that consciousness is indeed a strictly physical phenomenon and *not* algorithmic in nature. I believe I provide ample proof for that view and once we do that, the explanation of intelligence and thought become a much simpler prospect to understand. I start my presentation with two classical neuroscience methods of brain function.

Cognition, recognition and consciousness

Cognition or recognition (remembering what we were cognitive of in the past) and consciousness are two very different things. Cognition is being aware of new things. Recognition is the means at which we identify past things. Consciousness is the means by which we are aware of all things. I will explain the various theories of consciousness in detail in the latter part of this chapter as well as my own views. So I ask the reader to place consciousness on the back burner for the time being and the discussion of cognitive processes will come first. Cognition and recognition includes use of all the inputs humans use to detect the outside world in order to communicate with other humans and for survival which are: Sight, hearing, touch and taste. The main outputs humans use are: Speech and physical manipulation of objects with the hands and feet. The outputs are included in cognition because we need to be cognitive of our physical actions in real time.

The term used for the entire set of actions humans do is called *cognitive processes*. The way cognitive processes are produced by the brain has been studied and sometimes explained by two main methods: Neural networks and Cognitive Neuropsychology. The misconception that may arise in using the term "cognitive processes" is that one may surmise that these methods provide explanations for cognition, recognition and consciousness; but that is not the case. Cognitive processes only attempts to describe the attribution level of actions that humans are capable of. For example, the study of the attribute of color recognition as the mechanism or the pathways the brain uses in that attribute is one cognitive process.

Other examples of attributes might be: Speech recognition and interpretation, speech production though external processes such as reading, manipulation of motor processes with eye coordination, etc. In other words, all the defects people can become afflicted with because of brain trauma or disease can be modeled in an attempt to identify which area of the brain and what specific pathway is responsible for each attribute. The underlying root processes of cognition, recognition and consciousness are not addressed in these methods at all. In other words these methods do not explain how the brain actually produces cognition, recognition or consciousness. They only identify specific pathways the brain uses to accomplish these attributes. However, this is not a concern for the purpose of this exploration into intelligence production because I am only using this aspect of brain function mapping (that's one way to name it) as a debarkation point to start the journey to intelligence production. We need to start somewhere, and this provides an understandable foundation.

Two methods of cognitive processes modeling

The first method is usually called computer neural network modeling. It can also be thought of as connectionist modeling. The connectionist moniker arrives from the many connections of the many neurons that comprise the whole structure. This method attempts to explain brain function by use of computer programs known as neural networks. These are simulation programs in which a representative section of the brain is modeled after the exact way the brain is thought to be wired. This method has limited capabilities in that only small functional areas of the brain can be simulated. This is due to the vast number of neurons and the many connections between each that are required to complete even the smallest functional area.

Functional areas are things such as speech and face recognition, depth perception, motor control and coordination are a few examples of function areas that can be modeled. Up to the time of this writing I am unaware of any successful attempt at neural network modeling of the entire brain that would be of use in explaining how intelligence or thinking is produced.

The second method is known as cognitive neuropsychology and is an attempt to explain brain function by breaking the brain up into functional areas and by applying some common sense rules to those areas. The functional areas are labeled "modules". Modules are categorized with respect to the attribute of function as accomplished in a real brain. Brain function is then postulated by the intercommunication between modules. Nearly all brain function has been explained with this method except for the most important functions of all: Cognition, recognition, consciousness and what we call "thinking" or i.e. the production of intelligence.

In summary, we have two basic methods for describing how the brain does its job. The connectionist approach has value mainly for research into the micro functionality of the brain. In other words, simple single functions, not macro complex functions can be modeled. Cognitive Neuropsychology has more promise for explaining how the brain actually works. I elaborate on each next. I reiterate that neither of these methods yet has any capability of describing how the brain produces cognition, recognition, thought or consciousness. While this may seem strange given the medical profession's lofty position as the authority on everything that is the human body, the fact remains that these basic functions, which comprise intelligence, put medical science at a complete loss at this time. It could be that a modified view of cognitive

Chapter 3- The Brain

neuropsychology may have some promise of describing how intelligence is produced at some future date but that is a matter for discussion which I will undertake shortly.

The connectionist approach

The connectionist, neural network explanation is by far, the most complicated and difficult by any efficient means to be easily understood. Medical science has had a difficult time in mapping the various brain functions using a purely connectionist approach. This is largely due to the complex nature of the brain's structure. The brain's circuitry is made up of some 100 billion neurons with an estimated 2 billion connections between each! Well, that's pretty much it for neural networks! There is really not much to say about this as it is doubtful it will ever be used to describe what my goals are here, which are to describe cognition, recognition and thought.

The functional area approach – Cognitive Neuropsychology

My goals in this writing are to provide a plausible explanation for thought. I want to stress that the way I will later be describing brain function is not necessarily exactly how the brain does what it does. I present my theories of brain function from a somewhat philosophical approach that could be the way the brain does things and if what I am describing seems to have logical roots, then it just may be that what I conjecture here might actually be true! I have done much research on neuroscience and there is at present very little in the way of understanding on how exactly the brain does what it does. I am talking about rational explanations for cognition, recognition, thinking and consciousness. I present an explanation for how the brain does these things but I will concede that my explanation may not be the only explanation but it is certainly one that works! That said, to continue the start of this journey, my opinion is that the right way to go to understand brain function is; the Cognitive Neuropsychology approach. This does not provide an exact description of how the brain does these things; it only describes *what* the brain does.

Modules

Cognitive neuropsychology is basically an interfaced functional area explanation of brain function. The functional areas are called modules. I have not yet explained what a "module" is. A philosopher by the name of Jerry Fodor is not responsible for the term but proposed the properties of brain modules. Fodor recognized that certain areas of the brain had to have a certain functionality, to do a specific job. There are nine properties proposed by Fodor but we only need to look at five which are the most interesting for this discussion:

Fodor's module properties

1. Information encapsulation – Processing within modules is unaffected by the information processed elsewhere in the brain. i.e.; modules are not interactive in their processing.
2. Domain specificity – Each module is specialized to process input from only one kind of stimulus domain.
3. Mandatoriness – Modules process whenever they receive input and process must continue until completion.

Chapter 3- The Brain

4. Innateness – modules are not formed through learning but are inborn (hardware).
5. Fixed neural architecture – Modules are associated with dedicated neural hardware, so different modules tend to call on different physical resources within the brain.

This sure looks like a description for a piece of human made technology, doesn't it? In fact when I first read about modules, I was taken aback by the similarity to embedded processors in electronics equipment I had worked on. In computer science each module could be represented by what is known as a "process". A process is a self-contained program that has a specific task.

We can view modules as areas of the brain that have distinctly different functions and the important aspect of this is: We are all born with these modules in place. Another way of stating the same thing is modules are hard wired in the brain; they are hardware. That means if our brain was assembled correctly when we were in our mother's womb, we will all have the exact same modules fully functional at birth, or at least at some later developmental stage, if the formative process continues after birth. This is property number 4 – innateness. I now briefly cover the other four properties:

Property 1 – Information encapsulation means that for example; your vision depth perception processing module should not interact with your hearing perception processing module. If it does, you will have problems with vision every time you attempted to view and listen to any stimulus simultaneously.

Property 2 – Domain specificity means for example; that your depth perception processing module (and all the other modules) was designed for that one job and that one job only. Once damage is done to a module, the chance of another module taking over that task is non-existent.

Property 3 – Mandatoriness means that whenever you are not sleeping and you open your eyes, your depth perception processing module for example, should be working. If it isn't, you will notice it the first time you try to pick something up and are unable to do so because your fingers do not end up where the object actually is. Unless you have some physical brain damage or you don't suffer from migraine headaches, this module (and all other modules) should be there working for your every waking moment.

Property 5 – Fixed neural architecture means that the same modules are located in the same physical localities of everyone's brain. For example "Broca's area" is known today as the area of the brain responsible for speech because of the findings of a doctor by the name of Broca.

The one caveat to property 5 is that there have been attempts to prove the total physical localization of modules and they have all been proven false to a large extent. This is most likely because of the brain's physical connectionist three dimensional layout which spreads out the functions of single modules over a wide physical area of the brain. For example, many doctors believe that the back of the brain is where all the vision processing takes place. In reality, over 70% of the brain is involved in vision processing in some way. The back of the brain may be where the majority on the processing takes place but that view doesn't account for a few rare cases happening in which the patients have problems not found by looking at activity levels in the area thought to be the only one. There is no doubt that modules exist but it seems that the

Chapter 3- The Brain

functionality may be spread to multiple locations in the brain. The important point is that whatever the physical layout of modules actually is, everyone is born with the same layout. This is property 4; innateness, which I started off with several paragraphs back.

Cognitive Neuropsychology is not an explanation for thinking

Fodor said he was cognizant of the inability of Cognitive Neuropsychology to explain things like thinking, reasoning and problem solving. I would be remiss if I didn't add to that list; cognition, recognition and consciousness. Consciousness was never addressed at all in Fodor's discussion, to the best of my knowledge. These functions can be viewed as the responsibility of what can be thought of as "central systems" in the brain. Fodor said that central systems are not informational encapsulated nor are they domain specific. Fodor admitted that it is doubtful whether any cognitive science will ever be able to explain how central systems produce "thinking"; hence - intelligence.

The last point made by Fodor is where I need to disagree with his assessment of the central systems utility as being referred to as a module. There may be a process (module) responsible for cognition, another for recognition, and a third module dedicated strictly for thinking. I refer to all as "central systems" for the remainder of this discussion. It is these three possible modules (perhaps more) that enable the production of intelligence. Fodor's opinion was obviously based on what was known about at the time, in terms of how the brain does the things it does. Later on in this chapter I propose a logical description of just that. Once we view the brain in a different perspective, we may change our attitude about what "central systems" are and exactly what they do. But first we need to examine modules and how they tie in to the whole picture.

Modules – what they do

Vision

Perhaps I should have labeled this section as: Modules - what *don't* they do, because they do everything for us to ensure that whatever stimulus inputs the brain has input to it; is in a form the brain can use. In other words, modules process raw data into an enhanced form that the brain can interpret. Raw data is: All the light that has bounced off of objects, sounds from everywhere, smells of foods / environment and all of tactile senses.

Throughout this presentation I will use vision as a descriptor for how the brain works. It is the simplest way to give examples on the brain's function. For vision modules, a good example is the visual depth perception processing module. In order to better understand how our depth perception system functions, it will be useful to examine how holographic images are recorded and displayed. While on a trip to Disneyworld over thirty years ago, I was amazed by the holographic images displayed on one of the rides in the park. One image was an attractive princess dressed in renascence garb about 18 inches tall and she looked completely solid when the projector was turned on. She looked completely real; as if you could touch her.

I did some investigation on holographic projection and I found some interesting facts. Holographic images make use of the fact that our vision system is designed to work in 3 dimensions. We not only make use of the light that is reflected off the front of objects (as in a computer screen) but we use the light that bounces off the tops, bottoms and sides of everything in our field of vision. The brain takes in all this raw data and processes it into a useful form and the net result is that we have depth perception; not from having two eyes but because of the depth perception module in the brain. A commonly held misconception is that we get our depth perception from the stereo effect of having two eyes. The stereo effect does contribute some of our depth perception but only about 30 – 40 %. If you close (or lose) one eye you still possess enough depth perception to move through the world and even drive an automobile.

The light reflected off of objects cannot be used directly since it contains light that originated from the sides, tops and bottoms of objects and *in between* the sides, tops and bottoms are what we call corners or in computer science terms; "edges". The back of the eyeball and retina is hemispherical. This means that light from edges (corners) of objects will not fall in a sharp line on the curved retina but in a band of possible correct locations for that line. Without depth perception processing our vision would be too blurred to be of any practical use to us. Edges, i.e. corners of everything would not be sharp but would be a thick band of edges that would appear as if they were vibrating in a blur. The brain has to process that visual information and sharpen up the lines that comprise the corners or in computer science terms; the "edges".

This is exactly what image processing software does. If you have ever used photo shop or any other image processing program, you now will learn how it sharpened up your photo. The software breaks up the entire photo into pixels and assigns a "container" for each one. Each container has all the intensity and color information for that one pixel and can be accessed and compared to all the other containers (pixels) which when combined is a complete pixel map of the entire photo. This is accomplished by using only three variables; the Red, Green and Blue variables (RGB) stored in each container, for each pixel. If each variable was represented by two bytes (a byte is 8 bits and a byte can store from 0 to 255) there would be 256 possible levels for each variable and when all three variables are combined, they give approximately 16 million color possibilities. If all three variables are each zero the color would be white and if all three are the maximum of 255 each then the color would be black. The values of everything in between the two extremes define the various colors that can be represented. When a photo file is selected for enhancement, the software puts every pixel into a container that has all the information that is required to describe the pixel, such as color, location in memory and its relative memory location in respect to all the other pixels in the photo file.

The program then looks into each container and does this doing a sweep of the containers from left to right and from top to bottom one horizontal line at a time, until the entire photo file is stored temporarily, pixel by pixel. Each pixel is then compared to the adjacent pixels and a table or record of all the parameters is kept. As the pixels are compared to their neighbors a decision is made to either decrease or increase the intensity and color based on the table of stored data just compiled. The program then changes the intensity and colors of the pixels closest to the perceived edges so that there are fewer pixels with the higher intensities and colors which are representative of an edge. The result is that edges are sharpened up by the program selectively lowering the intensity and color in the pixels leading up to the edge and intensifying intensity and color in the pixels that have been determined to be the edge.

Chapter 3- The Brain

Image sharpening software works by concentrating pixels in areas where the edges are determined to be. Our own depth perception processing module does the same thing! We are way more machine-like than we can imagine. Most of our depth perception is due to the depth perception module's image enhancement capability in processing the light that originates from the sides, tops, and bottoms of objects. When we are viewing a photograph or a flat screen television, our retinas only receive light from two dimensions, width and height. The light that originated from the sides, tops and bottoms of the original object has been lost in the recording of that visual information.

When we view a real three dimensional object, and everything surrounding that object in our field of view, the hemispherical retina is able to obtain all the incident side, top and bottom light data. If we didn't have image enhancing capabilities, the edges of every object we view would be blurred and not sharp. The depth perception module uses incident light data from the tops and sides to present the brain with an image processed for *distance* by using a comparison of real time data and archival data that was obtained and stored in an "evolutionary algorithm" (**A-3**) learning process. "Evolutionary" in this case does not mean Darwin's theory. We learn distances through a learning process and an enhanced image system.

Evolutionary algorithms are *not* algorithms that we obtained through the process of human evolution. On the contrary, they are algorithms that *evolve* in magnitude responses as we move through the world and learn about it. Our depth perception is as proficient as it is because we have learned since birth that objects are a certain distance away and that vital information is stored for use throughout life. If you have never spent any time in the vast outdoors, and then experienced being submerged in a continuous outdoor experience, you will notice that your long range depth perception improves with use. I have personally experienced this phenomenon. We are able to calculate distance because of the relative dimensions we see in the tops and bottoms compared to the sides of objects. This is a learning process that begins as soon as we begin picking up objects and moving through our world. The brain uses real time image data and stored image data and a historical record of 3 dimensional sizes (length, width and height) to determine current distance. The images are sharpened up to reduce confusion for further comparisons.

Face recognition is likely another separate module that works to identify other human faces for various reasons. As humans we are always looking for anything shaped like a face. This is hardwired into all of us, but why? It could be that it is the result of a module that works only to read the message that a face is sending. We communicate with a lot more than just words. Body language plays a large role and facial expressions are nearly as important as words. You cannot tell someone you love them while simultaneously looking at them as if you want them killed. They will know you are lying and completely insincere.

There has been much research done on facial expressions in several monkey species and this is their main method of communication. Humans also communicate with facial expressions but it sometimes goes consciously unnoticed by the both the sending and receiving party. We have expressions for happiness, love, hate, sorrow, fear, surprise and probably several others that I am omitting. The point is: we are all born with these. It is sort of a built in language that we don't need to learn or ever think about because it is all contained in a module. Think about this. We are all born with the innate automatic ability to smile if amused, frown if angered, etc. This is equivalent to possessing a built in language that is there automatically when we are born. A module is responsible for this processing and is an excellent example of the characteristics of modules. On the receiving end, and interfaced with the vision system, there must be a module that recognizes the expression on the sender's face.

The vision system is probably the most complex and process intensive modules of any in the brain. The reason for this is simple. We obtain most of the vital information about the world around us through vision and it is by far humanity's number one essential survival tool. It is doubtful whether anyone born blind would be able to learn enough about the world to survive without external help. I have profound admiration for blind people who lead active lives and are able to be successful in a variety of careers. It is the ultimate challenge for any human.

Hearing

My example of the depth perception module is only one of many built in programs the brain has that make outside stimuluses' useable to the brain. Hearing is another stimulus that is processed. The human hearing response "chops up" or compresses sound so that a small portion of what is presented to the ears actually reaches the central system(s) is utilized in real time and consequently gets stored. This is very similar to what the MP3 algorithm does and its development was enabled by the human hearing response. We all have a nature designed MP3 algorithm in the auditory module in our brain! I have done research on the human hearing response pertaining to the mechanisms involved. The information I have been able to obtain says our hearing response is not due to the mechanical aspects of ear canal design. The ways in which selective frequencies are eliminated would be all but impossible to do in a purely mechanical system. Since that is the case the only other plausible explanation is what I am presenting here. It is the auditory module that does this job.

The MP3 algorithm was developed by utilizing a model of the human hearing response. When auditory stimulus such as music is presented to the human ear, only about ten percent of what is actually presented to the ear is necessary hear the entire spectrum of music that was produced. This is what allows your teenage daughter to download a hundred songs a day (that you pay for) and keep them all on that tiny MP3 player you got her for Christmas. The MP3 algorithm is a program "routine" that reduces the size of any audio file by identifying the aspects of the music that humans don't hear anyway and it simply eliminates them.

Auditory researchers discovered the human hearing response through a series of experiments with real humans. Unfortunately, no one has ever addressed the purpose of having a hearing response such as humans possess. The researchers discovered something very important about human hearing but to the best of my knowledge, no hypothesis about why we have this response was ever made. No need to despair, for I have such a hypothesis! I explain it next. This may be an example of not seeing the forest through the trees.

There is a property in computer science called "entropy". The easy explanation of entropy is that it means the *simplest way to convey information is the best way*. The rationale behind this paradigm is that the fewer information points used by the sender to convey some transferrable usable information, the higher the probability will be that the described information will be

Chapter 3- The Brain

understood by the receiver. This is largely because the receiver has fewer information points to attempt to recognize and therefore the probability will be greater that the correct interpretation will be made. Another way of saying this is the "signal to noise" ratio will be increased by reducing the noise.

The reader may be asking, "OK Frank, so how does this enter into the picture of the human hearing response and the hearing module?" I'm really glad you asked. Think about how hearing would have been used for all but the last several thousand years of human existence. A real advantage to people in not so long ago times would be communicating at distance by simply "yelling". Yelling to your wife with some vital information like, "There is a bear behind the cabin!" might have been useful to have been heard correctly. If our hearing was designed to acknowledge the entire spectrum of sounds rather than the compacted version that we are programmed to accept, the chance of recognizing something yelled at a distance would be much less. This is only a hypothesis but it fits in here nicely as one of the important modules we have working for us full time; the auditory recognition module(s).

What I have just described could be thought of as part of speech recognition and there may be a separate module that uses processed auditory data from the human hearing response module and attempts to match the auditory data with data we call "words". If you have ever attempted to understand someone from another country with a heavy foreign accent you have an idea of what the speech recognition's module job is. Your hearing may be excellent but you still may not be able to understand someone's speech because of the inability of the speech recognition module to "recognize" the sounds that are supposed to be words. It is helpful to have known someone with the same type of foreign accent sometime in your past history.

Tactile

There needs to be modules that condition input stimulus in the form of touch, heat and cold to be presented to the central systems. For example, if you move from a warm climate to a very cold one, it will take some time to "acclimate" to the cold. What seems freezing a few days before becomes comfortable once you "get used to it".

What is really happening is the module that controls heat and cold sensing level is adjusting to conditions while your body adjusts its physical parameters. The way the tactile module adjusts for heat and cold sensitivity has to work in concert with physical systems such as circulation. As the physical body adjusts to cold climates, by restricting blood flow to extremities for example, the module will allow for a greater and greater exposure to colder temperatures. This requires a complex system that compares the temperature of the blood in the extremities and compares that to the temperature of the skin in the extremities. As the body is able to maintain the temperature of the skin, the module allows for longer exposure at lower temperatures. This is a real advantage in a survival situation and that's what we are all about; survival.

Taste and smell

The taste and smell modules are two of the most important survival tools mankind is endowed with. There is no doubt that our primitive abilities to identify possible threats in foods have been

Chapter 3- The Brain

largely subdued by modern lifestyles and civilization and the subsequent lack of experiential episodes. I believe this is partly due to the evolutionary aspect of the taste and smell module programs sensitivity that will adjust to current conditions and also due to the level at which we ignore things we are initially alarmed by but learn to "live with". It is important to note that what is going on with these changes are not algorithm procedural changes but changes to limits or levels that the system responds to. The programs in modules cannot be changed as they are hardware.

We ignore our olfactory senses and this trains our olfactory module to evolve to conditions we are regularly exposed to. We may be unfortunate enough to necessarily accept a job in a manufacturing plant that our sense of smell tells us we should not be there. In that case, we have little recourse but to accept the repugnant odors and get paid for our sacrifice. We are told that things that smell bad are not necessarily bad for us and we believe that. We usually have little choice, we have to believe that. I know that if I have a choice I will not subject myself to odors that I find offensive. Your brain is telling you something, you should listen.

Besides odors that may be harmful immediately to some physical bodily function, (like acids, corrosives, etc.) there is also the prospect of being exposed to strong smelling perfumes, after shave lotions and other man-made substances that may trigger severe reactions in some people. We believe that the odor itself is causing us to be sick but in reality it is what the olfactory module is reporting to the central systems. There may be some component in the perfume that the module is hardwired to identify as dangerous, and so the module prods you into believing you are getting sick so that you will remove yourself from the threat. In some extreme cases the extremely sensitive may become physically sick which demonstrates the power of the central systems over the physical body. Of course there is always the possibility that inhaled chemicals can actually make us sick whether they can be smelled or not. This is because the offensive chemical can actually enter the bloodstream by way of the lungs or skin. In this case the illness of the body is telling the brain that something is wrong. We perceive that as "being sick".

Our sense of smell and our taste buds can "acquire a taste" for things even if we are repelled initially by them. The necessity to consume things we don't find palatable initially may have some value in the game of survival. The brain learns to ignore the alarm signals in favor of survival. This is yet another module at work and although we never think of our taste buds being controlled by a computer program; that is exactly what is going on.

Miscellaneous Input Modules

There must be a pain module which monitors various physical body systems and outputs a pain signal to the central systems. There must be a fatigue module which outputs a fatigue signal to the central systems when bodily systems detect certain conditions. There must be a nausea module which monitors things like stomach activity and digestive systems and reports a nausea signal to central systems. There may even be a psychological depression module which monitors the central systems and reports back to the central systems with a depression signal.

The idea is that when you "feel sick" it is because a module, which is nothing more than a computer program, i.e. an algorithm; is telling your central systems that you should feel sick.

Chapter 3- The Brain

Your body cannot tell the brain directly to "feel sick" because it is way more complex than that. The modules are essential in that they have one job and one job only to do. Modules also have to be connected to dedicated resources. The "nausea module" would need to be connected to digestive systems only in order to detect a fault condition (need to throw up for example) so that it can report this condition to the central systems and you will "feel sick" and possibly regurgitate whatever it was you ate prior.

If the reader has noticed anything about what I just described above, it is that if any of the modules were to report in error that pain has occurred, or perhaps fatigue has occurred or even depression has occurred, the *central systems will respond as though it actually happened!* This is an astounding concept in that it identifies the source of many problems associated with real people today. Depression is a leading cause of disability and it could very well be that much of it is caused by nothing more than a computer processing mistake.

Another viable aspect of all of the above is that migraine headaches can mimic any brain problem that can occur because of disease or damage of any kind. It is not inconceivable that many problems with fatigue and depression are due to the same underlying cause; the migraine headache. Migraine headaches are most likely due to a lowering of activity in one module and that lower activity spreads to other modules that are interconnected through shared memory (explained shortly). This is what causes migraine aura, and all the smart neurologists in the world now recognize that it is low activity (they call it low metabolism which is actually a low stimulation rate) that is the root cause of the migraine head pain, not bulging veins, or any other cause.

Modules; like the rest of the brain and nervous system needs *and loves* stimulation. Some European counties have the right idea of sweating in a sauna and directly afterwards jumping into an ice cold lake. This provides so much stimulation to the brain that anyone doing this on a regular basis will be very unlikely to ever get a migraine, or feel depressed or fatigued for no apparent reason. That's why those people do it; it makes them feel great.

Besides all the ancillary problems migraines can cause, they can also produce head pain, which if you happen to be a migraine sufferer, will say that is the worse part. I believe that the low neurological metabolism caused by insufficient stimulation spreads to many areas of the brain and when the pain module is affected it causes the pain signal to be sent erroneously to the central systems. There is no physical reference point for the central systems to connect the pain to, so it manifests itself as head pain. This is my hypothesis so I cannot provide reference but it does make sense and it is at least *some* hypothesis.

In neurological terms, low stimulation is called "depression" not to be confused with the psychological term. Neurological depression means low activity (low stimulation rate) and in computer science terms, that would equate to slow processing ability. When one module experiences low processing ability the interconnected modules do not receive the stimulus they need to maintain a high processing ability. The net result is what is called "spreading depression" and this can eventually involve the whole brain and will render the migraine sufferer incapacitated.

Chapter 3- The Brain

Output modules

Since this book is about intelligence and stupidly, a discussion of output modules is not entirely relevant. The one exception to that point is to reinforce the concept that we are all born with innate brain functions and that definitive point is more proof that high intelligence is mostly a choice. It is unlikely that we are born with every module that allows us to survive with an absence of the most important survival tool hardware; the hardware that enables and produces intelligence.

Besides the facial expression control module I mentioned above there are many other output modules to consider. There are modules that control every muscle in the body including everything from constricting arteries to lifting weights with the legs. They control all the minute intricate control functions with the fingers which allow people to be surgeons, watchmakers, welders, artists and auto body technicians. Whenever you use your fingers to manipulate a tool to make something there are modules at work in your brain to perform these tasks. As the hardware for modules is in-born, the skills acquired amount to learning distances just as we do when we begin picking up things as a baby.

Those of us interested purely in the intelligence aspect of the brain will not be interested in the output module functions unless they are planning on building a cyborg type of intelligent machine. The only requirements would be vision and possibly hearing as input and perhaps a speech synthesizer as an output for a useful intelligent machine.

It should be noted that none of the described modules do anything that could not be accomplished by the programming of a modern computer. I do not profess to know how the brain performs any of the module functions and I have no reason to speculate on how they accomplish their tasks. The reason for my attitude is that I am not tasked with the duty of repairing anyone's brain. The main reason I have for any explanation would be to convey that concept into a manmade version at some point in time. I think it is safe to say that the depth perception programming would be the most challenging since it involves three dimensional image processing which is orders of magnitude more complex than the two dimensional type. It would also involve the use of a hemispherical shaped image detector for a camera. While these two things are a challenge, they are by no means nearly impossible to explain which cannot be said for the central systems which I describe below.

Central systems are far more difficult to explain whether we are describing the brain or duplicating brain function with artificial intelligence. I do need to at least propose some type of biological brain action theory for the explanation of cognition, recognition and thinking. I attempt to do that below. Before doing that, I need to explain the most important aspect of the brain's production of intelligence and its main enabler: Memory (storage).

One important aspect of output modules with respect to motor control (nerves controlling muscles) is the possibility that these types of control actions are also utilized by the brain to control memory locations. We have no problem understanding the way the brain controls our fingers but we have a tough time relating that type of action to the way we can locate stored artifacts in memory. I elaborate on these principals shortly.

Chapter 3- The Brain

The brain's storage architecture

Up to this point, I have given the reader a logical description of how the brain handles input stimulus and I briefly commented on some output functions that may play a role in the production of intelligence through memory access location control. Now I will attempt to present a logical view of how the brain stores input stimulus and some output information such as distance data (for depth perception) and perhaps even memory location data (for locating anything in memory). I base my assumption, on the way information is stored; on a purely logical viewpoint. What I am saying is; this is the way it has to be. If it were not this way, we would not have the capability to produce any sort of useful intelligence. Although what I am saying is an assumption, it is based on actual human capabilities and is a viable explanation for why we have the capabilities that we do.

One of the main hypothesizes in this book is that the amount of memory and the architecture of that memory is critical to the production of intelligence. In other words: Intelligence is dependent on size and structure of the brain's storage or memory device. There can be no production of intelligence without a memory structure that lends itself to that production. The size of memory is directly proportional to the level of intelligence. A small memory size will produce a lower level of intelligence than a large memory size; given that both have the same correct architecture (pathways) to begin with. In order to properly present this concept I will need to enter into the topic of human made computers.

Just as your human made computer has what is known as primary memory, the brain has to have "primary" memory just to manipulate information and operate all the storage functions necessary for intelligence. In the brain this is known as "working memory". In your home computer, this is the primary memory which is dedicated to the operating system which controls everything including control of all input and output data flow, scheduling of all tasks and programs running on the computer. Primary memory (sometimes referred to as main memory) is the solid state hardware that is usually in the form of integrated circuit devices called Random Access Memory (RAM). These usually plug into the motherboard of your computer. Secondary memory is the memory that is used for archival storage of anything you want to keep including software programs. This type is usually in the form of a hard disk drive (HDD).

The two types usually work together in what is known as "virtual memory". Virtual memory is orchestrated by the operating system of your computer. It is the amount of memory a program "believes" it has. What happens is that many transfers of data from the hard disk to the main memory take place and vice versa to give whatever program is running (such as a game) the impression that it has way more primary memory available to it than it actually does.

The main idea behind the two main types of memory is that the primary type is the type that the Central Processing Unit (CPU) can talk to. Primary memory has the speed that the CPU needs to keep up with data transfers in the form of instructions and data. Secondary memory such as the hard disk is too slow to directly interface with the CPU and thus needs to have a "dispatcher" to control the data from the hard disk secondary memory to the solid state primary memory which is directly connected to the CPU. The dispatcher is the virtual memory process contained in the operating system such as MS windows, Apple IOS, etc.

Chapter 3- The Brain

Virtual memory programming is and has been a topic of much research in computer science since the beginning of the digital computer. There are many different designs for how the operating system handles this important task and there is a huge disparity in performance of various designs. Hard disk drives have also been advanced to the point where it is physically impossible to make them any faster than what they are now.

It is more than interesting to note that all of this research on virtual memory software and hardware is due to one thing and one thing only: RAM is expensive! That's pretty much it; RAM costs way too much to implement a useful economical computer system with RAM only. The entire virtual memory paradigm could be completely eliminated if costs were not an issue and we used nothing but solid state memory without mechanical disks of any kind. There is also the issue of volatility which if power is lost; RAM loses the data it had stored in it. But in reality, hard disk systems could be used to store everything on shutdown only with large amounts of RAM used as the only memory devices for all data transfers during operating system function.

If you are a computer enthusiast then you are already aware that the size of RAM in the machines of today is astronomical compared to just a few years ago. The amount of RAM that is included or available is steadily increasing with time. You should also be aware that the RAM requirements of nearly all software have also increased dramatically in the same amount of time. For example, as the performance of games increases, so does the amount of RAM necessary to run those games increases in step. Why do you suppose that is so?

The simple answer is that high performance (like in gaming) requires a greater number of data exchanges between the CPU and whatever memory structure the computer has available as a resource. The term "data" can refer to anything stored in memory including the things that tell the CPU what to do (instructions) with data (numbers). All these data exchanges need to be done in the shortest amount of time possible. The only way to do that is with fast memory; the more fast memory, the better chance the virtual memory process will have of providing the gaming program (in my example) with enough fast memory that the gaming program needs. If you have been paying attention, you should note that the fastest computer with the highest possible performance would be one that has no secondary memory at all. This would be a machine that has only a large amount of primary memory, which would be fast enough to handle a CPU that is fast enough to do the intended job.

This is the basic concept behind my hypothesis of the role of a specific memory structure for the production of intelligence in the human brain. The production of intelligence is likely dependent on very high data transfer rates. There is really no way around that. The brain, just like any computer, simply has to use memory to manipulate data. While there are no instructions to be "fetched" from memory as in a human-made computer, the brain's hardware instructions in the form of cognitive neuropsychology modules (including the possible "central system module") provides all of the instructions on what to do with the data. The number data (information) is all the things we get from the input modules; pictures, sounds smells, tastes and physical sensations.

The big question is: What exactly is the architecture of the brain's memory system and is that the enabler of the high data transfer rates required for the production of intelligence? Another question might be: Does the brain rely on speed or architecture or both to achieve the required level of data transfer? I answer these important questions with an explanation of my theory of brain memory architecture. It turns out the architecture lends itself to high speed data transfers and so is the big enabler of speed as I posit below.

A shared look-through memory

To answer the questions in the above paragraph, we might attempt to analyze how the memory system functions. What is obvious to me is that the human memory system is what I call a "shared look-through memory". I will explain the look-through part first before moving on to the shared memory concept. These are both my own theories and the proof I have to substantiate them is pure logic. I don't know or care exactly how the brain accomplishes what I am hypothesizing; I only care what it does.

The look-through memory

I will again use an example of vision to illustrate this point. Human memory is very much like looking through a number of classroom projector transparencies every time we use our vision. The transparencies are an analogy of the brain's storage architecture and were created when we observed and stored the important objects in our life. They contain all the things we have seen in our past that are stored in our memory. Somewhere in your brain there is a "transparency" of perhaps your mother and father, your house where you grew up and every significant person's face you ever dealt with. There is a theory that proposes we may actually record the face of *everyone* we have ever seen in our entire life! Whether we can readily recognize those faces is the topic of another discussion best left to psychologists. I personally don't buy that theory because as we shall see the things that we remember are stored by a very specific mechanism I call consciousness intensity level. Routine boring memories are short lived. Painful, exciting or traumatic memories it seems are the ones easily remembered because they have been stored rather permanently. I will cover this in depth when I describe consciousness shortly.

Additionally, there are other things stored on those "transparencies". Things like what kind of feelings you have for that person, place or house you grew up in. Smells associated with the house and the woods behind your old house. If you hit your finger with a hammer while talking to someone that is also stored, along with the pain involved. Every sensory input you experienced will be on a "transparency" somewhere in your look-through memory, provided the criteria for storing that information was met at the time.

I now present an analogy that may be helpful in understanding my hypothesis. Imagine a high rise commercial building with a perfect square floor layout with about 900 floors. Imagine that the pupil of your eyeball is as large as an entire floor of the building. You are at the top and looking down through all the floors because the floors are made of glass. You have at your disposal a controller that can turn on the lights on each floor in sequence from top to bottom. If you want to find which floor has the office furniture arranged in the word "frank" you simply turn on the sequence switch and allow each floor to be lit up in succession. It is only a matter of time before you locate the floor with the letters "frank". This is a look-through memory and I believe this is essentially how mammalian brains are structured. Human brains probably have much more office space per floor and many more floors than say, a chimpanzee does, but the idea is the same.

It should be apparent that it is essential for all categories (sounds, smells and touch) of processed input modules data to be stored in the same physical location, i.e. the same transparency (floor in our high rise building analogy). The reason for this is that we need to access the entire attribute data of the main object and any relational data associated with it. When you are recognitive of someone's face, you know "who" that person is, what they have said to you, what the relationship they have to you is, if you have a like or a dislike for them, what their name is, etc. All of those attributes of the face you are looking at are essential or otherwise any memory you have of just the face would be meaningless. This is true for anything stored in memory. This has been theorized as being what is called the Object-Attribute-Relational (OAR) model of human memory, by AI researchers. **(A-2)**

I personally do not understand how any logical mind could disagree with this model. As I stated above, it is basically essential for any meaningful use of learned, i.e. stored information to have all relational and attributable data stored in close proximity to the object data. In addition to individual objects being stored with their attributes and what the relations are to other objects, we should realize that some of these relationships may serve to put objects into categories to simplify the brain's task of connecting a large number of objects as being in the same or similar category.

For example, we are all familiar with the automobile, and we also know instantly that there are other objects we refer to as "vehicles". Anything with wheels and an engine is instantly known to be some variation of the automobile. We don't need to ponder that relationship; it is already there and understood. Part of that understanding is because we have stored it, through what we call a learning process. The learning process is just a refined method of storing the information that is presented to us. The other part is how that information is stored, and that is essential to any beneficial use. This means storing a description of all objects such as the descriptors necessary to identify someone's face for example. Is the face someone you know and if so, is it a relative, neighbor, co-worker, etc.?

Shared memory

To summarize, I said that just as in a human made computer, the brain uses memory to store (temporarily or permanently) all the processed data from input modules for use as central systems needs arise. The question is: How do the central systems get access to processed data from input modules like visual, auditory, tactile and olfactory at the same instant?

For example while we are reading a book, we are accessing the words we read in memory and the meaning of those words (we shall see later that it gets stored as a concept) must be stored physically adjacently to the word symbol itself and this combined information is available to the central systems for recognition and interpretation. If we are reading aloud it is necessary for our speech producing module to have access to the very same memory locations that the visual module is using at the very same time. There is really only one way all these things can be inputted and outputted to a central system while simultaneously having an ability to compare real time data (temporary) with archived (permanently stored) data which is the primary function of recognition:

The way I'm talking about is: "shared memory". Shared memory is a commonly utilized technique in computer science that allows several processes, sometimes running on different machines, sometimes in different parts of the world to have access to the same data stored in the same memory location and on the same memory device.

Shared memory is what makes e-commerce and banking on the internet possible. Two computers, often located on the opposite sides of the world need to have access to the same data in order to perform any useful function, like balancing a checking account. Two or more processes running on your home computer often need access to the same data. The most efficient way of doing that is to simply allow both processes, to use the same memory. The two processes share the same memory, hence the term; shared memory. Duh!

Our brains utilize shared memory to make all intelligent behavior possible. The reason the central systems need access to stored archival data is so that we can "remember" or recognize things. We need the ability to "recognize" what we have seen, heard, felt, tasted and smelled in the past. The functional layout of the brain is obvious if thought about. This all means that central systems have access to a very specifically designed memory that is shared with all the modules. The central systems can access real time data and it can also access archival data for recognition. It is necessary for two or more modules to have access to the same data to produce the coordination between modules that result in useful functions. Some of these functions are speech, reading, driving an automobile, etc.

To repeat my above example, vision modules work in conjunction with speech modules when reading aloud. They both need to access the areas of memory that store the words (object), the meaning and pronunciation (attributes) and what category they are in (relation). The central systems simultaneously share this memory location with those modules in a supervisory role. I ask the reader to make note of this for the next chapter where I attempt to duplicate the brain in electronics hardware.

As a side note, all of this interaction between modules needs to be synchronized somehow, in order to provide timing. Without timing, the brain would have difficultly doing anything of a useful nature. Neurons work by "firing". If we can imagine a lattice (or network) of neurons all connected in a basic connection scheme that we are all born with this may provide some understanding of how this system works. The brain necessarily has a mechanism that a "wave" of neuron firings "sweeps" across the entire network. This wave probably starts in a central physical location of the brain (possibly the base of the brain) and sweeps across the entire macro neural network. This would provide a central timing mechanism which would be necessary in any system like this to synchronize the many different modules.

As the wave sweeps across a stored image for example, the synapses that are bridging the spaces between neurons the group of neuron-synapse families "output" whatever it is that happens to be stored there. Continuing with the vision example, the most likely scenario is that the rods and cones of the retina are connected to neurons in the brain that represent rods and cones in the memory structure. In other words, the places that store visual information are most likely just extensions of the receptors (the cones and rods) which are the originators of the visual information, whatever that information might be. Of course my interpretation of the brain neuron sweep is only a representation of what I feel would be necessary for a biological computer such as the brain to function correctly. I reiterate that I don't care exactly how the brain does what it does; I only care what it does.

So, when the "transparency" of neurons holding a loved one's face is output we don't consciously see the output; only we "see" it internally. This is an example of non-conscious **(A-1)** viewing of stored information. That internal visualization is used for recognition of the viewing in real time. The non-conscious image is compared to what we are consciously looking at and if a match occurs; we "remember". This probably happens because of a "recognition signal" that the brain understands. If you recognize anything, that means it has been stored somewhere in your memory. Images are probably stored in exactly the same form as we view them in. The term "non-conscious" is used to differentiate between the term "sub-conscious" which promotes the connotation of being somehow subordinate which it definitely is not. I will now explain conscious and non-conscious processing.

The mystery of consciousness

Consciousness has nothing whatsoever to do with intelligence. The reason many people connect consciousness with intelligence is due to the belief systems we operate under as humans. Consciousness is not the ability of "self-awareness" as many people believe. It is actually the ability to be aware of *everything*. Consciousness is the ability of the "mind" to "see" things and be cognizant of all things, including one-self. The truth be told, there is actually no requirement of "self-awareness" in consciousness. There are many other animals that probably employ consciousness; some of which may not be self-aware such as alligators. It is also possible that any animal that sleeps will be endowed with consciousness. I explain this in more detail below. In order to provide the reader with a simple explanation of what consciousness actually is, I will turn to a Hollywood movie.

The alien inside the alien

If you saw the movie "Men in Black" there was one scene in which a tiny alien was inside and at the controls of a human appearing robot. For all intents and purposes it appeared that this robot was indeed a real person. However once the "hatch" was opened the little alien could be seen sitting in a little chair, operating the little controls. One way of looking at this is that the alien was the robot's conscious "inner self".

Recall my explanation of how the brain processes, stores and presents visual information. This will provide an easy way to understand that the real time visual information stored also gets presented to "something" so that we can "see". The question is: Just what exactly is that "something"? The only way of creating a straightforward simple understanding of how an image is actually "seen" is to imagine another entity looking at whatever was presented to the inner self (the little alien in the above example). We would need a little alien inside each of the little aliens. This could go on forever and it is obvious the process has to end somewhere. As President Harry

Chapter 3- The Brain

Truman once said, "the buck stops here" and we need the buck to stop at the very first alien for to continue would only be postponing and never solving the problem. This is the difficulty in understanding consciousness.

One very large mistake that is routinely made by CS AI people when discussing consciousness is that they include more of a logic aspect to the problem than they should. A very compelling reason for them to believe that consciousness is algorithmically derived has roots in an incorrect or distorted ideology of what consciousness fundamentally is. One of the reasons why we have a problem with consciousness is that the name throws us a curve ball. A better term would be: "World Interface".

Consciousness in humans is not a logical or algorithmic phenomenon at all. It is simply the physical "boundary waters" or "interface" between some physical stimulus and some acknowledgement of whatever that stimulus is. When we "see" things we say that we are "conscious" of things. What is really happening is that light has bounced off of the things that we see and has struck the retina in the back of our eyeball. The vision modules then process the image into a more digestible version and it is this processed image that is presented to the neurons in the brain that are subjected to or possibly ultimately responsible for the phenomenon of consciousness. The exact mechanism of consciousness is a subject for conjecture and I make an attempt at explaining that shortly. The point is that consciousness has to be a physical process and I do have reasons for believing that, it's not only my opinion.

The light from the objects we view has been converted into internal neuronal signals in the brain. It is only the conversion of those neuronal signals into a viewable image in the brain that encompasses the phenomenon of consciousness, nothing more; nothing less. It is a purely physical property and as such does not require the moniker of logic whatsoever. Any logic applied to the images we "see" is done after the process of consciousness has done its job; not before.

If the hypothesis of a totally physically enacted consciousness is true and I believe it is, we are now left with a somewhat simpler problem to solve, which is: How does the brain convert the patterns of light which have been reflected off objects; into a viewable image that we see? Any attempt to prove that this phenomenon happened because of some logical or algorithmic function will undoubtedly prove to be an intractable problem. Any purely algorithmic explanation of consciousness will impose the undeniable fact that we would not be conscious to ourselves but only have the attribution of consciousness to others, and we know that is clearly not the case. What this means is if consciousness *was* purely algorithmic, humans would only *appear* to be conscious by other humans. We would act and react in the same way, only our internal experience would be no experience at all and as I just alluded to, we know that is clearly not the case.

If we were not physically conscious we would be very different creatures, indeed. For one thing; we would not actually "see" things. We would react to things just as we do now. We would appear to have emotional feelings like anger, love and hate only we would not actually "feel" these emotions; we would only have the "attribute" of feeling these emotions to others. In other words we would appear to others just as we do now; but our own experience would be drastically

Chapter 3- The Brain

different. Others would appear to be conscious through merely the attribution of consciousness but we would not appear to be conscious to ourselves! We would all be just like robots that were programmed to act intelligently. While this may sound perplexing, it is not vastly different from what we are. We are programmed to act intelligently and just like a properly programmed algorithmically conscious robot, we do have the power of choice and making decisions. Since consciousness is not a logical phenomenon, we would make the same choices and the same decisions.

We also need to remember that being human does not make us members of some exclusive club which provides as part of our membership the exclusive club benefit to consciously see, hear, touch, and experience emotions. All higher order animals, most certainly mammals such as field mice have the same benefits of consciousness. I also believe some very primitive animals such as alligators and crocodiles possess consciousness, simply because they sleep and they are cognitive and recognitive. I explain cognition and recognition in the next chapter. All of these paradoxically sounding ideas will be clearer as I explain what consciousness is for.

The purpose(s) of consciousness

Biological physical consciousness must have some benefits over a purely logical, purely algorithmic mechanism. The reason I say that is simply because we are here, we exist and we possess consciousness, along with many other animals; so there must be some advantage. The question is: Why do we have a physical system for our interface with the rest of the world when it seems that a pure algorithmic albeit more complex system might work? One key piece of evidence lies in what I just said. Simplicity is the normal mode of nature, not complexity. There are many very complex things in nature that are enabled by very simplistic underpinnings. The mammalian brain is a prime example of the simple concepts underlying complexity of systems paradigm. A pure algorithmic system would need to be way more complex as I explain by exploring the possible reasons for consciousness.

Consciousness as a peace and quiet controller

Perhaps one answer to the above question and one of the possible purposes is that consciousness is the brain's simple automatic shutdown/startup mechanism. As we wake up in the morning, brain activity; which is controlled by an internal biological clock begins to increase algorithmic processing activity intensity of modules in the brain. The input modules begin to process stimulus activity from the eyes, ears, olfactory and tactile sensors. At the same time the central systems begin to increase processing levels. As the activity or in other words; stimulation (brain metabolism) increases, the physical consciousness mechanism turns on and we begin seeing, hearing feeling and smelling external stimuluses' again. It is similar to switching on a light bulb. During the shutdown phase when we are falling asleep, processing activity in all modules and in the central systems decreases until the "fire" of consciousness is extinguished, all the sensory inputs are turned off for peace and quiet and we are sleeping.

In both cases of shutdown and startup, it is the stimulation *rate* of neural network metabolism which controls the turn-on and turn-off, of consciousness. High metabolism or fast stimulation rate turns on the consciousness "fire" and low metabolism turns it off. It is nature's way of

Chapter 3- The Brain

providing a way to decrease brain activity so that vital neurotransmitter replenishment mechanisms work unaffected by external nuisances. It permits a total shutdown and corresponding rest and relaxation of the brain without being disturbed by sights, sounds, smells or feelings.

Consciousness as nature's mitigation device

Another possibility is that consciousness is a property of life itself and is necessary in biological computers such as the brain because of the shear variability that the brain is subjected to on a regular basis. Consciousness may be a necessary mitigation-normalization-compensation technique that helps keep brain function on an "even keel". When we consider how much everyday substances like coffee and alcohol change the capabilities of everyone, we can get a feel for how neurotransmitters can be affected by just the foods we eat or don't eat. Consciousness may be a way to deal with nutritional deficiencies and other threats to neurotransmitter balance.

Consciousness might be due to a type of field which is produced by the brain and in turn the brain reacts to. A hypothetical example is that the field produced by stimulation of neurons acts as negative feedback to oppose any further stimulation which can occur in a small time period. It may limit the spread of overstimulation which could cause as many problems as insufficient stimulation. This is analogous to inductance in the movement of electrons through a conductor. Movement of electrons creates a magnetic field and that magnetic field momentarily inhibits electron flow. I cover the concept of a field induced consciousness in greater detail below with a discussion of the Rodger Penrose theory.

Consciousness as a memory controller

A major problem in a storage and retrieval system like the brain are the decisions on what gets stored and what doesn't get stored in memory. Consciousness may provide a simple mechanism for storage selection by only providing long term storage for objects that are input at a high level of consciousness. This would require a simple "consciousness level control" that cranked up the "intensity" of consciousness with the level of concentration, excitement, agitation or stress.

Concentration for example, requires an increase in processing and the increased metabolism intensity results in an increase in consciousness level. Low intensity means low consciousness and high intensity means high consciousness. With this paradigm, the only time the objects in the "working memory"; i.e. things we can consciously see; are stored, is at a high consciousness level and a high consciousness level only happens with a high level of concentration, excitement, stress or trauma. This provides a simple way to conserve memory. The simple act of observing something new and interesting may trigger a high processing response and a corresponding high consciousness level to get the new object stored.

This is why we need to concentrate on things in order to remember them. When we are exposed to routine things that we have been exposed to over and over, this low activity does not invoke a high consciousness intensity. Therefore this lower activity does not push the consciousness into a higher intensity level. This means that once we have seen something more than a few times, like the houses we live in, we have no need to store it any more than it already is. Since the act of viewing the same old stuff invokes no increase in processing speed the consciousness intensity level stays low and memory is conserved.

This is why we remember dreams which always occur when we are either falling asleep or waking up. We don't remember anything that happens when the consciousness "switch" is turned off, i.e., when we in deep sleep and are unconscious. I use the term "switch" because this is the terminology used in a clinical description of consciousness in several medical journals. A change in algorithmic processing iterations cannot by its own merits, explain the way in which consciousness turns off and on. An analogy is that when you turn up the volume on an MP3 player, the music becomes louder but it is the same music. The programs we are born with are hardware and the code contained in those programs cannot autonomously morph into changing algorithms. The "switch" phenomenon defies explanation for any logic based algorithmic theory of consciousness. Something turns on when the processing levels get to some threshold and that something has to be a physical mechanism.

I believe it is safe to comment that people, who have many disturbing dreams throughout the night, are probably not getting a beneficial restful sleep. This is because in order to remember a dream, we must be coming out of a shutdown phase and going into an increase in consciousness intensity. This means that stimulation intensity on average is way too high for neurotransmitter replenishment mechanisms to be effective and beneficial. If my hypothesis is correct, the best night's sleep is uninterrupted and dreams should only be a phenomenon during shutdown at bedtime and wakeup after many hours of sleep (current research says at least 7). This also reinforces the notion that we don't remember anything unless the consciousness intensity level is high enough. This is why we remember dreams only during wake-up or shut-down. This also explains why people who have had very traumatic experiences have a hard time forgetting what they would love to purge from memory. The level of consciousness intensity during those experiences was at very high levels and whatever happened was stored rather permanently, unfortunately.

The phenomenon of dreams leads to many unanswered questions, however. There is a conundrum of why we are able to actually "see" and "hear" our dreams when these should be non-conscious events. Dreams are actually more mysterious than consciousness when these facts are brought into the mix. We are in some state between the conscious and non-conscious state but in this case, instead of internally visualizing as we do when we are fully conscious and thinking about someone's face, we can actually see things like faces and hear things such voices and music.

It must be that the thalamic switch (I explain this below) is like a main circuit breaker on a power panel so that when opened, nothing gets through to the area of the brain that accepts the conscious picture, sound, tactile or smell. When this switch is turned off entirely we are totally out and don't remember the dreams that are apparently occurring on a regular basis, unknown to us. This means that while dreaming there must be a third mode the brain operates in where high local activity results in a consciousness intensity that is even higher than normal awake consciousness intensity in memory areas but the main circuit breaker is off so we don't

Chapter 3- The Brain

remember anything unless that main circuit breaker begins to develop a short and we actually begin to wake up.

This may happen to some people while in a full conscious state and would explain why routine hallucinations are possible in some people who are deemed to have some type of mental illness. People who suffer migraine headaches also can experience hallucinations and I am one of them. I speak with firsthand knowledge of this phenomenon and there is no doubt in my belief system that what I have just described could very well be the truth.

Consciousness as a comparator register

As conscious beings who can "see" and be "cognitive" of objects, we need to identify the objects we are recognitive of and the "world interface" of consciousness provided physically displayed image makes the identification process much faster and is requisite of fewer memory and control resources. This might be another benefit of consciousness in that it is the part of the brain that we are currently cognitive of objects and then compare those to objects in archival data. Archival data are things we have learned previously and are stored in memory. This is a convenient way for a biological system to differentiate the present from the past, even if the past was only a fraction of a second prior. In other words, another benefit of consciousness is that the conscious "lit up" area of the central systems acts as continual buffer area for quick comparisons to be done between current real time data (which is constantly dynamic) and recent to very old historical, archival data.

When we are viewing anything, we know instantly if we are viewing that object for first time or if we have viewed it many times or even just once prior. We can do this because the current compared artifact key is in the lit up area of our consciousness. It is the object we say we currently "see" or in other words; are cognitive of. Without consciousness, the brain would to process everything in an algorithmic fashion, and of course we would only have the attribution of being conscious to others who observed us reacting to that object.

In an algorithmic system, the brain would necessarily need the same type of architecture found in human-made computers. There would have to be a dedicated area of memory reserved for only current real time object artifacts and that area would necessarily have some sort of pathway for easy comparison to any archival object artifacts stored in other memory locations for recognition. There would also need to be a complex controlling mechanism for storing any pertinent objects presently in the real time memory location by a transfer mechanism to archival memory. This is the kind of complexity typically not found in nature and is not necessary in nature's look-through memory I described previously. Nature's method provides us with a quick and efficient method to compare what we can "see" (conscious) to all the other stuff we have in memory that we can't "see" (non-conscious).

If you want to experience the difference between consciously viewed information and non-conscious stored information just think of someone's face. You can internally visualize it but you cannot actually "see" it. This is non-conscious viewing of archival memory. What I have just described is a prime example of simplicity being the underlying mechanism for very complex performance. Simplicity is a hallmark of nature. If we were conscious of archival objects in

Chapter 3- The Brain

memory (as we are in a dream; which is merely the accessing of memory), we wouldn't know what the real time information was and what prior information was. This would be big time confusion on a royal scale.

Would an algorithmic system work?

A purely algorithmic system of consciousness in a biological computer like the brain is in itself a paradoxical proposal. Nature works on simplicity and a system that accomplishes exactly what biological consciousness does would be necessarily super complex. In the next chapter, I will propose a method for doing just that and when the basic functions of biological consciousness are analyzed for emulation it becomes clear just how much complexity that endeavor would entail. If we use the purposes of consciousness I have just proposed, it should become evident that there are some that have no true algorithmic substitute.

For example in the consciousness as a peace and quiet controller, doing this in a pure algorithmic system would be impossible. I challenge any CS expert to write an algorithm that would perform the same function with no hardware control requirement of any kind. The same thing can be said for the mitigation aspect of consciousness, if in fact that theory is correct. That is a description of hardware inadequacies and no software solution could work for that either. Consciousness as a comparator register is theoretically possible but as I have alluded to would be necessarily complex.

The one aspect of consciousness that could possibly be implemented in software and the most complex part of an algorithmic alternative would be the conservation of memory paradigm in the consciousness as a memory controller purpose. I have proposed that the brain conserves memory by only permanently storing the information that is important and that is done with consciousness intensity levels. In the biological brain there is always some element of emotional guidance that provides passion or interest in things that we decide are important. Traumatic things such as life changing events are recorded permanently and this is because an emotional component of thought caused a corresponding increase in consciousness intensity during exposure to that event.

The big question is; how could memory conservation be done in a strictly algorithmic system? It is not easy by any means and I will address this topic further in the next chapter. Suffice it to say that the complexity of the needed algorithms is way beyond what is normally found in nature and if in fact we discovered that humans actually operated that way we would have to give credence to the theory that space aliens were responsible for programming us. I find the comments I have read pertaining to consciousness and why we have it rather than an algorithmic system to be laughable at best. The so-called "experts" who make comments such as that are making one of the cardinal sins of not following the intelligence algorithm in that they are commenting on topics they really have no firsthand knowledge about.

Writing a program that emulates the storage controlling aspects of consciousness would require that entire sets of concepts of all the attributes and relations of every object we were cognitive of (another complex algorithm) were somehow judged to be placed in orders of *importance*. The objects judged to be of high importance would be the ones to be stored. I believe it's safe to comment that nature's way of doing this is the better way, at least for a biological computer and that's what we are.

Purpose(s) of consciousness – summary

To summarize, consciousness may have several highly beneficial purposes including:

1. Peace and quiet controller to eliminate disturbances during the brain's important shut down neurotransmitter replenishment mechanism.
2. May be a mitigation-normalization mechanism needed for inherent variability in biological systems.
3. A memory storage controller in which information only gets stored in times of high concentration by controlling consciousness intensity levels.
4. A real time buffer for comparing to archival stored information in order to perform cognition and recognition. I explain both of these modes of thinking later in this chapter.

How is consciousness produced?

So far I have only proposed what turns the consciousness mechanism on and off (intensity levels). I have also provided some interesting possibilities for the purpose of consciousness. The next logical question is: If brain activity is the cause, what is the mechanism that produces the result? In other words, what exactly happens in the brain to produce consciousness? The consciousness mechanism produces one of the most mysterious phenomenons ever presented to humans as a problem to solve. It is the "alien inside the alien" forever problem. When we "see" something what does the "seeing"? We say it is "us". Perhaps it is evidence of a soul.

The soul hypothesis really is a convenient explanation and it answers a bunch of questions at once. If in fact we really possess a soul, we have no need to do any further explanation of what does the "seeing". If it is the soul that comprises our consciousness, we could say: "Case closed." However there are some indisputable facts that tend to counteract this hypothesis and they present themselves in the form of medical symptoms. This explanation requires some background:

When we are sleeping and not dreaming we are said to be in a "sub-conscious" state. We could say that consciousness is the opposite of sub-consciousness but that is not entirely true. It is more correct to say that consciousness is the opposite of "non-consciousness". This is an important distinction to make because non-conscious activity is what drives (or enables) conscious activity. It is not subservient in any way; in fact the exact opposite is true. There are basically two types of non-conscious processing. The first type is exactly like conscious activity (thoughts and thought trains) only at a lower intensity level. The second type is module processing which we should never be aware of and aren't unless there are problems. What I am about to present has to do with the second type.

The fact that we are not readily cognizant of all the processing going on in the background does not make it any less important. I discussed the various modules as being program processes that clean up and enhance the outside world for the central system to be able to use. We are not aware of this processing unless something goes wrong. When people experience a visual migraine headache aura, they are witnessing firsthand what the vision processing modules do for them on a continual basis.

Migraine headache auras are visual disturbances that can literally punch holes in a migraine sufferer's consciousness. Recall that I described a migraine as the result of low processing in modules which can lead to low stimulation and a resulting "spreading depression", again not to be confused with psychological depression. When visual modules lose processing capability; the result is that the person will actually see (be conscious of) the processing errors that the modules are making. This can manifest itself in many ways, including what is called "mosaic vision" where every object in the field of vision is no longer "cleaned up" with nice sharp edges. The objects will appear to be "constructed" out of blocks; very similar to a child's building block set.

The reduced processing in the visual modules that result in mosaic vision can progress into more and more severe vision calamities. As processing slows down, so does stimulation and eventually this results in that module experiencing severely reduced firing rates of the neural networks in that module. This can lead to a condition known as "scotoma"; which is usually a very jagged black hole in the field of vision. In really severe cases, the migraine aura sufferer will not even know that they have a hole in their vision. In other words the migraine sufferer will not be conscious of the hole. This is called; "negative scotoma" and has been documented in several migraine patients.

In one of these cases, a woman suffering from severe migraine for several days was hospitalized because of the complications that can arise from not being treated. Some of the complications can even include the migraine aura becoming permanent; as is the case with me (I explain my sob story in chapter 7 – The Medical Profession). In the reported story of the woman's case; she complained that she was going to be hungry by only getting a half plate of hospital food, when in reality she indeed had a full plate of food in front of her! She was only cognizant (conscious) of the left half of the plate and what was more; she was not even aware that the entire right half of her vision was missing!

This medical case study example backs up the hypothesis that consciousness is a physical property. When processing levels reach a certain low limit, there is not enough energy in that part of the brain to produce consciousness. There is a continuum phenomenon here. Scotoma occurs with some low processing rate and then the more severe form of negative scotoma, can occur with an even lower processing rate. This last type is the negative kind and is named thusly because it can actually negate consciousness.

I believe these documented medical cases shoots down any notion of the soul being the originator of conscious activity. It also casts serious doubt on an algorithmic basis of consciousness. The reader is invited to believe anything they want but I would suggest always taking the most logical path. Conditions like migraine aura also back up the theory that consciousness is produced by physical local activity on possibly the atomic level which I will cover shortly.

Chapter 3- The Brain

Dr. Oliver Sacks claims that there is probably much more negative scotoma happening than is what is known about, since the people that have this problem are totally unaware of it when it happens. I have some advice to people with any type of migraine headache whether you suffer vision problems or not. If you have a migraine or migraine vision problems, stay home, don't drive, if you do you are taking a big risk. The spreading depression from a migraine can also cause severe low processing of the central systems, which means you may be making bad decisions, making incorrect assessments and generally you may be prone to making lots of mistakes. You don't even need to have a headache to suffer from "brain fog" that is a result of low processing in your non-conscious and conscious mind. Yes, pain in the head is *not* a requirement!

Non-conscious activity is activity that "runs in the background" and is responsible for all of our underlying intelligent behavior. It is running all the time but we are totally unaware of its existence. This is a difficult concept to grasp but it makes total sense if it is presented logically. For example, is it possible for anything to happen without an underlying cause? Can an airplane take off without the wings producing lift? Can a car roll down the road without some sort of engine powering it? Can a light bulb produce light without electricity? All of these things have underlying causes and our intelligence is no different.

We cannot produce spoken words without all the processing necessary to produce those words taking place, prior to that speech. It is impossible for us to accomplish any task without some prior processing taking place beforehand. This is just common sense if you think about it. Everything we do is pre-processed by all of our modules including central modules (or central systems) before the task at hand actually happens.

We could say that all of us have dual personalities. There is our conscious outer self and there is the non-conscious inner self that really is controlling everything. There can even be conflicts between what the conscious decides and the non-conscious believes may be a wrong decision. Much of this behavior is dependent on the level of brainwashing an individual has undergone.

If we were brought up by our parents to believe certain things are immoral, this will manifest itself in a non-conscious belief system that will attempt to make us feel guilty if we stray from those teachings. For example, even if our logical mind tells us it is OK to eat meat on Friday, we still may feel pangs of guilt if we were brainwashed sufficiently as a kid by our parents who were following the tenants of the Catholic church and the ritual banning of eating meat on Fridays. This behavior will be stored in memory forever for use by our non-conscious mind in pushing the conscious mind to make our decisions.

The non-conscious mind can also help us in many positive ways. I have often done home improvement projects in which I have been amazed at how things turned out without me consciously thinking of everything I was doing. It was my non-conscious mind doing all of the figuring. For example, things like amounts of Portland cement needed for a specific masonry job turn out to be so close that very little is wasted after it is mixed. If you perform a skilled task enough times, things just seem to work out as you do it again. Ask any skilled tradesman and they will tell you of similar experiences.

Chapter 3- The Brain

To understand what the non-conscious does we only need knowledge of what logical iterations the conscious does and accept that the non-conscious iterations are responsible for the conscious iterations. As in the above example we can also acknowledge that the non-conscious does much more than the conscious as it requires much more processing running underneath to support what is apparent on the surface. This may be a difficult concept for many people to grasp but it really is not difficult when we examine consciousness itself and come to the realization that it has many intensity levels, the highest level being the level that makes us aware of everything. The lower levels are the ones that are responsible for the non-conscious mind.

Consciousness theories

There have been many theories presented that have attempted to explain how the brain produces consciousness. One theory is that consciousness is nothing more than an illusion produced by the brain. I have been a proponent of this theory only to change my mind when I realized that any "illusion" would require "something" for the brain to present that illusion to. It is this "something" that is the big conundrum. Stating that consciousness is just the result of an illusion is a complete denial of the complexity of the problem and is a giant cowardly ruse. We can take the easy explanation way out, but that would change nothing and it only accomplishes a convenient side trip to wasted time and energy.

We usually label the "something" "I" or "us", "we", "me", 'you", etc. The problem with this labeling is that there is no "I", "you'" or "me" or any of the other labels, there is just the brain. If the brain produces any illusion, it is the illusion "we" have of our "selves". The act of producing consciousness is what produces the illusion of "self", but that still doesn't explain how consciousness itself is produced.

The neuroscience theories of consciousness

There are currently three main theories of consciousness that neuroscience takes seriously. These are:

1. Higher Order
2. Global Workspace
3. The Biological Theory

1. Higher Order

This theory makes use of the HOT acronym for the term, "higher order thought". This theory basically says that stored representation of anything combined with a current real time example of the same or at least similar stimulus is what produces consciousness. The problem I have with this theory is that is fails to explain how consciousness is actually produced. It merely is a description of what happens during the recognition process. The people that promote this theory are not cognizant of the fact that in order for us to "have thoughts" we must have something stored in memory to "think about".

Chapter 3- The Brain

In other words, this theory requires some memory or storage of artifacts in order for there to be consciousness produced on any logical level. This is abjectly false because we can and are regularly conscious of all kind of things we have never experienced before. In fact if this were the modus operandi of the human control system we would have never survived the first few hundred years let alone one hundred thousand. Even if we are totally ignorant of what is presented to us we are always conscious of it. To not be so would be very dangerous indeed. As I said previously; any computation or algorithmic action takes place after consciousness has done its job, not before.

2. Global workspace

The global workspace theory of consciousness is one of several theories known as "functionalism" and it does not account for any true neuroscience per se. These theories can be implemented in computer hardware just as well as any imagined biological theme. As such, they follow many CS professionals' beliefs that consciousness is the result of some computational mechanism or in other words; an algorithm. Another theory based in functionalism is called the "integrated information theory". This theory basically says the level of consciousness in a system is based on how many possible states it has at that time and how tightly integrated those states are. In this explanation, the term, "states" refer to "information" or in other words; the things we can be conscious of.

This theory has parallels to an "integrated theory of intelligence" and as the reader should be aware of by now, consciousness and intelligence is *not* the same thing. All of these theories are abjectly false in my opinion because as I mentioned, consciousness has nothing to do with intelligence, as there are many animals that probably possess consciousness and are not intelligent by any measure. In my opinion these theories are poor attempts at rationalizing away a highly complex phenomenon by means of an overly simplistic explanation; an explanation that fits intelligence, not consciousness. Explaining how the brain deals with information is just that, and not at all an explanation of consciousness. As in the higher order theory, we are conscious of everything prior to any information processing that might take place.

3. The biological theory – the thalamic switch

This is a theory that says consciousness is the result of neurological activity in the brain. This is the most promising theory as it allows for many different possible brain functions and interactions to be the underlying mechanism for consciousness. Exactly what these functions and interactions are is at the present time, unclear. The best chance of a valid explanation may be that active connections between cortical activity and the top of the brain stem create what is known as the "thalamic switch". When you go in for surgery and are given general anesthesia, the drugs used disable this thalamic switch. Also when people are observed going from a completely unconscious to a low level conscious state these connections are involved as increasing activity. This may be the "on switch" of consciousness. The "off switch" for consciousness may be a little more involved in that a large overall decrease in cortical metabolism is required to "turn it off". This is along the same lines of conjecture that I alluded to in my purpose of consciousness explanation for consciousness as a peace and quiet controller. I will reiterate an analogy to end this part of my discussion by referring to the volume control of an MP3 player. The player's output is the same music no matter what the volume level happens to be. There is no change in the music which would be analogous to algorithmic iterations; there is a change in power output in sound pressure waves which is analogous to neuronal activity intensity or stimulation. I hope this clarifies what could be a difficult concept to grasp.

Neural correlates of consciousness (NCCs)

The metrics that allow neuroscience to track brain activity with respect to consciousness are called Neural Correlates of Consciousness or simply: NCCs. NCCs are done through brain tests that either monitor electrical brain wave activity or are the result of nuclear medicine scans. The later involves injecting a radioactive isotope in the bloodstream and then taking what could be thought of as a "passive tomogram". The detector is positioned around the patient's head and pictures are taken from radioactivity from the inside out. This gives pictures of overall brain metabolism which is represented by high blood flow to areas of the brain with high metabolism and vice versa. This means that high activity uses up more energy than low activity and this energy usage needs to be supported with more blood flow because blood contains the gasoline of the body; glucose, and oxygen we get from the air we breathe.

Many studies have been done which map brain activity during the sleep, awaking and fully conscious phases. It has been shown that certain areas of the brain "light up" which are indicative of higher activity during the transition from sleep to wake modes. Unfortunately, medical science has been at a loss to explain why the areas of the brain that are known as functional module areas appear to have increases in neuronal activity during wakeup. In other words they believe they are witnessing an increase in *algorithmic* iterations and to them that is not an explanation of consciousness production. This must be patently false, if indeed consciousness is entirely physical. This may be a prime example of not being able to see the forest through the trees.

What medical science may be missing is: They are waiting to see some global area of the brain "light up" during the transition phase of non-conscious to conscious states and waiting for that may be a fool's errand. Perhaps what they witness in all the local activity is exactly what they should be witnessing. They are expecting something different to happen when they are witnessing the very process they are looking for! This is because consciousness happens at the local level not at some global level. This fits in nicely with the theory that consciousness is produced where the activity (consciousness intensity) is the highest and also limited to locality to prevent hallucinations.

Quantum theory of consciousness

A pretty smart guy by the name of Rodger Penrose has a theory on consciousness production that I believe is close to being true, if not the actual explanation. He says that consciousness is produced on an atomic level in the neural structures of the brain as a type of energy field. This energy field then has an effect on some of the other neural structures and this is what produces consciousness.

Chapter 3- The Brain

It is sort of a "closed loop" control system explanation of consciousness. The brain produces a field which is modulated into waves and these waves in induce the phenomenon of consciousness which in turn can produce different varying fields, which begins the entire process again. It could be that since we (and all other animals) were constantly exposed to gravity, we evolved for an environment where we also made use of this fundamental field. If this hypothesis is true, this lends credence to the claims of paranormal activity including physic powers.

In other words, the brain produces some kind of field (it may actually be a form of gravity waves) and it is this field that in turn induces consciousness in the brain. This all happens on very small structures called "micro-tubules" that reside in neuron extremities. This is just one of the myriad brain theories that will be tough to prove or even test. However, this is the one theory that makes any sense to me and I believe it is either correct or at least very close to being correct.

This is the only explanation that is needed if indeed, it is correct. The arrangement of neural structures that have consciousness induced in them could very well be all that is needed to do the job we all experience on a daily basis. The fact that we all (technical people included) have a hard time in understanding how this could be possible means absolutely nothing. There are many things in nature we don't fully understand. As I said previously, we don't really need to understand consciousness in order to be able to understand how the brain produces intelligence, for that is just pure logic.

What this theory also proposes is that if we could produce the energy field that our neural networks produce with an adequate amount of processing activity, we should be able to induce consciousness, even in a sleeping brain! This may be possible but if it happens on the size scale that Dr. Penrose theorizes then it will be very difficult to detect and possibly analyze for any initial research. We are talking about things like gravity waves which have not been proven to exist, even on a cosmological scale. Detecting gravity waves on the atomic scale will be a daunting task. We will have to wait and see.

Consciousness in machines

What I have just described about human consciousness would not be valid if we were to design a computer that does the same thing our brain does. We could assign a specific register (a holding place) for the current information and then use that to compare with all the previously stored information. An algorithm (albeit a very complex one) would suffice to determine what got stored and what didn't. Consciousness in the sense we experience it would not be possible. Since the brain is a nature designed biological computer, we cannot expect to produce a computer the way nature would. The way the biological consciousness system works is the most efficient system nature could produce using very simple underlying principles. I will provide ample proof for the proposal of conscious acting intelligent machines in chapter 5. These machines will only possess the attribution of consciousness which to us will seem no different than a real living human to humans observing them.

Chapter 3- The Brain

Summary

I believe I have presented an accurate functional representation of the human brain. The phenomenon of intelligence is enabled and produced because of the architecture we are all born with (most of us anyway). The functional areas of the brain are comprised of a look-through memory structure shared by input and output modules. Modules can be viewed as separate computer programs (processes) running independently and providing the brain with processed, cleaned up versions of sensory inputs and processed, refined versions of output control signals I referred to as the result of evolutionary algorithms. In the next chapter I hope to demonstrate that the phenomenon of thought is not as big a mystery as it appears to be. The biggest mystery of thought is how humans are able to control it. and I hope to demonstrate that this can be explained just as easily as explaining how output modules control the hands and fingers.

Chapter 4 - The mystery of thought

I now begin the presentation of my hypothesis of how the brain produces useful intelligence or what we call "thinking":

Central Systems

I believe the central systems Fodor referred to are in reality modules themselves and the physical locality may be even harder to prove than any of the subservient modules. This is because the central system module(s) are probability spread out over the whole brain and have access and are partially part of; all input and output modules. It is these central systems that are responsible for consciousness and all the fundamental functions of intelligence I laid out in the first chapter.

It is obvious to me that the central systems are what all the modules "report" to for inputs or are controlled by for outputs. In other words, for example, your depth perception module takes information stimulus from the eyes, performs processing and the central system partakes (passively) in this "edge sharpened" version. If there is enough activity in the central system then the phenomenon of consciousness will be turned on and you will "see" and be cognitive. The central system is the brain's equivalent of the "CPU" of your home computer. The CPU is the central processing unit and it does all the logical functions of your home computer. It can be considered as the "executive" of the entire computer.

The home computer CPU is the place where all the decisions are made, hence the executive moniker. The central system of the brain is also where decisions are made along with all of the preliminary steps that need to take place before any decision is possible. A review of the basic algorithm of intelligence is in order. The basic tenants of intelligence are:

1. Assess all new information – store temporarily or permanently if important
2. Analyze all new information – store temporarily or permanently if important
3. Decide what to do with new and/or old information – store temporarily or permanently if important
4. Transcend what is known to solve problems of the unknown – store temporarily or permanently if important
5. Survey the known for possible solutions for present problems of the unknown – store temporarily or permanently if important

I have simply added a "store" after each major step since that is exactly what the brain does. From the time our conscious system starts working we begin storing everything that is presented to us. We also store the decisions we have made, the emotions we had and every detail of our lives that we were conscious of. This continues until the day we die. The total sum of all these objects is what we call our "personality".

Chapter 4 – The Mystery of Thought

We could easily develop a flow chart based on the simple foundation stones of intelligence and in doing that will have laid out the algorithmic functions of the CPU of the brain or what we can call the Central Systems in figure 1.

FIG. 1

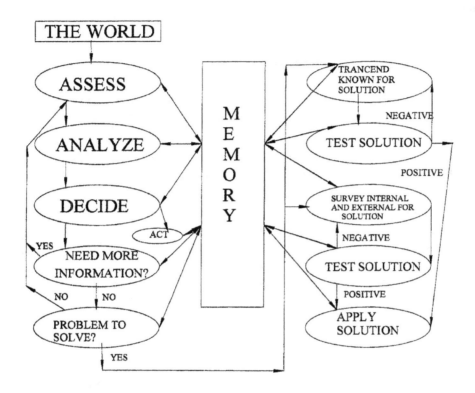

We can follow the flow of information from the upper left (the world) and the logical steps required to produce intelligence flows down, over to the top right and down again. On the right side there are two possible problem solving techniques, the Transcend and the Survey which can be used simultaneously or individually. You will also notice that everything has a common connection to memory. This should tell the reader that intelligence is memory based. That is, everything we do as intelligent creatures depends primarily on the brain's ability to store information.

I mentioned Ray Kurzweil previously. He is the futurist who believes that it will be possible to upload everything in a human's memory and store that until a machine that would replicate the brain could be constructed. If this all comes to pass; we could in theory upload ourselves into a new body! Remember, I said, "If all this comes to pass", in other words, if it is indeed possible to access all the memories in a human brain. We can become the recipients of a new body someday with the notion of "self" intact and exactly as we are now. This is entirely true because everything about "us" and the experience of "who" we are is the net result of a lifetime of information storage that is uniquely "us".

Chapter 4 – The Mystery of Thought

This is a tough concept to grasp but it makes perfect sense if we think about it a little. Everything that defines "you" as a "person" is just the result of your brain being able to access all of the information that was stored since birth. The brain accesses this collection of memories every second of every day. If the brain wasn't continuously able to access all the memories that make up "you", then "you" would not know who you are, what kind of person you are, your likes and dislikes, the people you love and hate; i.e. everything about you. This collection of stored "parameters" is the definition of "you", no more, no less. It is what we call our personality. The main reason I allude to all of this is to make a point, which is intelligence is based (enabled) on memory which is one of the main focus points of this book.

In the example of downloading and uploading everything that comprises "you" we should also be cognizant of the fact that the information downloaded and uploaded would not only contain information about "who" you are, it would contain information about all your abilities. This includes all of your skills, concepts, understandings, decisions you have made, results of acting on those decisions, knowledge of all subjects you are proficient at and subjects which you have only a perfunctory knowledge of. In other words; everything that makes you intelligent. Now you should have a better understanding of why I say that intelligence is memory based.

Just as many other complex processes in nature are based on relatively simple constructs, intelligence is no different. Intelligence is based on the efficient management of information. This includes the storage, retrieval, comparison, and traversal of information, all done at the fast rate necessary for any worthwhile benefit. The brain's ability to recall anything you ever experienced in your lifetime at any instant is a demonstration of the brain's capability. All you need do is "think" about a subject and there it is! The most important information management tool the brain has is the ability to *traverse* all of the information stored there in an advantageous manner. We call this phenomenon, "thinking".

Is thought really mysterious?

Actually thought is not so much of a mystery as it is a misunderstanding about what thinking fundamentally is. It's really not all that mysterious and is relatively easy to explain if viewed from a memory (storage) and conscious and non-conscious mind viewpoint. In other words, it's just not that big of a deal. Thinking is basically the ability of the conscious mind to direct the non-conscious mind to traversely look at the things that are already stored in memory whether the storage is temporary or permanent.

To get a better grasp at what thinking actually is, consider that even animals such as dogs are conscious of their surroundings, their master and their chew toys. This means that they also have some primitive level of conceptual thinking because they "understand" or "know" what that chew toy is. They are cognitive, re-cognitive, emotional, and they even have some facial expressions. They are capable of making decisions such as whether or not they will bite another dog or perhaps a human they have decided they are not fond of. To them, that is the extent of their thinking capabilities.

In contrast, humans only need to add some more complex stored information pathways to add to those dog capabilities. If we don't consider high level concept and language thinking, the dog is

Chapter 4 – The Mystery of Thought

not that far behind in the thinking attribute. Humans possess the same primitive capabilities as dogs but the human brain has much more storage capacity and is structured to take advantage of that extra resource. The extra memory resources allow for much more complex information to be stored which is required to support the advanced modes of thinking humans need for survival.

Thinking can be viewed as the internal playback of information that was pre-recorded whether it was purposefully learned or by some casual means. Information gets recorded first and then during the thought process, it gets played back. It is really that simple.

There is also evidence that we can think non-consciously. Since everything stored is non-conscious (we can't consciously see this information unless we are hallucinating or dreaming), it is not difficult to accept the notion of non-conscious thinking. If you want a clearer understanding of non-conscious thinking just think about a subject you became competent in. This could be cooking, working on cars, basically anything humans become proficient at. If it's cooking, you probably can assemble your favorite dish without ever consulting a cookbook or your own notes. The information is obviously there, somewhere, because you are able to call on this information whenever the need arises and it's also obvious that you cannot actually see that recipe, can you? We may have thoughts about the sequence of events necessary to assemble the ingredients, but where does that information in the thoughts come from? Non-conscious thinking drives conscious thinking. This is something we do every day of our lives and never give it a second thought as to the underlying process driving this ability. The phenomenon of thinking and how humans produce "thought trains", should become a little easier to grasp during my presentation of the modes of thinking which follows.

I now present my hypothesis of how the brain produces useful intelligence or i.e. what we call "thinking". This is undoubtedly the most difficult aspect of human intelligence to explain or understand. Humans have many belief systems and one of those is to believe that all human thought is a special, almost miraculous aspect of human behavior. In order to begin my explanation of how the brain produces thought, I will break thought up into its basic components and in doing so, make use of the "divide and conquer" strategy. I start my expose with what I believe are the fundamental human modes of thought. When viewed this way, thinking becomes much less of a formidable problem to understand.

The 6 modes of thinking

1. Cognition thinking

Cognition may be and I surmise that it is indeed the most primitive of all thinking modes. Primitive animals such as alligators, fish and even insects display cognition regularly because if they weren't cognitive they would not be able to hunt their pray. At the very least, they definitely possess the attribution of consciousness because they also have the attribution of cognition. I believe I provided an adequate argument as to why a purely algorithmic consciousness would not be the way nature does things. So in that regard, we really do need to believe these primitive animals are conscious and thusly cognitive in the same way humans are. Humans use cognitive thinking regularly in conjunction with more advanced thinking modes that primitive animals don't have but that's only because our brain has more structure. Whenever we

Chapter 4 – The Mystery of Thought

encounter something we have never seen before we should be cognitive of it provided everything in the brain is working properly. The current real time information is compared to fractions of a second prior information and if anything changes (a new object appears) and we have never stored it previously; the cognition module outputs a cognition signal to the conscious and perhaps non-conscious mind. The cognition signal can be considered to be a primitive thinking construct. This mechanism makes use of consciousness as a comparator register purpose of consciousness. The real time information is compared to all recent (a fraction of a second old) and all archival stored information.

2. Recognition thinking

Recognition requires a slightly different brain structure, in which *all* stored information has to be compared to current real time information and if there is a match, the recognition module outputs a recognition signal and we then know we have seen whatever it is before. It is actually a little easier to do than cognition, since the entire memory structure will not need to be searched once a match is found. The recognition signal can also be considered as a primitive thinking construct. Humans routinely use recognition in combination with all the other modes. Cognition and recognition are used exclusively in the assessment stage of the intelligence algorithm.

In the case of human recognition we not only receive a recognition signal but we can sometimes get a full conceptual picture of the object in question if there is enough background information stored with that object. We call this "understanding" and I will attempt to explain this in more detail later. For now I will just speculate that this is partly possible because of the large instantly accessible memory size of the brain and the see-through memory structure. It is not difficult to understand (no pun intended) how humans accomplish this remarkable feat if we accept the notion that non-conscious thinking is exactly like conscious thinking only we are not conscious at the same level as we were when the understanding about the artifact was recorded. We must remember that the recorded understanding contains the chronological record (the object's description) of our existence up to that time. We first understood the object because of the information we had already recorded at some prior time. During the recognition process, we "know" what we are looking at. It pays to accept the fact that animals such as dogs routinely recognize objects so intelligence wise, recognition is not a big deal.

The big difference between dog recognition and human recognition is the richness of the understanding that happens when the recognition signal gets sent to the conscious mind. When a dog is cognitive of something he is familiar with he may understand that the object is his master, possibly a human that is has had contact with or maybe inanimate objects such as "chew toys". However, the understanding doesn't get that involved. The human on the other hand, will understand in richer, deeper ways the objects that have been presented to them in the past. The amount and level of understanding that happens in concert with the recognition signal is dependent of whether the human understood the object when it was first introduced or perhaps over a course of time. Humans have an advanced capability over animals such as dogs because the human brain has more storage capacity and the architecture to make use of that capacity. The higher level of understanding is possible because of the stored relations and attributes that get stored with every object and the relational links that further describe the object. This is where relational links comes into play and is a main intelligence enabler. Human understanding does not happen without the training to enable that understanding and humans have the hardware that make that training possible.

3. Emotional thinking

The emotional thinking mode was probably one of the first forms of advanced thinking in primitive man, before the invention of languages. It worked well enough with facial expressions to communicate until some of the actions that we were attempting to communicate could no longer be supported and then invention of language filled in the gap. Unfortunately (from an intelligence standpoint), we still use emotional thinking in combination with the all of the other modes. It is not difficult to comprehend what emotional thinking is about, just recall the times you felt, love, fear, hate, etc. because of some situational conditions and no other complex thoughts such as words were immediately apparent.

Many animals have the capability of emotional thinking. If you spend enough time around dogs as I have, you will begin to appreciate the fact that dogs really do have many of the same emotional signals built in as hardware. I use the word, "signals" because when all the correct situational input conditions are met the module responsible for the particular emotion will output a signal that the brain understands as love, hate, etc. Dogs are capable of fear, hate, love, jealously, envy, happiness, loneliness, sadness and possibly many other emotions that humans are also born with. Even animals such as alligators appear to exhibit the property of anger and possibly fear when they are threatened in any way.

The phenomenon of humor

William Shakespeare used "comic relief" in many of his plays to break up the tension associated with the maiming and killing of many people. I often wonder if he understood the significance of the term and if he knew he was describing the purpose of humor in humans. Humor has been used as one of the definitions of intelligence because we are the only species capable of laughter. Humans need humor because of the complex social situations that can arise and it is an advanced method of dealing with situations that place stress on the nervous system. We need humor simply because we understand everything at a much higher level than any other animal does. It is not just a nice thing to have, it is a necessity. Intelligence brings with it the burden of understanding all the really bad things that can happen to us. We need a way of dealing with that and humor fits the bill nicely. I believe humor is accomplished by the use of a dedicated module. Situational factors (inputs) determine whether we find something funny or not. It is the variability of the accepted input parameters that can change, not the algorithm itself.

Emotions as a threat assessment tool

Emotional thinking allows us to determine when situations in daily life routines are beneficial, threatening or non-concerning. I believe emotions are implemented by individual modules since we are all born with these innate functions. The individual emotional modules must have different conditional input values that when correctly correspond to the module's requirement will result in the particular emotion to be output to the conscious and non-conscious mind.

Chapter 4 – The Mystery of Thought

For example, someone of the opposite sex pays a lot of attention to you, gives you gifts and compliments, believes in the same things you do and you just happen to find them physically attractive. All of these things combined, just may cause the love module to send the love signal to your conscious and non-conscious mind. It should be noted that there can be very severe errors in the decisions you make about the genuineness of the input factors. In the case of faulty decision making the love signal may be sent erroneously, generating many social problems. This is proof that many of the decisions we make are done by the non-conscious mind. If you have ever found yourself to be in love, you know it was not something you made a conscious decision about.

It should be noted that emotional thinking is almost entirely automatic with the only real decision effort expended by the person is usually the just the validity of the input conditions. Usually not much effort is placed in the analysis of those vital input conditions and many people rely strictly on superficial appearances to readily accept the perceived truth of conditions. I provide an example of the way the brain processes such conditions by giving a young man who has repeated social contact with a young woman.

The man's love signal might be thought of as a light bulb with a number of on-off switches wired in series with a battery. In order for the bulb to turn on, all of the switches must be turned on. Here is a list of items that must be true in order for the switch (a combination of all conditions) to be on:

1. The young woman is attractive to the young man.
2. The young woman seems to regularly pay attention to the young man.
3. The young woman laughs at all the stupid jokes the young man tells
4. The young woman smiles repeatedly at the young man.
5. The young woman smells nice to the young man.
6. The young woman always talks to the young man, regardless of the situation.

If all these input conditions are met, the love module of the young man will probably send the love signal to the conscious and non-conscious mind every second of the day and night. That's the way emotional modules work and you can recognize the fact that responding to the inputs require the use of an "acceptor language". This mechanism is called a deterministic finite acceptor. This terminology is used in computer science to describe the workings of what are called "automatons". The best example of this type of automaton is the old coin operated Coke or Pepsi vending machine which required $1.00 in coins to purchase a bottle of the soft drink. That machine was actually a determinate finite accepter and would accept any combination of coins containing 5, 10, 25 or 50 cents that added up to $1.00.

In the case of the love sick young man, we can see that some of the inputs are relatively complex situational conditions. These involve entire situational concepts that the brain stores as they are learned and then at some later date are used in the comparison process. It should be noted that in the six conditions listed, three of them are conditions the man doesn't need to think about. Number one, four and five are all instinctual primitive inputs which the man responds to on a very primitive level and are built in as hardware in all of us. We might even say that the other three inputs (two, three and six) may trigger a primitive built in response mechanism because what appears to be complex behavioral pattern may reduce to some simple response signal in all of us. In my example, I could have specified a non-determinate acceptor to do the job but in my opinion the love emotion does not work with any sort of decision, in fact we usually do not have much to ponder about the validity of the inputs, it just happens automatically. A non-determinate acceptor is one in which some type of decision is made before acceptance.

We routinely use emotional thinking in combination with all the other modes. Emotional thinking can be used as an aid to analyze what we have just assessed in the analysis stage of the intelligence algorithm. For the most part we would all be better off not using emotions in our routine decision making because as we can see, the validity of the input conditions is paramount in the validity of the output emotional signal. Many of the concepts humans attach to words in language thinking are emotionally based. This is one way understanding is accomplished and I will elaborate on this shortly.

4.   Internal visualization thinking

This mode of thinking could also just as well be labeled as "non-conscious visualization thinking" because this in fact describes what non-conscious thinking is; in part anyway. I believe humans have the ability to think in a non-conscious manner exactly the same way we think consciously and this mode is an apt description of the entire phenomenon of non-conscious thinking because it demonstrates something most humans can relate to; the viewing of visual information. This mode of thinking is the internal visualization of pictures, shapes, scenes, numbers, objects, people and anything that was input with the eyes, that we have stored in memory. Just as in every other mode of thinking except emotional, we need to have things stored before we can think about them. Even cognition requires us to be aware that we are in the current situation, by comparison to all the past life experiences (including those which are only fractions of a second old) we have stored which is the definition of "us".

This mode is how we can internally visualize the shape, size, color, spatial location, and any visual parameter that we have ever been exposed to. We cannot visualize things in which we have no building blocks in which to construct them out of. This is yet another illusion that we have about our own capabilities. We assume that we can be "creative" but nothing could be further from the truth. We don't actually create anything in a "something from nothing" sense. When we say we are creating something what is really happening is that we are assembling pictures or images that we have stored in memory and it is very much like using a "Lego" set to assemble our "creation" from smaller components.

This mode of thinking has a non-conscious component and a conscious component to it. The non-conscious part is the internal visualization, which of course we cannot actually "see" and the conscious component is the actual use of the things we are internally visualizing. We can understand how this works by simply thinking of any visual stimulus we have ever encountered. If we are given a simple arithmetic problem to solve, many people will be able to internally visualize the written equation in order to solve it. This is very much like writing the problem on a sheet of paper only instead of writing it we generate it internally. Many people such as me have a tough time doing these internal visual operations because the visual processing centers of the brain are not working up to speed. People who have lots of visual migraines may also be in this category.

The brain can internally visualize by calling on stored information which is searched for by using the key that was provided in the description of the problem. We could not write out the problem internally if we have never done that on real paper at some earlier point in life. We also could not paint a picture or sketch out a simple drawing without stored representation of pieces of that painting or drawing first. This is not difficult to explain how the brain does this in logical terms and it only requires the non-conscious searching for whatever the externally provided keys has given. Once a key is provided, whether from an internal or external source, the memory search uses the appropriate images that are relationally and conceptually linked to the key, to construct an image useful to the problem at hand.

There are two possibilities, which are internal and external search keys which are also used in conceptual and language thinking (the next two higher modes). The first is a result of random call ups of any visual information stored in memory or the non-conscious could have been working on the problem in the background with no conscious awareness; both of which we consider to be a spontaneous thought but that is an illusion. The second would be a result of an externally induced problem key which begins the starting point for any thought process stream. I cover thought process streams in detail in the next two modes. We routinely use internal visualization thinking in combination with all the other modes.

5. Conceptual thinking

This is the mode of thinking that enabled the human race to excel in technology. Without the ability to think in concepts, man would never have developed tools, mathematical constructs and understanding of the physics necessary to perform the technology that has propelled humanity into the 21st century. A concept string is a concept strung along with an enabler that when linked together provide a useful description of the concept. Concepts generally do not stand on their own to provide a useful explanation for their existence. It requires an attachment of these concepts to an object in order to provide any real meaning. Concepts are always related directly or indirectly to the physical.

For example, we cannot think about the concept of speed (velocity) without attaching a noun (object) like a car, boat, airplane, rocket, gamma ray, light, etc. to it. So, even if our thought is apparently purely conceptual, upon closer examination, it most definitely is not. The concept of velocity means nothing without the necessary object to be doing the speed. We accomplish this mode of thinking by calling on our stored experiences and in the case of my velocity example you may have learned about velocity in a class you have taken but there had to have been an example of some object at velocity. I believe this is where many people fail to grasp mathematics "concepts". The artifacts thought in math courses are really not concepts at all if there are no physical practical examples to attach them to. The best math teachers are the ones who provide many real world examples of everything they teach. This is one reason why some people have difficulty with math; they need physical real world examples and many instructors don't do enough of that.

Chapter 4 – The Mystery of Thought

Humans need some ability at internal visualization in order to be proficient at this mode of thinking. The reason for that statement should be obvious because if we are able to internally construct a picture of a car speeding down a highway, the concept of speed is immediately understood. If we never were exposed to anything that moved, we would have a tough time in understanding what velocity was. It has all got to do with our life experiences and then connecting new concepts to those.

Albert Einstein was able to postulate how the planets and stars in the universe were held together by a force we always called "gravity". He hypothesized that gravity might be just a result of some other process that was universal in the universe. Through the use of internal visualization and conceptual thinking he was able to internally visualize "the fabric of space" as being warped by the masses of all the bodies in space. The larger the mass of the bodies, the more space got "warped" and this acted like a downhill slide for other smaller bodies which were then pulled towards the larger ones. Mass warps space and warped space tells mass what to do. These are all concepts which require links to physical objects or in other words, "things we already know about". A concept, such as "warped space" is difficult to grasp unless linked to a visual image such as a ball in the middle of a large piece of fabric, pulling the fabric down in the middle in a type of trough where things like water would flow from the outside in towards the ball in the middle.

This is a prime example of our ability to transcend the known into the unknown to solve problems. It is one of the prime problem solving tools humans possess. I believe this mode of thinking is built in as hardware and as such does not require a learning process. In other words it is part of the algorithm of intelligence. We all have this capability but some humans are more inclined to make use of it. I believe the reasons for this are entirely due to personality differences, the largest being a general disinterest in solving problems.

Early humans needed this mode to make tools such as stone axe heads. For example, an axe maker had the ability to recognize a fault line running through a piece of stone as a potential problem. This would enable the axe head maker to discard that piece because of past experience at faulty axe heads because of faulty materials used in their construction. Just making the connection at why the head failed previously is a demonstration of conceptual thinking. A fault in a piece of stone was known to crack and fail if stressed so that was the known. Discarding a piece of stone with a fault was enabled because of the human capability to transcend. The unknown was guessed at because of the known.

The people who develop expertise at conceptual thinking are routinely tasked at solving problems and so have experience to draw on from past experiential processes. Some humans use this mode of thinking on at least an occasional basis. It should be evident that humans cannot make use of this important strategy without the necessary stored background knowledge base to draw comparisons from what is known to what is not known.

5. Language thinking

Language thinking can be used as the most effective model for how the brain actually produces thought. It is the most productive mode and also the most difficult mode of thought to explain.

Chapter 4 – The Mystery of Thought

Language thinking is by far, the most utilized form of thinking for technology because it assigns terms to concepts which helps categorize and transfer highly complex subjects. In fact even simple concepts can be difficult to transfer without the use of a natural language.

Humans attach concepts which are simple physical and emotional traits to words during the learning process. I reiterate that concepts are always related either directly or indirectly to the physical or emotional. Even dogs "understand" or "know" their favorite chew toy. While this comparison may seem to be a drastic oversimplification of what seems to be a complex problem, it really is not. The important thing to grasp here is that when the word training is happening we get a "feel" for that word and a "feel" is always physical or emotional. "Word training" is learning how to read and write. We don't need to internally look up the definitions of words such as like, hate, good, bad, heat, cold, fast, slow, bottom, top, sides, front, back, up, down, sideways, left, right, blue, red, orange, bright or tense mean. They are all connected to the physical or the emotional in some way and are instantly "understood" because of the attached concept that happened during the learning process.

In order to get a grasp of how humans develop or understand language thought trains (sentences) we should not overlook the training involved. When we are thinking or speaking in our native language, we may be using memory "ladders" or "scaffolds" that we have accumulated throughout our chronological existence in the use of that language. We have heard countless numbers of people speak and we have spoken back in our language. When we were first becoming proficient in our language, we made mistakes and if the training was adequate we were corrected. The correct way in which words are used and the order in which they are used were deposited in memory. We could call these *usage* records as sets of "examples" or "proofs" or "models" or "samples" or ladders. These ladders contain references or relationships to the words and the semantic meanings (concepts) that connect these words to other words. Since the semantic meaning (actually a simple concept) is automatically located physically adjacent to the current word because of the OAR model of human memory storage, it is another of nature's simplistic answers to complex problems. To get a better "feel" for what understanding is I turn to a classic AI thought experiment.

The phenomenon of understanding

A philosopher by the name of Jon Searle said that a computer could be taught to translate a language but there would be no understanding going on in that case; ever. He was a proponent of the "machines will never think" crowd. I believe that what follows here is suggestive that Mr. Searle identified the one aspect of intelligence that differentiates humans from all other animals. That difference is what humans call, "understanding". I will elaborate on this aspect of intelligence later. For now I need to concentrate on what Searle proposed. In order to demonstrate his hypothesis he proposed a thought experiment he called:

The Chinese Room

This was an attempt to prove that a computer program could not be made to "understand" the way a mind does. The Chinese room consisted of a room with only a small opening to the outside and an English only reading person inside and a stack of cards that have Chinese symbols written on them and some blank cards. There was also a rule book, written in English which represented the computer program. The person represented the CPU and the cards which represented the instructions of a program of a human made computer.

Chinese symbols on cards were fed into the small opening and the person would match the symbols in the rule book and follow instructions. Some instructions in the rule book might include writing some symbols on blank cards and passing those to the outside world, rearranging the stack of cards, and finding more symbols in the stack of cards and repeating the process again. The net result would be that the Chinese room would act as if it were a Chinese reading and writing person. Chinese would be fed into the room and a Chinese response to the input would be output to the outside world. This system would pass "The Turing Test" in which a computer and its program are tested to determine if there is a computer or a human talking to the human who is doing the testing. Searle argued that even though this passed The Turing Test, this did not constitute "understanding" of the computer. His rational was that there was no understanding in the person and not in the cards either, therefore there could be no understanding.

There are several problems that I have with Mr. Searle's assessment. One problem I have is that he assumes that humans are some sort of mystical creature whose actions cannot be explained purely in algorithmic terms. I agree with part of that assessment because I believe that consciousness is a purely physical trait but I differ with Mr. Searle by believing that all of the important logical functions explaining intelligence in humans are strictly algorithmic. This has nothing to do with the free will I alluded to previously because I believe it is possible for a purely algorithmic system to also have free will. So, if it is true that free will can be achieved by a purely algorithmic system, the phenomenon of "understanding" should also be possible as the result of a purely algorithmic system. This begs another question.

Will computers ever be able to truly "understand"? Is it some fundamentally complex process that we will never be able to reproduce in an intelligent machine? If we do not have the knowledge necessary to construct a machine that understands, then we have little hope of ever explaining how the brain performs understanding and vice versa. I believe the answer to that question is that we can build an understanding machine. Understanding is just another facet of the phenomenon of thinking albeit the most important facet. Since thinking is just a displayed conscious view of the orderly call up of stored information, understanding must be the same basic process, only slightly more refined in the types of attribute information stored in close proximity to the objects in use.

Humans are without question cognizant (conscious and cognitive understanding). We need to admit that many animals also have this ability even if they only have it on a primitive level. The term cognizant actually means that we *understand* what we are cognitive of. We don't usually consider some of the animals who possess cognition and recognition as being very smart. Dogs can be cognitive of a MP3 player and they may even recognize that it belongs to you because of the smell but is very unlikely that they understand what an MP3 player is. Cognition plus understanding requires a higher level of intelligence which must be achieved through algorithmic processes. However, dogs do understand and therefore are cognizant of things such as their chew toys. Granted, this is a very simple ability, but it is *an ability*, nonetheless. Taking this line of

Chapter 4 – The Mystery of Thought

reasoning to humans, when we understand the meaning of a word, it is not much more complex of an operation than what our dog did when he understood his chew toy.

When we are reading any language we have mastered, the process of reading is a simple process of locating the read word in memory. The act of locating the word automatically locates the meaning or the attributes of that word, which is displayed to the conscious mind by the non-conscious mind as a concept. The concept was connected to the word and stored next to the word at the time of learning perhaps as a child and the learning process could have taken what we now consider to be large amounts of time as adults. Days or weeks were spent when first learning our native language and as we became proficient it gradually took less and less time to digest new words into our vocabulary. This is because we were connecting words we knew to words we didn't know just as in conceptual thinking. What we are doing is actually connecting the stored concepts of words in our lexicon to new words we want to become part of our lexicon.

It is difficult to grasp how the brain instantly "knows" or "understands" the meaning of each word as we hear or read a train of words as in a sentence. We don't immediately have a dictionary definition of each word displayed to us consciously or non-consciously. There is no internal visualization with more words describing each word we have just been presented with. To do so would be just an extension of the basic problem and that process could go on forever, much the same as the consciousness paradox. There is a perceived mystery with this process, there is no doubt. I believe that we are able to immediately understand the meaning of words because as I just alluded to; we store the meaning of words as concepts.

As I alluded to, even dogs "know" or "understand" what their favorite chew toy is and this is conceptual thinking at a very primitive level. We don't need a dictionary definition displayed to us for physical things we were exposed to and learned about. Once we see a vehicle and have ridden in that vehicle at zero to 60 MPH in 5 seconds we know the concept a vehicle and of acceleration. At some later time, when we read or listen to the word acceleration we connect the concept and there is instant understanding of that concept. Concepts are always related directly to the physical or they indirectly relate to something physical in one way or another or they relate to basic human emotions. Every word in the English language can be traced back to something directly physical or something related in some way to the physical or to a human emotion. We attach physical or emotional traits to every word and we use those concepts to immediately identify the word's meaning. A word concept can the viewed as a type of "code" much like a cryptographic code used in securing the unwanted sharing of words. It is a code that once the brain has learned and stored will instantly convey the semantic meaning of that word.

So, to summarize: Understanding is no big deal and just as with consciousness it is a primitive ability that has little to do with intelligence. It is more accurate to state that intelligence uses understanding to accomplish its mission but it cannot be described as intelligent behavior since animals like dogs possess it. This is yet another example of nature's simplicity. When we are babies and hear and see well enough to begin to store a sufficient amount of information about our world, we begin to associate spoken words to actions to physical objects and our emotional response to the word. We learn our native language as a matter of relating what we don't know, (the language) to physical things and emotions that we do know and these connections must be repeated a number of times. We listen and observe our parents speaking and we also observe actions, emotions and objects that frequently are associated together with the words being spoken. This combination builds a knowledge base with which we can draw on later so that when a word is spoken we automatically access the definition of the word in the form of related concepts and emotions. In other words our conscious mind is directing the non-conscious mind in accessing the area of memory where the actual concept of the word is located and stored. I reiterate that the understanding takes place during the *learning* process, not at the time of reading, listening, talking or thinking.

How the brain accomplishes thinking

I hope to have established the fact that intelligence is based on memory, the next logical step in explaining how intelligence is actually produced is to examine the functional (not the physical) architecture of the brain. I do this with purely a functional approach. I do not care *how* the brain does what it does, I only care *what* the brain does what it does. It is not difficult to become aware of what the brain does, the only requisite is to pay attention to what humans do.

The brain is often referred to as a computer. The very definition of a computer is: "A device that computes". The problem people have when they think of the brain as being a computer is that they place too much comparison towards the home computer that they are familiar with. Nothing could be further from the truth. The brain is as similar to any human made computer as much as a duck is similar to an F16 fighter plane. They both fly and that is where the similarity ends. There are far more un-similar attributes between the brain and modern computers than there are similar ones.

Differences between the brain and modern computers

The modern home computer uses several different types of memory which are categorized into speed capabilities. There are the "cache" memories that are very fast and are able to match the speed of the CPU. The latest CPU designs have several levels of cache memories usually called the "L1, L2, L3 caches" with L1 being the fastest and L2 and L3 being a little progressively slower. The next slower memory type is primary memory and this is the largest solid state memory used by the CPU while running any program. Primary memory is where a large proportion of a program must reside in order for the program to have any real beneficial use. I alluded to virtual memory previously and the basic function of the virtual memory paradigm is to maintain a usable program content in primary memory. The next slowest and the slowest of all memory types is secondary memory which is usually implemented in the form of a hard disk drive. The operating system uses its virtual memory sub-program to pull little sections (called pages in a paging type system) of the program out of secondary memory and loads these little sections into primary memory where they can actually be used by the CPU.

In striking contrast the brain has only one type of memory, the equivalent of the L1 cache. This is one reason why we can access anything instantly any time we want. The brain has a dedicated memory as fast as the CPU's capability with no waiting involved. Nature would not do this any other way; the name of the game in nature made things is simplicity. Another component of the simplistic design of the brain is the number of information points it can process at any one time.

Chapter 4 – The Mystery of Thought

A modern CPU is what we call a 32 or a 64 bit machine, which would be common for the standard home computer. There is an IBM processor currently in the works which is supposed to be a 128 bit machine. The number of bits a CPU is designed with is the primary architecture of that CPU. It is the size of the computer "word" that can be accepted by the processor at one time. Obviously, the more bits a machine can load into itself at one time, the faster and more processing it will be able to do. Computer words are called a "machine word".

The bigger the machine word is, the more powerful the processor will be. For example, the CPU is processing an image enhancement program and the image enhanced is a photo file with a total of 6 mega pixels. If each pixel can be represented by one byte (8 bits), this means 6,000,000 X 8 / 64 = the number of transfers (roughly) that a 128 bit machine would have to make just in the transfer of the image to another memory location. The 128 bits is reduced to 64 because the other 64 is reserved for an instruction and things like the "metadata" which describes the location and other details about the contents of the "container" that the pixel information is in. In this case the answer is 750,000 transfers to just move the image from one memory location to another. In the case of a 32 bit machine word; the answer jumps to 3,000,000 transfers. The main difference in performance between the two processors is the amount of time required to do the same amount of work.

By very stark contrast, the human brain CPU (I have called this central systems) must be at least an approximately 1 Giga bits (one billion bits) machine. I arrive at this probably conservative number by making a few simple assumptions about what gets stored. I use the vision system exclusively since that is unarguably the most memory demanding of all human senses. First of all, there are 120 million information points from each eye. 120 X 2 = 240 million for two eyes and I multiply that by what I believe is a conservative 4 giving 960 million. I then round this off to an even 1 Giga bit for simplicity sake. I multiplied the 240 by 4 because I guess that is what is presented to the memory system after processing by our depth perception module. We see and store things in 3 Dimensions and the resulting 3 D image would probably require 4 to 5 times the storage space of a 2 D image.

It should be noted that a "bit" in the human brain does not have equivalence to a "bit" in a digital computer (bit = binary digit). A bit in the case of the brain is only an information point and has no placement value as in computer bits. I use the terminology purely to give contrast to the size of the brain's storage compared to the human designed counterpart. In keeping with the spirit of coining new terms for newly transcended concepts, I now take the liberty of coining the term BIP which is an acronym for Brain Information Point. From this point onward, I will use my new term, BIP to describe the brain's storage capacities. BIP is in capitals because it is a true acronym whereas bit is not.

The one G BIP described is only the "footprint" or the machine word size of the "CPU" or the central system of the brain. It is the number of BIPs that the brain can access at one time simultaneously. I will attempt to tackle the problem of how much total memory an intelligent machine actually needs to produce intelligence in the next chapter. For now, I believe we can postulate that the total amount must be very large.

Chapter 4 – The Mystery of Thought

To summarize, the brain far surpasses the computer in the number of information points that can be accessed at any one time or in other words, the size of the "machine word". The reason is again, simplicity. The brain would be necessarily complex on a basic level in order to do what the human-made computer does in the assembling of a 1 G BIPs composed of a visual field with all attributional and relational artifacts to 32 BIP chunks. Nature just doesn't work that way. The brain stores real time information (if at a sufficiently conscious intensity level for storage), in whole, not in pieces. This means the entire field of vision, the smells associated with that, the way we felt at the time, what we were thinking emotionally; basically everything. This requires a lot of memory and it has to be in a very specific architecture to be of any functional value. The shared look through memory fits the bill to a tee.

In addition to storing information from the input sensors, we also need to store our past experiences, decisions we have made, things we have assessed and analyzed, new concepts we have created, and even searches we have done through our memory in an attempt to solve problems at hand. This is what we can consider to be our "knowledge base" and this is the main enabler of intelligence. I said this before and I reiterate: Intelligence is based on memory or the storage of information. It just stands to reason that the more information we have to draw from the greater chance we have of making a correct conclusion about related objects or even objects that have a small similarity.

This is something I alluded to in the first chapter: Learning does not make you smart. It only increases the probability that you will make smart decisions. This is why I say that intelligence is not static, it is dynamic. In other words, intelligence is not automatic; it requires a precise series of directed steps (and accompanied decisions) in strict order and performed at every opportunity to produce the desired result. The size and structure of our memory system lends itself towards the storage and retrieval of vital information that we need to take those steps. If we wanted to define intelligence this could certainly be one definition: Intelligence is the result of the correct storage, retrieval and usage of information.

How the brain assesses and analyzes information and produces what we call thought:

When we view the memory structure of the brain as being a huge repository for information that the conscious and non-conscious mind can access at any instant of time, this view simplifies what thinking is; drastically. The big mystery is consciousness which I have tried to shed some light on, even if the light was only a dim candle. If we accept that certain areas of the brain, when sufficiently activated with metabolism, will become conscious; then we can postulate how that consciousness is able to witness the phenomenon of thinking. Thinking is merely the conscious and non-conscious mind traversing the vast reaches of the human brain's memory structure in a serial stream of related information.

Prior to providing the reader with a continuation of my look-through memory example, it is requisite that I define the method the brain must use to store information as it comes in. Following the "nature is simple" paradigm, I believe it is safe to say that we use up storage space in sequential physical locations as we go. That is, as we move through the world and experience life, our brain's memory capacity gets filled up in sequence, just like filling up a jar with water. As the water is poured in, it takes up space and approaches the limit of capacity of the jar. This

Chapter 4 – The Mystery of Thought

begs the question of how we are able to link related artifacts that get stored in memory if everything is stored in a simple first-in-first-stored, next-in-next-stored manner. The answer to that question is dependent on how we store things in the huge 1 Giga BIP machine word of the brain. When we store objects all the relations and attributes of the object get stored in the same physical location. It is a simple matter for the brain to do a subsequent search with the key for the new search being some relation or attribute of the original object (the original search key) contained in one machine word. I call this memory leap frogging and the new acronym, MLF describes how the brain produces thought trains. I expand on this in the next chapter.

In order to provide the reader with a stronger sense of how the thinking process is produced I will return to my example of a very tall office building, with perfectly square floor layout. As before, all the floors in the building are made of high strength glass and each floor is the equivalent of a single "transparency" or perhaps "frame" of memory. In other words, each floor contains a one G BIP human brain machine word (BMW) – I take the liberty of coining a new acronym). This is a complete set of information that was stored in some prior learning process, either through a casual (volatile) or purposefully learned (high consciousness intensity level and permanent) process.

The information contained on that "floor" could be a song that fits the fancy of the personality of the brain, i.e. "you". Remember, (no pun intended) that we will easily remember things we are fond of and not things we don't necessarily like. This is the same as saying we store things we are fond of and not things we don't necessarily like. Again, this is due to the activity of the conscious intensity level being higher when we are exposed to things we like. The floor could also contain visual information such as members of the band that produced the song as well as other ancillary information that you may find interesting.

Floors can contain any information we have been exposed to in our entire lifetime and they will have any relational and attribute information on the same floor that connects to the same category of object somewhere else in memory. That relational link could connect to an adjacent floor or to a floor some arbitrary distance away. This may explain why "memory joggers" like the deliberate assignment of some relational attribute of any subject will assist in helping us to remember something that we have a tough time in recalling about that object. "Memory by association" works because of this memory structure. This is done by adding an object we can easily identify to objects that have a small relational richness to the object we are attempting to remember. Smells have also been known to be memory joggers and my theory for this is because the smells that were present when the storage took place are also stored directly adjacent to the primary object. Here is an idea for an entrepreneurial minded college student: Create a collection of pleasant odors in small vials that someone cramming for an exam can smell and apply to their fingers to assist them in remembering things while taking exams.

Now, getting back to my high rise example, if we can imagine being at the top floor in the elevator car of our "memory tower" in which all floors combined possesses all the information that we have accumulated in our lifetime. In reality if we imagined a representative building equal to human memory capacity, it would probably go out to the distance of the moon. Each individual floor has a specific category of meaning that is related to objects stored on that floor and those objects have the relational links to objects that are stored on other floors. Attributes of individual objects are also contained on the floors which contribute to the richness of the meaning of those objects and can also be used as relational links to other objects. We are on a transparent elevator car which can arrive at any floor in an instant and we can "see" all the information available on that floor by looking down into it when we are directly over it.

The elevator car has the remarkable ability to traverse instantaneously to any floor and "hover" anywhere or swing up and down from anywhere to anywhere. This is what goes on during the process of what we call "thinking". The brain is not doing anything miraculous; we are simply a miraculously designed machine that is based in simplicity. If there is an illusion about anything; it is that we are living under the illusion that we are something that fits in the realm of mysticism.

The reader may have a tough time in understanding how the conscious mind traverses the huge memory the human brain is endowed with. The conscious (and the non-conscious since the latter is just operating on a lower level of consciousness) mind can literally zoom around to and fro to anywhere it wants to go in the brain's memory system. How is this possible?

Since we are imagining an elevator car, there must be an elevator shaft, so I now add that to my high rise analogy. The inner shaft of the elevator that runs from the very top to the very bottom of the building and the cables from the car represents a chemical/electrical connection to the brain stem at the top; the brainstem in all likelihood is where consciousness ultimately is transferred to. I say this because consciousness appears to be a very primitive phenomenon and this also agrees with neuroscience theories of consciousness. Animals that possess very simple brains appear to be conscious. They have one thing in common with humans. They have a brain stem.

How the conscious mind controls memory location access

Now, posit that consciousness is the result of the connectionist neural networks of the brain attaining enough activity to induce consciousness locally and then transferred to the brain stem. Non-conscious activity is consciousness at a much lower level of intensity. During dreaming for example, as the intensity increases the non-conscious activity in any floor of our imaginary tower, that non-conscious activity turns into conscious activity at the brain stem but the thalamic switch is off so we are not aware of it. It is only during wake up or shut down that we can remember these instances because the thalamic switch is in some smaller state of "on". During fully conscious times when we are awake the algorithmic activity increases that accompany the acquisition of new or interesting artifacts cause increases in consciousness intensity and that produces storage.

High intensity happens during the storage phase and lower intensity happens when we are accessing the things we think about during the retrieval phase but we are totally unaware of this. In between those two extremes there is an intensity high enough that allows us to be conscious of the lower intensity non-conscious activity (like imagining a loved one's face). Thinking in our native language is a combination of conscious and non-conscious thought. We are conscious of the non-conscious acquisition of words and connected concepts but we cannot actually see or hear the words so that can be described as non-conscious thinking observed by conscious thinking in the intermediate level of consciousness intensity.

Chapter 4 – The Mystery of Thought

I reiterate that non-conscious activity is probably just conscious activity on a lower intensity level and since this is an explanation of language thinking and not language learning (storage) I will not address the highest level of consciousness (required for storage). So in my example, wherever the elevator car happens to be is where the non-conscious attention will be and activity will have increased there above all other areas of the brain's storage (memory). So non-conscious activity is not zero activity, but is it much higher activity than in all other storage areas. It is this higher activity of the non-conscious mind that takes control from the conscious mind for where that higher activity proceeds to next (the elevator car), by increasing and decreasing activity anywhere along the elevator shaft.

The conscious mind is the elevator car operator and that determines what memory location (floor) is accessed by the non-conscious; the analogy is that the elevator car cables serves as a conduit for the flow of information to the brain stem where the information gets transformed by the "world interface" of consciousness. It is actually the conscious mind that directs the non-conscious mind's location but the non-conscious does all the work in traversing the storage areas. There can also be a combination and cooperation of non-conscious and conscious processes to accomplish the desired task which is usually to solve a problem by locating pertinent information for the task at hand such as language thinking. I would be remiss if I didn't repeat myself one more time; non-conscious thinking is the same as conscious thinking but it goes unnoticed by us because we are not conscious of it. We can become aware of it but that is *not* the same thing as being conscious of it. Being conscious of it would freak most people out to the point where they would believe they are insane.

I want to add one more descriptor to the paradigm of non-conscious and conscious thinking. As an aid to understanding how the non-conscious mind works, it is helpful to come to the realization that the way things are stored in the brain makes the non-conscious mind capable of viewing exactly what was earlier a real time event. If we can accept that we are cognitive of real time events then we should also accept that we can be cognitive of those same events at some later time if they were recorded and played back. This is basically what thinking is.

I believe that the brain's method for directing from the current memory location to an appropriate relationally connected location is that the non-conscious finds that relationally connected location for the conscious a priori. It is very much the same as what we call "motor control" for an output module's role in controlling hand and finger movements and we know that the conscious mind does control that. Even animals such as alligators have conscious motor control skills. In humans during language thinking, instead of controlling finger movements the conscious mind directs the non-conscious mind in controlling memory location which are in fact, different physical locations. There may be a dedicated output module whose job it is to direct the non-conscious to appropriate storage locations. This is not a big deal by any means and is somewhat easy to explain. The big hurdle is accepting the simple explanation for this.

The brain is very likely, a system that operates very close to a state of chaos. In chaos theory, there is always an "attractor" which is usually the cause of the beginning of a destructive instance. In the human brain, the attractor is the high neural activity metabolism (consciousness intensity) associated with consciousness (or non-consciousness) which directs the non-conscious with regards to memory location. If high enough neural activity occurs in multiple memory

Chapter 4 – The Mystery of Thought

locations at one time, this can result in confusion and possibly what we call, "mental illness". A highly stable system would ensure that only one floor would be accessed at one time. A chaotic system would not ensure this stability as the location of non-consciousness could be vacillating over a number of floors at any instance of time. If this hypothesis is true, this could be an explanation for many mental illness problems. The bottom line here is that we want the system to be stable because the more stability, the less confusion the conscious mind has to contend with. If the stimulation (non-consciousness) is highly locality stable, the conscious mind will have more of a chance to avoid confusion, stupidity and mental illness.

As I have alluded to, we may lose sight of the fact that assessing various memory locations at any instant is really no more complicated than simple muscle movements we employ on a daily basis. Instead of moving a specific muscle, such as the muscles in the fingers I am using to type this book, during language thought the neural networks direct the flow of nerve pulses and increase metabolism to a memory location by means of commonly used pathways (also a type of evolutionary algorithm) that were established through learning (use). The pathway is itself a stored memory. It is much the same as finding physical objects we have placed on shelves.

In this hypothesis of thinking, it is requisite to believe that non-consciousness is not a global phenomenon but is produced locally, and where appropriate and the information stored at the memory location of non-conscious higher intensity gets presented to the conscious. Another way of explaining this is to say that when the "mind's eye" traverses our cavernous memory, we access the local contents of that memory location and those contents only. Since we don't consciously "see" or "hear" anything we access in memory during the thought process, it is the non-conscious mind doing this. When we silently think with no spoken words, we can "hear" the words but not as if we are listening to sounds created by sound waves and picked up by the ear. We hear the words internally and that is another example of non-conscious language thinking.

The phenomenon we label as "thinking" has many facets that can be explained by what I have laid out here, so far. Information is deposited in our brain's memory; the conscious mind accesses the contents in various ways by directing the non-conscious mind. Recall that I said every action has to be enabled by a cause. The conscious mind directs the non-conscious mind but logically that cannot happen instantaneously. There has to be a lag time for the non-conscious to do it's "thing". There has to be much more activity beneath the surface to support what is on the surface. What I am suggesting here again is that there must be more than two consciousness intensity levels. I will use words as a descriptor, since I am describing language thinking. Conscious activity is words we can hear with the ear. Non-conscious activity is words we can hear internally. The third level of consciousness intensity is the activity that happens below the surface to locate the correct words for placement in the thought stream. We are totally unaware of that processing but it has to be there.

If the reader is paying attention, I am using the word, "mind" to describe the consciousness that gets produced by some unknown process at the brain stem (probably). The "mind" is the same for non-consciousness only we are only aware of objects and we cannot actually "see" or "hear" them. The word "mind" is not a descriptor for intelligent thought. The mind can "witness" intelligent information streams such as language thought streams or it can witness primitive thought modes such as cognition. The terms "mind" and "intelligence" are not synonymous by

Chapter 4 – The Mystery of Thought

any means. I believe that primitive animals such as alligators have a mind because my definition of a mind does not require advanced thought modes.

Language thought can be considered to be a serial stream of related information. In order to give an example of what this means, we will need to think about how we think. When we think in our native language, is it a flow of disjointedly meaning information points (words) or do the words flow in a relationally, systematic way in which every word is preceded and is followed by a word that has a relational connection semantically? Of course, we think in exactly the same way we talk. If we didn't talk in a semantically flowing manner in which each word had no or very little relationship to the preceding or post ceding word, our speech would sound like the babbling of an idiot.

Talking is merely thinking out loud. The same process that produced the word train for speech also is responsible for our thoughts. We think in the languages that we normally use in everyday life. What this means is that as we are thinking or talking in a language thought stream, each stored word in memory had to be linked in a semantic relationship at the time of storage and then in real time during the "assembly" of the thought stream, chosen for its appropriate place in the stream. This means that every word added to the thought stream is the result of a decision. The result is complex but the underlying mechanism is actually pretty simple. The main reason language thought seems to be so mysterious is that we forget how much time was required for us to collect the information we have stored and also the way in which that information was stored (learned).

There are two main types of language thought streams. The first is internally generated and always relates to some problem or condition we have been dealing with in the not so distant past or in some cases long term problems which we can think about for decades. The main point I am attempting to make is that thoughts about the subject did not just happen spuriously from nowhere. There was something ongoing prior and if you had new thoughts about the problem they were just a continuance. The second type is the language thought train that is externally generated in the form of presented question or problem. In both cases, there should be (if we are eloquent enough) background information to formulate language thought trains or what humans call "sentences". The one million dollar question is: How do we do this?

I believe the answer to the perplexing question lies in the way the brain stores and retrieves information including language thought streams. The brain does not just "take pictures"; it takes full motion videos of everything. Language thought streams are one of the things the brain records as a video with full audio and we are able to play back small chunks of the recorded thought stream audio and assemble these chunks into what we call sentences. We either speak the words we have assembled or we keep them internal and we call that language thinking. The mystery of language thinking is a mystery because we forget how we learned our native tongue to begin with. It was a long slow process to say the least.

Every new word that is presented to us undergoes a preliminary requisite learning curve in which we use the word in a number of ways. That process places the word in a category and depending on how complex the semantics of the word are; the category can be placed in sub-categories and the sub-categories in sub-sub-categories, etc. Since we don't need to read a dictionary

Chapter 4 – The Mystery of Thought

description of every word we place into our thought train, there has to be another way the brain does this. I believe the answer to this important question is the brain attaches concepts to each word during the learning process. An explanation of concepts is in order.

Word derived concepts

Language thinking is probably mainly enabled by the way the brain connects the semantic meaning of words to concepts. Concepts are simple physical and emotional constructs that are easy for even a simple brain such as a dog brain to be cognitive of. For humans it provides a simple method of instantaneous understanding of words. I go into this in the next chapter in detail where I attempt to provide mechanisms that could be technology based to duplicate what the brain does.

The process of language thinking is not as mysterious as it appears. We are able to find objects we have placed on shelves in the home and workshop. We know what shelf these items are on and when we go to that shelf we can find an individual item. Finding words in memory may not be any more of a mystery. Even dogs can locate things they have stored (hidden). When words are used an adequate number of times in thought trains, the brain gets trained by algorithms that evolve and "remember" the pathway to them. These are the evolutionary algorithms I mention so often in this writing. I also called these pathways scaffolds or ladders.

The fact that all of the pre-processing is done by the non-conscious mind gives rise to the illusion that thought happens spontaneously and this is clearly not the case. I reiterate that the chronological memory, the non-conscious mind has access to may contain entire thought stream scaffolding to aid it in preparing a new thought stream. This is analogous to using a "template" or "style" assistant in a word processing program. The various thought stream scaffolds are like skeletons ready to have meat applied to make them complete. These structures are a learned phenomenon and individuals who do public speaking about many diverse and complex subjects have developed and stored a complex set of thought structures for their use at any time a need arises. It is common knowledge that public speaking competency is a learned skill and the more humans do it the better they become. The structures I call scaffolds are merely "to memory location" pathways that have been used multiple times and this becomes as a foot trail is in high grass. The more a pathway gets used the easier it is for the non-conscious to follow and then the resulting contents of the located memory gets presented to the conscious. It is yet another use of evolutionary algorithms and another illusion the brain fools us with.

Algorithms that evolve in us over time

Evolutionary algorithms are the nature's way of setting up a "directory table" for the brain's memory system. In your desktop computer, the operating system has to have a way to know where the physical contents of memory are stored. If there was no directory, it would be unable to locate any programs or data and your computer would be no more than a fancy paper weight!

Evolutionary algorithms are simply a set of steps that the brain has connected into a semi-permanent circuit by which the often used pathways are transformed from software to hardware. I say semi-permanent because as everyone has experienced, when we do not use our stored

Chapter 4 – The Mystery of Thought

knowledge on a regular basis, it becomes more difficult to "call it up" at some later date. There are theories about why this is so and they involve the mechanism of storage that the brain uses at the root level.

It has been hypothesized that memories are stored in synapses between neurons and not the neurons themselves. A synapse can be considered to be a "short circuit" between neurons. The more a pathway is used the more permanent that pathway (a short circuit) will become. If that synaptic pathway happens to be part of an evolutionary algorithm, the more that algorithm is used the more permanent the connection will be and the access time (to a memory location) will also be decreased. This is common knowledge for anyone who has had a sabbatical from some complicated subject. Upon returning to that subject, we find that the information is still there, it may just be very hard to find!

Summary

If everything I have presented sounds completely convoluted, it only makes sense to me that most people would feel that way. This is because we have been brainwashed into believing that the things the brain does are so complex and mysterious that we will never be able to have a complete understanding of how the brain works its magic. One of the "holy grails" of brain function is the concept of "thinking". Thinking is believed to be impossible to understand and thus explain in any logical layman's terms. This is categorically wrong as I have attempted to prove in this chapter. I have attempted to present the reader with a paradigm of the non-conscious and conscious mind with an information friendly memory system. This system explains every aspect of the phenomenon of thinking except one; consciousness production, which has nothing to do with thinking anyway.

I have no real explanation for consciousness and I do not believe anyone does at the present time. We are coerced to accept the theory that it is a physical process and, that happens to be stimulation, metabolism, neuronal activity or whatever you wish to label it, will induce consciousness in the brain stem of most animals that sleep. We are then left with the somewhat simpler task of explaining the algorithmic, logic manipulations that are responsible for the production of intelligence. Since I am a computer scientist and not a neuroscientist by any means, I am best suited to explaining the logical, algorithmic processes of intelligence and I leave the biological explanation of consciousness to the medical profession.

The biggest obstacle people may have in understanding how the brain produces thought and how thought is directed by our conscious mind might be in the realization that these questions can be answered in relatively simple terms. The process of directing our thoughts may be no more complex than the process of directing our muscles in what we call motor skills. Very primitive animals such as alligators which have been around for millions of years probably possess consciousness and if you have ever been attacked by one, you already know they can certainly direct muscle action to perform useful tasks such as moving rapidly towards you!

If we take a leap of faith and accept that we are *not* some miraculous creature that can only be explained by mysticism, we will be a little closer to understanding the simple underpinnings of the mind. Thought is basically the non-conscious mind traversing the large expanse of human memory storage space and that action is sometimes controlled and experienced by the conscious mind. The location and directing of that transversal is no more complicated than is the use of our arms, hands, legs and feet. We use our arms, hands and feet to store physical things on places we call "shelves" and at some later time we go back to those shelves and we are able to locate all the things we placed there prior. Finding things in memory is no more of a mystery than that, and works basically the same way.

As we develop in our very long childhood, which is a requirement of high intelligence, we develop what I refer to as "evolutionary algorithms". Perhaps a better and more easily understood term would be "evolving learning algorithm". When we are first learning to pick up, move and place things with our hands, the instructions for doing those things gets fine-tuned. And, after a period of time sufficient to complete the corrections in muscle movements necessary for the precise placement of things we become proficient at these precise tasks. Some of us go on to be professional athletes when the picking up and placing of things like a major league baseball is practiced over and over. What is happening is the algorithms that control muscle movement are being refined to act in coordination with the eyes and all the parts of the body such as sensation in the finger tips that contribute to that muscle control. This is the reason a major league baseball pitcher can place a baseball in a 1 foot square box at 100 MPH. His control algorithms have evolved to the point of precision and by the way, that happens to be the non-conscious mind doing the control.

We do the same type of algorithm refinement when we begin to access information in our memory. The whole process of memory content location procedure takes years to refine with use but when we use our memory the process of thought control always appears instantaneous. The control and "creation" of thoughts is an illusion that we are tricked by on a moment to moment basis. It is not, by any means, a mysterious or complex process. As I have alluded to, the creation of spurious thought may be entirely random. We can call up anything for our past instantaneously, and when the artifact in question is being thought of, it becomes a key for any subsequent thought. We wonder how we were able to call up that one artifact from literally nothing but what we don't realize it that we could have called up anything from our past. We also could be thinking non-consciously of an ongoing problem and our conscious mind became aware of that. Our memory is a continuum from the present to our very first memories in life.

Notwithstanding, I believe I have presented a sensible biological explanation for how the brain works. My further belief is that the process of explaining how the biological brain works will enable humans to construct a machine that does basically the same thing. It is said the copying is the sincerest form of flattery and I intend to copy nature's design to propose a human level intelligent computer design in the next chapter. If there are still questions in the reader's mind about how the human mind works, perhaps the next chapter will clarify that. We cannot truly understand how the brain works until we attempt to duplicate what it does.

Chapter 5 – Computer Science and AI

Chapter 5 – Computer Science and Artificial Intelligence

In the last chapter, I presented a possible technical biological mechanism of the brain's production of intelligence. In this chapter I shall attempt to present a valid electronics based mechanism for artificially creating an equivalent level of intelligence. In order to do this, I will explain the various concentrations of computer science (CS) which lend themselves towards this ambitious goal. CS is the field that is best suited to the development of any future human level intelligence since it is the science of computing and the brain is most definitely a computer. However, since I believe the pathway to a real Artificial Intelligence (AI) machine is mostly in hardware design, computer engineering could also be the field that will accomplish this goal. In keeping with the theme of this book, I coin and present another acronym for Real Artificial Intelligence; RAI. This differentiates the current lackluster weak and the theoretical "strong" AI known in AI circles today to what I propose will be *real* and not contrived artificial intelligence. Since either form of currently accepted or proposed AI is not what could be called real AI by any stretch of the imagination; the RAI label is fitting.

The brain is a computer; however it is far removed from the computers we are all familiar with. The architecture of the brain is completely different from the computers mankind has concocted and science is at a loss to explain how the brain's architecture produces intelligence or even if the physical layout has anything to do with it. In the last chapter I made an attempt to break free of the deadlock that is present in today's science by providing some possible explanations for the brain's architecture and how that architecture produces human intelligence. I will concede that the ideas I have presented in the last chapter are purely hypothetical. However, we need a debarkation point to begin our journey into the unknown and if during the course of our journey we discover that copying this model of the brain actually might result in a RAI machine, then it won't amount to a hill of beans as to the validity of my original hypotheses.

We are all familiar with "digital computers". Digital computers use discreet "on and off" variables to follow precise instructions which result in precise actions. Since the smallest unit of control in a digital computer can only be on or off, there is no room for error on the micro level. If errors occur in digital computation, they usually happen at macro levels in complex program errors, not at the micro levels of ones and zeroes.

Although digital computers are "all the rage" now, analog computers were some of the first computing machines utilized by humans. The famous "Nordon Bombsight" of World War Two was an analog computer. The operator (bombardier) only needed to put the target in the crosshairs of the sight and press a trigger. The sight would input airspeed, aircraft heading, cross wind, altitude, air temperature, humidity and probably some other inputs I am not aware of and calculated a release time for the bombs. The bombsite even took control of flying the bomber during the computation phase and until all the bombs were gone.

Chapter 5 – Computer Science and AI

This form of computing involves the use of input and output micro variables that can not only be a one or a zero as with digital computers, but anywhere in between. The theoretical number of possible levels is infinite, since if plotted on a number line, will be represented by geometric points which are infinitely small. It is this large variability of micro level control points that allows for errors that are not a problem in digital computing. Analog computers are adequate for many applications and were used in the past with satisfactory results. It is better suited to simple applications and as the system it is attempting to control becomes more complex the rate of errors also increases. In other words, it has limitations.

The brain is neither a digital nor an analog computer but is a combination of the two. The brain's physical hardware as a digital computer is simple compared to even the earliest human made digital computers. The neuronal synapses may act as digital micro level storage devices, whether the storage is temporary or permanent. That is the extent of the brain's comparison to a digital computer from a hardware aspect. The brain processes information in much the same algorithmic way with the use of modules as a digital computer does, albeit at a lower certainty of correctness at the micro level. A digital computer has a correctness certainty of 100% at the micro level, provided there is no malfunction present. In the brain, there can be a great disparity in effectiveness in the storage of micro information throughout the brain's entirety.

Since storage is dependent on brain metabolism and in turn metabolism is dependent on stimulation and neurotransmitter balance and correctness, there is always the possibility of variability, just as in an analog computer. There is also the problem of locality stability of the activity of metabolism which is responsible for correct memory location acquisition. These are some of the many biological pitfalls of the brain and it is the main reason that AI has the potential to "outsmart" the brain many thousands of times. Add to that; the emotional roadblocks humans are born with and usually have a very tough time controlling and you get the picture why AI is needed.

Why AI is the most important milestone in human history

I truly believe that not only will RAI be a nice thing to have, it will be a necessity. I don't envision how humanity will survive without it. We seem to be coping with the problems we have always faced as a species, but what about the unknown? I am talking about the one predominant event that is just over the horizon and will end up blindsiding and ending us as a species. This could come from any number of sources. It could be an asteroid or comet that is just way too big for the earth to tolerate. It could be a new unforeseen virus that just pops out of nowhere. There is also a very remote possibility that we get invaded by extraterrestrials! I personally do not believe that but it would be foolish to ignore that possibility. I cover that in detail in chapter 8 - UFOs.

In addition to all the things that may put an untimely end to us, there are a plethora of items we could fix to make life easier for those of us that survive the "great zombie apocalypse". How about an unlimited supply of cheap energy? How about space travel that does not involve the use of fossil fuels? How about medical science that actually knows everything there is to know about the human body? How about RAI doctors that are so knowledgeable that your medical problem is diagnosed correctly at least 99% of the time in a few minutes? The other 1% will take a few more days. Sounds a little like Obama care, doesn't it? I'm kidding of course. It may sound like propaganda but in this case it will be true! RAI has the potential for humans to enjoy a complete understanding of everything! Every problem we now face whether it is social, political or scientific can be solved.

If this all sounds very similar to a communist utopia, it will be a utopia, only communism will have nothing to do with it! It will simply be; making decisions that are based on every bit of information that is available, all the time, with absolutely no emotional component. The decisions made will have the highest probability for success. Eventually socio-economic issues will improve. There will be less crime and that will evolve into no crime. There will be less poverty and that will evolve into no poverty. There will be less hunger and that will evolve into no hunger. We will be able to solve every problem we currently have.

The only requisite will be that we follow the advice of our RAI machine friends. That may be the biggest stumbling block in the entire process; human willingness to listen to a higher intelligence. We don't do that now; this is evidenced in the continuing war between the smart and the stupid which I cover in detail in the next chapter. There is no more hope of the stupid listening to or believing intelligent machines than they would smart people. Perhaps RAI can cure stupidity (a stupendous accomplishment) and then there would be no opposition to trying out the ideas of our RAI machine allies. I believe eventually every problem we now contend with can be solved. This will be part of the continuing advancement of humanity, and the alternative of doing this may be to regress or maybe fail altogether. As I said, I do not think we have a choice. In the survival game, we either advance or get ready for failure.

Strong and weak AI

Just about anyone who has used a computer has as some point made use of what is known in CS circles as a weak AI program. The spell checker on a word processing program is one example. Anything that functions as an aid and acts like a helping hand is probably got some element of weak AI In it. It is safe to say that at the present time, all AI is of the weak variety. This is because strong AI is considered to be what is known as "human level" intelligence. The methods that are currently proposed for attaining the "strong" type, will all predictably fail because the proponents of these ideas fail to consider one important key point: The brain does not function as the proponents of these methods advocate.

The brain does not work by using any human invented logic systems programmed into algorithms but it works on supreme simplicity as I attempted to explain in the last chapter. Some examples of the human invented logic systems taught in CS AI classes today are: first-order, fuzzy, higher-order and propositional. A great deal of importance is placed on these topics for the utilization of these systems in weak AI. The professors who promote these ideas have some distant dream of strong AI but it seems to stay just out of reach for them and the reason for that is understandable: The brain does not work that way. The bottom line is: These are nice things to have but they do not explain how we get our smarts in the first place.

Chapter 5 – Computer Science and AI

I know of no actual strong AI program or machine in existence at the present time. I also foresee no "Strong AI" in the near or far future, at least using the hardware and the logic systems we have available now. What I am trying to say is that if strong AI is ever achieved, we will accomplish that goal through the use of radically different hardware and not using classical logic systems as the main enabler. In other words I do not believe that we will be successful in designing a "strong AI" machine (an RAI machine) by simply programming any type of computer that is currently available and not even any type of supercomputer.

Review of how the brain produces and controls thought

I use language thinking for this discussion since that is the premier mode of intelligent thought. Interests are the key driving force in understanding how the brain controls thought. "Interest" is the term humans use for what are actually *key artifact locating directors*. Where does the "interest" that ultimately causes the control of memory "drifting up and down trees and ladders" come from? I call that memory drifting; "thought" or "thinking". Interests are what? This may sound like overstating the obvious but; *it is the things we are interested in*. If we have an interest in any subject, objects, i.e. anything we may want to think about, we have already established "paths" to those locations. Evolutionary algorithms have, through a learning process, established paths that the non-conscious has followed and may follow in any future thought process. Another way to look at evolutionary algorithms is that they are simply a memory of memories accessed in the past. Interest creates high metabolism which is equal to high neuronal activity first during the storage phase and later at a lower intensity during the playback phase. When we get emotionally excited that translates to high levels of activity neuron wise.

It helps to recall that the non-conscious works in coordination with the conscious and it has a view of the possible relation and attribute pathways to be taken by virtue of what I termed the "scaffolds" of thought. This is part of how the non-conscious pre-programs the paths that the conscious mind will take. Recall that in order for anything to happen; there has to be some underlying causal affect that happens a priori. Since we are not conscious of the relational pathway selection that is going on in the non-conscious, we only are aware of the results of that pre-selection and we term that phenomenon: "Thinking". Understanding the mechanism of pathways to memory locations should be no more confusing than understanding common human acts of locating objects we have placed on shelves.

Interests can also be new ones in which we have no prior experience or have never had a single thought about. Then the control of where to go in memory must be from a purely relational mechanism, in which the most closely related match to the currently viewed context is taken. What do we usually do when we have an insufficient or perhaps zero knowledge of a subject and the subject seems interesting? We try to enhance our knowledge of that subject by reading or some other learning process. This establishes relational links and provides pathways for use in subsequent thought(s).

When we think, it is always a flow of relationally rich information. In the language thinking mode, it is a flow of concepts that are always related to each other in some respect. Another important concept is that language thought is a serially produced and almost always a non-deterministically accepted individual word and subsequent train of information. It is never information that is not linked from word to word relationally and a decision is made at every word as to what the next word will be. This is an important clue as to what thought is. It is the non-conscious mind, with direction from the conscious mind, traversing memory areas that have strong relational connections via scaffolds. I alluded to the possibility of "thought scaffolds" being a method the brain uses to construct language thought trains. These are essentially evolutionary algorithms that were established through learning of our native language over long periods of time. The pathways used to locate information are like thoroughfares to the information and are established with use.

The training that allows us to think didn't happen overnight. Again, finding information in memory is no more mysterious than locating items we place on the physical shelves in our workshop or garage. It is very unlikely that any human could generate a useful and interpretable thought train (speech) without ever having listened to and read a number of thought trains in the same natural language. In fact, the more listening and reading done before hand, the better humans are able to public speak, unaided with things such as "teleprompters". If the reader has doubts about the validity of my claim that speech is merely the playback of recorded speech; this small fact should quell those doubts:

Humans always speak in the accent that they were exposed to during the training process. British people all have that distinct British accent and they might retort by saying it is Americans that have distinct accents. We can break accents down to sub-accents within the U.K. and the same holds true for America. The Welch accent is very much different from the Cockney accent and in America, people in the Appalachian Mountains sound very much different than the people who grew up in Brooklyn, New York. This is all because speech and the thought that drives speech, is merely the orderly playback of previously recorded speech that we were exposed to during our development. It is definitely not a mysterious process and is completely algorithmic in nature and therefore we should be able to create an artificial version of the brain which would basically do the same thing. Things are usually easier said than done but we must try nonetheless. Of course we are not chasing a machine that can merely talk because we already have that. We want a machine that can "think out loud" and actually perform language thought.

The one million dollar question is: How do we build a machine that does what I just described? My personal opinion is that it would be difficult if not impossible with a modern digital computer. That is because the Von Neumann architecture machine simply does not lend itself towards this particular application. A bit of background is necessary to explain what I mean by "Von Neumann architecture". This is how all modern digital computers including supercomputers are structured. It involves the use of a "central processing unit" (CPU), memory and input / output devices.

An important aspect of this paradigm is that the CPU makes use of instructions. Each CPU has its own "repertoire" of instructions or in other words; a list of instructions built in as hardware *receptors*. This is referred to as "combinational logic" and it is actually hardware ones and zeros which is configured so that when a matching set of software ones and zeros is fetched from memory it will perform the task assigned to the particular combination of ones and zeros. The CPU will "fetch" software instructions from memory, execute the software instruction that is a match for the hardware instruction and store the results back in memory. Typical instructions do things such as load (contents of memory location), add, subtract, compare, store. These instructions when put in specific order as in a program make up what we call "machine language or assembly language" and relate directly to what I alluded to with the term "machine word". A machine word contains an instruction, and memory locations with which to retrieve data (load) or store data.

Programs can be entirely written in machine language but high level languages such as C++ and Java were invented to simplify what can be complex if done at the machine language level. High level languages provide abstraction from the logically complex and make management of complex programs easier. When a high level program is completely written, it is run through a "compiler" program and what comes out of that operation is machine language. This is part and parcel of the current methods used to implement weak AI and is the accepted status quo for any proposed "strong AI". In other words CS is stuck on the notion of using currently available hardware and high level languages to implement what they consider to be AI, weak or strong. CS researchers have been working towards the goal of strong AI for at least 20 years using Von Neumann architecture with high level languages with no results of any kind to speak of.

The brain also has instructions but they are all hardware as in the CPU's hardware instruction receptors. The brain never gets instructions through the use of software. Our brain is programmed once during our development phase (probably mostly in the womb) and that's it. Every action we take and everything we learn is accomplished with the original hardware instructions we were born with. What this means in common sense terms, is that intelligence is based on very simple instructions that are in-born and unchangeable. All of what could be considered as complex programming is done in input modules, the depth perception modules being the candidate for the most complex. If the reader has been paying attention, those instructions which are contained in an algorithm are also hardware and also not changeable.

This all casts doubt on whether anyone; computer scientist, engineer or otherwise will ever be able to create RAI solely with a modern computer; supercomputers included. In order to provide backup for my assertions I will need to provide a few comparisons between what is needed (what the brain does) and the modern computer. I leave the programming aspect for a later discussion and I now address the memory aspect (pun intended).

In the last chapter, in my brief expedition into the utility of algorithmic consciousness, I said the conscious area of the brain might be represented by using a dedicated register for all incoming real time data. This is the real time data or information that we are currently conscious of and we need to compare this to *all* the previously stored data in our memory. In order to do this, we need a storage bank of previous data in the form of frames (floors in our imagined high rise building). This is where problems begin to loom large for the modern computer. As a point of reference I use the one G BIP (brain information point) machine word size of the brain as a comparator. Recall that we store things that are of interest to us (high consciousness intensity) and that one G BIP (machine word) chunks need to be stored at certain intervals. The interval is a purely arbitrary value and we can use a purely philosophic method in an attempt to estimate how many memory frames will be stored in a lifetime of use.

Chapter 5 – Computer Science and AI

To that end, I will use the arbitrary storage interval of 15 seconds. I came up with this number using survival in an equatorial region as a guide to how much a hunter / gatherer would need to store to ensure a high probability of survival. The reader is invited to do their own "mind experiment" and create their own estimate of the proper interval. I came up with 15 seconds because of my own personal experience in the military and much experience in living outdoors. I could be wrong by a large factor but as you will realize, that will not matter much in the final analysis. Do your own estimate and perform a few simple calculations and you will see that it really doesn't matter much. The end resulting number will always be quite large.

Using my 15 second storage interval, this means that every 15 seconds the brain would need to store 1 G BIPs of current visual information, odors, sounds and tactile (sunlight heat through trees, how the terrain felt on the feet, etc.). I will assume that people had to be awake and active for at least 18 hours a day. I arrive at the 15 second figure by noting how much information that would be needed to be stored walking a cautious 2 MPH. Although humans have lost most of their survival skills at present, in the past we would have to remember the terrain covered because doing things like walking in circles would not be advantageous. I estimate at 2 MPH we would have to record visual information every 15 seconds to keep our directions and not get lost.

60 seconds / 15 = 4 stores per minute, 60 minutes X 4 = 240 stores per hour, and 240 X 18 hours = 4,320 stores per day. 4,320 X 360 = 1,555,200 stores per year. I now guess at the number of years one of the elders of the group might live to and I will use the conservative value of 50 years since the elders who made most of the decisions and were probably the smartest in the group would likely live this long. So, 50 years X 1,555,200 = 77,760,000 stores per lifetime. Since the individual store is one G BIPs this amounts to a grand total of 77,760,000 X 1,000,000,000 = 77,760 X 10 twelfth, BIPs. This is 77,760,000,000,000,000 BIPs total lifetime storage. This is 77.76 Penta BIPs. I will round this number off to an even 80 Penta BIPs since we want our human made machine to far surpass the human brain. For a comparison to human computer machines we divide by 8 for the number of bytes. This gives 10 Penta Bytes human made computer memory equivalence. This is not a direct comparison because of the large numbers a binary system this large would be capable of. Since the brain does not use numbers the way a human made machine does, the brain is at a disadvantage as far as storage of large numbers is concerned. But, on the other hand, the storage of large numbers is not needed in the brain's system of addressing because obviously, there are no memory addresses, only the look-through memory to store and locate artifacts.

If we wanted to implement a human made computer to emulate the architecture of the brain we would then need at least 10 Penta Bytes of equivalent storage and the most contentious aspect of this is the modern computer's storage at this level is always mechanical, which is either a hard disk or tape, both of which are considered secondary memory. These types of media will not work with the brain's architecture since the brain has nothing but fast primary memory and the fast traversal of any and all memory is absolutely essential to the production of intelligence. In addition, the structures of human memory contain many relational and attribute links that need to be accessed, otherwise the entire paradigm of memory access and traversal is broken and the phenomenon of thinking would be impossible. Recall I referred to this as MLF (memory leap frogging). The memory system I am proposing locates things by how relevant they are, not because they get accessed by a program with memory addresses pointing to them. That is a big difference.

I know many computer scientists will scoff at my assertions but this is perhaps because they haven't read or understood my explanation of the process of thinking which is dependent of the traversal of memory and that is dependent on relational and attribute links contained in those memory locations. Recall what I said about arrogance, narcissism and egotism being an indicator as well as a cause of stupidity. While the detractors of my hypothesis are rolling on the floor laughing, they just might want to take a one minute break and consider this:

The human memory paradigm I have been describing would be one of the most difficult, if not impossible, high level language programs ever attempted by anyone using current hardware technology. If however, you are a diehard conventionalist and you want to prove that my suggestion of a memory system can be done with a high level language program using any computer you can get access to, including supercomputers; I am pleased to have provided you with the blueprint for your efforts. If you believe it can be done, by all means do it. I am skeptical (not unfounded by any means) and unless I see a RAI machine pop up somewhere, I remain skeptical. The architecture and operation of the proposed memory structure which follows would streamline logical search, compare and response operations. This idea for a new memory system would eliminate billions of lines of code that would be required to accomplish basically the same thing, if in fact the human memory paradigm is not an intractable high level programing problem, and I believe it is. Of course, I'm sure there will be detractors who will say that the whole notion of this memory system being the key to RAI is nonsense. Well, if it is nonsense, then why does it make sense?

There is an additional reason why the human memory paradigm would be impossible to implement with only current computer hardware and clever software programs. It is the phenomenon of MLF (memory leap frogging) I alluded to in the last chapter. It is highly probably that when RAI machines are first developed they will not have the self-learning capabilities that humans generally possess. The first RAI machines will most likely be trained by plugging them into another computer and downloading things like lexicons of computer friendly words matched with the word derived concepts I proposed in the last chapter. In this mode of learning the MLF methods won't be needed. However, eventually we will need our new smart machine allies to learn autonomously just like humans do. In order for machines to act as humans they need to follow the human MLF method. This means that when one BMW is accessed a section of that BMW can be used as a search key for a subsequent search and when a BMW is found containing the search key, a portion of that can be used as a subsequent search key and so forth. This would be very hard to accomplish using only conventional computer hardware and high level languages.

The key to understanding how the optical memory hardware I propose below trumps any equivalent operational software is that it will simplify what would be super complex data manipulations if done entirely with software. Hardware is always faster than software and this is yet another reason why a software solution in conventional machines would be difficult if not impossible. Some of the data manipulations include: Searching the entire system of one G BIP frames of memory (a total of 80 P BIPs) for similarities in the key search object, storing any returned hit memory *locations* in some sort of register for future use and also storing any found relationships *locations*. Storing the location or address of a 1 G BIP frame is explained below. It does not involve the use of conventional addresses per se and only uses a miniscule number as far as modern memory systems are concerned. The whole memory can be accessed using 80 million "addresses" (not really addresses but they serve the same purpose).

There is no doubt in my opinion that RAI will be impossible using solely currently available computer hardware. It is just that simple. No amount or correct design of virtual memory management will cure this problem. Recall that virtual memory is the amount of memory the CPU "thinks" it has. The operating system has to constantly change the contents of primary memory in chunks called "pages" (in a paging system) from secondary memory. The operating system does this when a program too large to be contained entirely at one time in primary memory is run. Part of the program resides in primary memory for processing and is constantly refreshed with program content from secondary memory that will be used next. This is entirely useless for the purpose of duplicating the brain's functionality.

What is needed to duplicate the brain's architecture is a very large primary memory structure with a machine word size equal to that of the brain (1 G BIPs). It also has to be on the order of 80 P BIPs which results in 80 million frames (floors of our imaginary high rise) of 1 G BIPs each. We want as much memory as possible as we are attempting to far surpass the human brain's intelligence level which is why I increased the 76.76 P BIPs to 80 P BIPs. The only solution is a new, fast, reliable and modern, optically based memory system. It has to be optically based because if we attempt to make the number of connections needed, the old CMOS (Complementary Metal Oxide Semiconductor) will get overloaded and will not work. It is very much like pugging in too many toasters into the wall outlet in your home. Too many toasters and you blow a fuse! This is called "fan-in" and "fan-out" in electronics terms. Every electronic device has a maximum number of connections that can be applied to its output or input. That's why future memory structures will be optically implemented.

A proposal of an optically based look-through shared memory

Why light?

What I'm about to present to the reader may be a bit too technical for the average non-technical lay person. My advice is that the reader at least make an attempt at what I am suggesting to get a better understanding of what can be done with technology if we use our nature given abilities to transcend and survey. Much of what I suggest here is used in other areas of electronics, mainly in communications. If you ever used the internet, you most likely used what is known as a "fiber optic backbone" which your internet service provider maintains to provide its customers with high speed internet service connected to the whole world. The backbone is a thoroughfare of sorts in that it acts similarly to a superhighway for "packets" of internet protocol data transfers.

The words "fiber optic" may lead the lay person to believe that somehow light is used in the operation of the superhighway fiber optic backbone in question. This is a correct assumption and the reason light is the preferred carrier of information instead of electrons for physical lines and not through open space (air) is threefold.

Chapter 5 – Computer Science and AI

The first reason light is preferable to electrons for the carrying of information by virtue of light's high frequency. Light as you may recall from your science classes in high school is in fact electro-magnetic radiation. The big difference between light and radio waves is the frequencies of light are much, much higher. Just as radio frequency signals can be "modulated' with some useful information to be transferred over distances, light can also be modulated and the frequencies of light can also be varied just as the frequencies of radio signals can be varied. When the frequencies of light are varied that is usually thought of as differences in colors but what I am about to suggest would be impossible for a human to witness that color change. It is beyond our range of sensory response capabilities.

The big advantage that light has over electrons is that since light has an inherently high frequency, when the frequencies of light are varied, they can be varied in a much higher "bandwidth" than any of the lower frequency radio waves, such as the ones we call "microwaves". This is simply because when a higher frequency is increased by 10 % for example, the difference between the value before the 10% increase and the value after the 10% increase will be much greater than it would have been for a lower frequency. It's just common sense and a simple numbers game. If we have a 60 Hz sine wave and a 120 Hz sine wave and we increase both by 50% then we have 30 Hz increase for the first and 60 Hz increase for the second. There are also 60 one hertz "steps" in the latter example and only 30 in the prior. It's just that simple. This allows for a greater number of simultaneous signals to be carried over the same fiber "tube" and also a greater number of discreet frequencies for any given light frequency range when compared to any radio frequency (RF) range.. This concept will be advantageous in my suggestion for an optical memory so keep this in mind.

The second reason light is preferred carrier of information for a "land line" is that light does not generate magnetic fields as electrons do. This means that the possibility of interactions due to magnetic coupling between wires that are bundled close together is non-existent. When a signal (voltage and resulting electron flow) is induced in a wire as a result of the magnetic field created by electron flow through a physically close adjacent wire, this is commonly referred to as "cross-talk" in electronics terms. This phenomenon causes many problems as the complexity of electron carrying circuitry increases. The number of possible cross-talk related problems is directly proportional to the complexity (number) of signal carrying conductors in any given system. Optically coupled systems allows for more carrier "tubes" to be in close proximity to one another with no interference between adjacent tubes. This also will be of importance in my optical memory suggestion.

The third reason is what I alluded to in my beginning discussion of why light is the preferred carrier of information. Electron carrying components such as transistors have a maximum number of wires that can be connected to them. Again, this is called a component's fan in and fan out number. "Optic-isolators (called opto-isolators) are routinely used in electronics equipment to electrically isolate signal transmitting or receiving components to eliminate an actual electrical connection between the sender and receiver. They work exactly like the fiber optic backbone of your internet provider only on a much smaller scale. A signal turns a transistor on and off in various frequencies and at varying levels and the transistor turns a LED on and off at the same frequencies and at varying intensities. At the receiving end, a device known as a "photo diode" responds to the light coming out of the led and follows the frequencies and intensities by turning a transistor on and off. Whatever signal was applied to the input comes out the output, with no actual electrical connection in between.

In systems such as fiber optic backbones of internet providers, the LEDs' "color" i.e. frequency, is "modulated" by varying the voltage applied to the device. The "carrier" or non-signal applied frequency (basically its color) of the LED is the result of the manufacturing process used when the device is made. It should be apparent that many photo diodes could act as receivers for one transmitting LED. The only difficult aspect to this setup is the physical layout of the light carrying passageways such as fiber optic tubes. This concept will be an essential requirement in my optical memory suggestion because of the sheer number of devices accessed.

Optical memory structure

I said that the "machine word" of the human brain was one G BIPs. I also estimated the total memory capacity needed to be on the order of 80P BIPs. This calculates to 80 million 1 G BIP frames for the entire structure which if illustrated will look very much like the high rise office building I used as an example in the last chapter. The entire structure will be mounted in a superstructure in which the top master frame will contain the electronics needed to deposit and access contents in any of the 80 million 1 G BIP slave frames. Considering that the square root of one billion is not an even number I decrease the size of the BMW to 900,000,000 which has a square root of 30,000. This means that the BMW will be a 30,000 by 30,000 matrix of BIPs cells. I now need to recalculate how many frames I need and to keep things on keel for a total memory size of 80 P BIPs. I now increase the number of floors (slave frames) to 90 million which results in a memory slightly larger than 80 P BIPs but more memory can only mean better performance. To summarize, I have a 900,000,000 BIP (cell) matrix of 30,000 X 30,000 cells in a flat frame which is one cell thick. I will stack 90,000,000 of these cells in a superstructure or rack if you prefer (IT jargon) and these will be the slave frames. Then I will have one 900,000,000 matrix of 30,000 X 30,000 cells in another flat frame configured to be the master frame. In reality I could include one than one master frame in the arrangement and that would serve to add functionality. The master frame(s) are placed on the end or top of the superstructure (high rise building) of slave frames.

Each *cell* in the master frame(s) is directly associated with 900,000,000 cells in the 90,000,000 slave frames. That is, each master frame cell can communicate with 90,000,000 individual cells by writing and reading one BIP (per cell).The 90 M BIP cells (because each BIP is a cell) in each slave frame will be accessible through the flat side of the slave frames and will be accessible by optically shooting light through all the cells that align with each other in all frames in the stacked frames arrangement.

To reiterate, I call the topmost frame (would correspond to the top floor of our imaginary high rise office building), the master frame which contains the LEDs (probably the laser variety) that shoot through the entire assembly of 90 M slave frames. The master frame also contains photo diodes that receive information from all the slave frames. Each cell in a slave frame will hold exactly one brain information point, of data which is analogous to a bit in digital computers and whose purpose is to emulate a synapse in the brain. The slave frames and their cells have no wired electrical signal connections to the superstructure and will communicate signals strictly optically with light pulses.

A system with this amount of storage capacity and this architecture would have little hope of working with wired connections for signals. Each cell could be powered with connections to the frame and the frame wired (plugged into) to the superstructure or possibly entirely wireless through a refresh system where the pulses of light power each cell's power requirements through an absorbed light energy concept similar to photo-voltaic cells (solar panel cells).

The high rise office building elevator described in my brain consciousness level analogy is not possible since we have no hope of synthesizing human consciousness in a machine. So I need to eliminate the elevator car and everything associated with biological consciousness. We only have the ability for the attribution of consciousness and what we are left with is a somewhat more complex solution than is nature's simple solution of biological consciousness. We are now confronted to the problem of emulating human consciousness in a machine. Since consciousness does not enable intelligence, it only provides biological machines access to it, the underlying solution is algorithmic, which we should be able to do.

To that end, we need to stay as close to brain architecture is as technically possible and that means we need to be true to the brain's logical architecture in its memory system. Since the brain does not use memory addresses to locate information, we need to do that the same way. There is no conventional addressing needed or wanted in this memory scheme as slave frames are accessed only if there is a similarity between the contents of the master frame and itself or if there is a relation or attribute link between the two. The location of slave frames containing pertinent information is done using some of the properties of light as a carrier of information, rather than electrons. I explain this in detail below. One of the master frames (if the design designates this is the way to go) could act as the "consciousness register" and take the place of the "consciousness as a comparator register" in the biological brain.

The cells themselves each contain a simple tiny memory unit called a "bi-stable multi-vibrator" or "flip-flop" which can store an on or off condition. The circuitry of the cell also has a photo-diode to receive light messages down and a LED (probably the laser variety also) for sending responses up. Each slave frame could be programed to respond and reply with a single light frequency and there would need to be a total of 90 million discrete frequencies for the 90 million frames. It is possible that a new device would need to be designed to perform what I am proposing here for the master frame LEDs but I believe it can be done. The master frame would need to transmit a frequency sweep of all 90 million frequencies for a response of all 90 million slave frames, one at a time. In each response, a comparison for similarities between the conscious register and the accessed frame is made and when there is a sufficient amount of similarity, the frequency of that frame (the frame's ID) is stored and used to request adjacent and / or related / attribute link frames (I called this MLF - memory leap frogging) for their contents for more comparisons. This is the extent of addressing for this system.

An additional problem is implementing the consciousness as a memory controller function. How do we create hardware that will only store the important artifacts and ignore the usual and mundane? This won't be a problem until RAI machines become autonomous learning. This book

Chapter 5 – Computer Science and AI

was never intended to provide a complete blueprint for an RAI machine, autonomous or not and so I will save my ideas for that in a later edition, if there is one and that will be only if there is interest in this edition. The reader is invited to dream up a solution for this formidable problem. I omitted one important point in my explanation for how the brain uses up memory space. Recall that I believe the brain uses up memory space as it goes, filling up space as needed and storing relationally rich objects next to each other in each brain machine word (BMW). It is the problem of how the brain selectively uses up memory; one memory location at a time. In other words when we are presented with the problem of duplicating the brain's memory architecture with electronics hardware, this immediate problem presents itself to us. It is the problem of how to fill up our memory frames one by one and leave the others empty until needed.

I believe the brain has to possess some simple mechanism for a systematic fill up of the memory structure in addition to the use of consciousness intensity level. In other words, the brain has to have a way to use storage locations in a step by step manner so that the desired information does not go to all the available empty storage space but only the next adjacent empty space. I believe this mechanism is relatively easy to do for a biological system as every animal on the planet shares similar structures with plant life. I am referring to the veins and arteries in animals looking very much like the veins and arteries found in plants. It does not take much of a stretch of the imagination to link this mathematical construct (that's what it is) to the neuronal structures of the brain.

This means that as the synapses between neurons get "shorted out" and become an information point, the neurons adjacent and next in line become "shorted" and storage will go down to the next and next of what can be thought of as a vein or artery. And, when that branch is filled, shorting will progress down the next branch and so on. Of course this is pure speculation but the brain has to have some mechanism for preservation of precious memory resources and this is as good as any that we as speculators can imagine. I said before, I don't really care exactly how the brain does what it does; I only care what it does.

So now we are confronted with converting what I have just proposed into electronics hardware. This is not so difficult with the optical frame and superstructure memory system I have just laid out. The conservation of memory could be accomplished by simply providing an enable output and an enable input on each slave frame. So when two frames are plugged into the superstructure, the frame above will have its enabled output connected to the enable input of the frame below. When the above frame is used (filled up) the enabled output goes high and that permits the below frame to be written into. This would ensure that each frame gets used up one at a time and memory is progressively used as needed. Otherwise without this provision, all slave frames would be written into simultaneously and they would all have the exact contents on the very first write.

If we were utilizing addresses as in current technology machines this would not be an issue at all. However in the paradigm of copying brain memory structure, we cannot use addresses as that would add unnecessary and burdensome complexity to the whole nature inspired system. We don't want a memory structure where the use of any directory or registry is needed. Once objects are located, we find additional useful information with a purely relational system of locating related objects, much like a modern relational data base.

Chapter 5 – Computer Science and AI

The modern relational database has revolutionized the storage, categorization and retrieval of many diverse types of information in the last 30 years or so. Using relations as the linking objects for information has enabled the ecommerce we enjoy today as well as being essential to engineering and all other subjects of study or research. Today's business models would not be possible without the use of relational databases.

The relational database has become one of computer science's main concentrations, and Master's and PhD students can select it as their main area of concentration and in the process write their thesis or dissertation on this diverse and complex subject. Searching has always been a hot topic for research in computer science and it has taken on new complexities when applied to relational databases. Every time we do searches in a merchant's store website, we are using the search capabilities of a relational database. Every time we do searches in Google, WebCrawler or Yahoo we are searching through relational databases. Finding anything in today's complex world of trillions of pieces of information would be impossible without the use of relations as the linking structure.

The way this could work in my proposed memory structure is this: Memory gets filled up as experiential time elapses. As memory locations fill up, one by one, they fill up with contents that will be related with strong relational links to other slave frames, some of which may be physically adjacent but the physical location is not important. For example if 100 frames were used to store information related to automobiles. Then a hiatus of 100 frames was used up storing information on cooking hamburgers. Following the food break, the subject returned to automobiles again and this time 500 frames were used up. So, how would the original 100 automobile frames be linked with the later 500 automobile frames? The simple answer is by relations.

The odds are that something in the 900 M BIP master frame search key would relate and have similarities to at least one artifact (attribute) in both the 100 and the 500 frame sets. A frequency sweep and query of the entire memory would now result in slave frame frequency identifiers being returned for something in both sets. Once the frequency identifiers were known, the system could assess adjacent frames for additional content which would have a high probability of containing pertinent information. It should be apparent that the "central system" doing the queries would necessarily need some additional memory in the form of a few simple registers such as stacks, queues, etc. to temporarily store search keys. A stack is known as a "first-in-last out" and a queue is a "first-in-first-out" arrangement.

Of course, mimicking the conscious mind without the benefit of a biological system such as the brain would be a little more complex to explain than was the brain, since we can't duplicate nature's simplicity with electronics hardware. However, once the relationally rich information was made available in a similar fashion to commonly available systems such as "computer vision" systems, voice recognition systems, etc. we could begin to do some serious programming for the purpose of creating a human-made highly intelligent machine. This is where conventional computers could find a happy marriage with my suggested optical memory system and perhaps a specially designed peripheral bridge hardware linking the two.

Chapter 5 – Computer Science and AI

This would amount to the implementation of many determinate and non-determinate acceptors which would be the main structures in creating RAI. Once the memory system is perfected, the only things left are systematic comparisons between real time and archival data and resulting decisions using non-determinate acceptors or simple cognition or recognition signals for determinate acceptors.

In summary, designing and building a human level intelligent machine may be no further away than designing and building a memory system as I have described above. A conventional computer could be employed to act as the intelligence's Cognitive Neuropsychology processing modules and perform all of the cognitive, re-cognitive functions utilizing the optical memory as a vital non-replaceable resource. We could also write programs for that conventional computer to access our new memory system to mimic the brain's traversal of memory and enable a machine to possess the holy grail of strong AI; thought. As I have alluded to, I can envision an interface of the optical memory with a dedicated specially designed "bridge" circuitry designed to work with the new memory in concert with a conventional Von Neumann machine.

This all could be done, now. No need for waiting for 5, 10 or 20 years. We have at our disposal, all the technology we need to construct a human level intelligent machine, right now. It is only a matter of our will to do it. The memory system would be difficult to manufacture but when compared to modern integrated circuit manufacturing techniques, it would be child's play. I hope we see memories of this type with 80 Tera slave frames in the near future. It is my hope that humans get off their posteriors and do something about creating RAI before it is too late and we end up relegated to the dust bin of history.

I believe I have presented an adequate starting point for the intended goal of a RAI machine. We next need to establish a "shopping list" that defines the many capabilities of the brain. We then can use that in an attempt to establish what type of hardware will lend itself towards achieving those capabilities in a conventional machine that has the new optical memory and the new bridge hardware to take advantage of it. The best way to create a shopping list for human capabilities is to review the modes of thought and then make an attempt at specifying the hardware which would lend itself towards those goals. I also postulate whether we need to duplicate all of these forms of thinking into machines or if doing that would be advantageous or even possible.

Review of the 6 modes of thinking

I will explain each of these first with an abstract and I will then attempt to at least propose a viable, doable method in electronics hardware to accomplish the artificial method following this list. First I present the 6 modes of thinking as abstracts:

1. Cognition – This form of thinking has already been accomplished by machines and I explain that below. It is not very difficult to do, or hard to understand but is more time consuming than recognition because the entirety of memory must be searched.

2. Recognition – A little easier to accomplish in machines than cognition since the signal to noise ratio is a little higher because the odds are that the entire memory does not need to be searched for a match.

3. Emotional – This form of thinking would be extremely difficult to program into machines and there would be no practical reason as to why we would want to do it. There have been many speculations that one of the perceived threats to humanity is intelligent machines we may someday design. The theory is that these "thinking machines" will inevitably decide that they don't need us, because we are so stupid compared to them. This sounds a lot like what stupid people like to believe about their smart counterparts, doesn't it? What these "experts on the future" are not cognitive of is that this line of thinking compares the emotional thinking capabilities of humans to what they believe machines will just "automatically" possess. This is nonsense because as any computer programmer will tell you, machines do nothing unless you tell them to. I suppose if one wanted to design a machine that would attempt to eliminate humans, it would be possible but it would take a concerted and elaborate effort to do so. It would be a lot easier and more effective to commit suicide with a low tech piece of hardware we call a gun.

4. Internal visualization – Recall that this is the way our brain allows us to think about the visual things we have stored in our prior learning processes. It also allows us to pre-plan courses of action by imagining what things will look like if different actions are taken. In this mode it is all about the physical because if we can't see it, it is not physical. Internal visualization is one important way we store concepts and some stored concepts are connected to words. Machines will have a distinct advantage over humans because images can be recorded uniformly and with greater fidelity without the variability associated with biological systems.

5. Conceptual – This mode combined with a greater propensity for surveying all stored information is where a RAI machine would be of the greatest use. Machines can far surpass humans in this mode mainly because of the reliability and fidelity of information stored and machines don't have bad days of forgetting things. I believe the ability to transcend and survey will be greatly enhanced by machines with the comparing of the concepts of many seemingly unrelated topics. Recall that conceptual thinking is one on humankind's oldest. Concepts such as "I", "you", "we", "it", "fast", "Cold", "hot" always refer to human emotions or physical objects or some action by or on those objects. Although one might assume that we would need to program some human emotions into our RAI machine for the purpose of attaching conceptual constructs to events or words for language thinking, this is really not the case as we will see when I submit my idea of synthetic concepts in my presentation of language thinking in machines.

6. Language – Language is a human invention which increased the number and richness of concepts available for exchange between individuals. Language thinking is the predominant mode of thinking for modern humans, there is no doubt. I believe that in order to use any human level intelligent machine easily and efficiently, communicating with that machine in our native language would be a necessity. Programming a machine to think may also be a lot more straightforward if language is used as the semantic medium for the exchange of information. Any topic that can be explained can be conceptualized and transferred with a natural language. In fact, natural language may be the key in any successful attempt at RAI machines. I will explain the key to training machines to think in this mode is in the use of synthetic concepts as I alluded to in the conceptual thinking abstract.

Chapter 5 – Computer Science and AI

I will now provide an in-depth description of each mode of thinking and how each mode could be implemented in a machine.

Cognition and recognition

Just as cognition and recognition were probably the earliest and simplest forms of thinking used by humans, they are the easiest to implement in a machine. The human look-through memory can detect similarities between the object contained in the "conscious register" and the location in memory (any floor in my example) that contains that similarity. The optical memory will lend itself to perform the same basic function.

This would involve the use of a 900 M BIP matrix comparator register master frame that could be real time data which would be loaded directly. This is the current real time visual field and is to be compared to every archival memory location. In other words, every real time BIP in the real time visual field is compared to every stored bit of every stored visual field (frame) and when a sufficient number of matches are noticed, some type of signal is sent to indicate cognition or recognition. There is also a problem of the key object not being in the same geographical area in the square matrix of the 900 M BIP "conscious register" i.e. the master frame; and that could be mitigated by "side stepping" the contents in both axes for each complete memory scan.

If there are no similarities between the new real time object and all archival data and background noise (background noise is that last few frames recorded) then a corresponding cognition signal could be sent to a processor. If the similarity of the responding frame's content has close enough similarity to the conscious register's content then the language of the acceptor (I explain shortly) is satisfied, and in this case, corresponding recognition signal can be sent to a processor. Both of these simple modes of thinking are the equivalence of machine consciousness. The processor receiving cognition or recognition signals could be a conventional computer with properly designed software to mimic logical interpretations and actions of a human. So, in replacing the brain's structure in hardware for thought modes of cognition and recognition the main logic circuitry needed are non-determinate or determinate acceptors and the optical memory.

The brain is (mostly) a non-deterministic finite automation (a computer)

Recall that automata are the generalized term for all categories of automatons. An automaton is a logical system which when presented with the correct input will respond in one of two ways. The first way is called "deterministic" and the second way is called "non-deterministic". The term "acceptor" is used in conjunction with automata and it is analogous to a combination lock accepting the correct sequence of numbers to open the lock. This condenses to the terminology: Deterministic and non-deterministic finite acceptors. Since; "Nothing is infinite except the universe and human stupidity and I'm not sure about the universe" - (Albert Einstein), we can drop the use of the term, "finite".

The difference between a deterministic and a non-deterministic acceptor is that the deterministic type cannot make decisions. A good example of a simple deterministic acceptor is a soda-pop machine that I have alluded to previously. If and only if the correct combinations of coins are dropped into the coin slot, the language of the accepter is satisfied, and the machine grants you a soda. There is no decision making capability here, just acceptance when the input conditions match the acceptors' language definition. Put in the right combination of coins, you get your soda out the bottom.

All modern digital computer hardware is deterministic because the micro state they operate in at any given time is completely predictable. Cognition is strictly deterministic because no decisions are required to automatically know we see something we didn't see a fraction of a second prior or have never seen in our existence.

Recognition is non-deterministic and is more complicated on the micro input level. It adds the notion of a choice of moves for the automaton, or in other words; a decision. During recognition thinking, the human brain as acts very much like a non-deterministic acceptor because the conscious (and perhaps non-conscious) mind must make a decision about the closest similarity between the real time and archived data.

In summary, whenever there is a new external key in the conscious mind, it is compared to all memory locations and if there is a no match there is cognition or if there is a match there is recognition. In the case of cognition and a new object is appearing in the "noise" (a signal in a field of noise) we can say that is deterministic because we do not need to make a decision. It is clearly there and was not there some instance of time backwards. In the case of recognition, this can be the function of a deterministic or non-deterministic acceptor, depending on how much similarity there is between the current object and the stored object(s). If you are looking at your parents faces there is no doubt and that action is deterministic. If you are looking at someone who is a "spitting image" of your parents, you may have to decide if the people you are looking at are in fact your parents or perhaps just people who have some remarkable resemblance to your parents. This could be considered non-deterministic. In this case we don't get a firm, definite recognition signal. Instead we get a signal that warns us that what we are looking at is close, but may not be an exact match.

People who have brain diseases such as Alzheimer's disease have problems with deciding if they are looking at people they know or not. This could be a result of damage to memory locations or damage to the pathways to those locations. The language of the acceptor is contents of the memory location accessed which contain conceptual markers describing your parents and how they look. In the case of deterministic cognition, the language of the acceptor is all previous stored information *not* being similar to the current.

While human biological consciousness could never happen with an electronic machine, there are examples of computer consciousness programs in machines which have indeed already happened, but went completely unnoticed by the very people who designed them. The designers missed the significance of what they did.

During World War Two, the US Navy was introduced to the tactical benefits of air search radars. When first adapted to shipboard use, the main output device of an air search radar was simply a round cathode ray tube (a TV picture tube) in which a rotating line was watched by the radar operator. The line started at the center of the screen and that represented the location of the ship.

Chapter 5 – Computer Science and AI

The end of the line pointed at the azimuth or the bearing as it rotated 360 degrees from north to east to south to west and back to north again. When a "blip" appeared on the screen, it only happened when the rotating line passed over something that caused "a return". The return represented something that the radar wave had struck and bounced off of and back. The distance from the middle of the screen and the blip gave the range of the return and the bearing was determined by the azimuth of the line at the time of the "hit".

If only one "bogy" was detected it was not much of a problem to keep a record of that by the operator. When many bogies were encountered the tracking and logging of each started to become a problem. The Navy constructed large clear plastic windows with grid line marked maps and installed them in rooms they called the "combat information center". This created a new "rate" or occupational specialty in the Navy and their job was to plot bogies as reported to them by the radar operators. When initial contact was made the plotters would mark the location in ink and repeatedly log the progress of the blip in range and azimuth. The "target" could now be calculated for speed and heading which resulted in drawing a path for the bogy on the readily viewable clear plastic window.

Sometime in the 1960's the old system of the big clear plastic plotting board was replaced with more modern hardware. This involved the use of computers to do the tracking of bogies once the operator had "clicked" on the target (all returns are considered as targets) just as we "click" on things with our home computers in the present day. The target was clicked on twice for an initial range, bearing and speed calculation. The computer would also generate what was known as a "leader" which was a line that began at the target return blip and the length represented the speed and the direction the bearing of the target.

In the 1980s there was a new modernization of the existing hardware called Automatic Target Acquisition and Tracking. This was in reality an early example of what we call "computer vision" in CS today. The computer doing this job was probably 1000 times less powerful than the smartphones we carry with us today. It was not very powerful and this is a perfect example of what can be done with a very small amount of computing power. The computer basically did the job of the operator in that no "clicking" on the target was required for a target to be acquired.

Once a blip appeared on the screen, the computer was "aware" of that instantly. It accomplished that feat by keeping a map of the entire swept screen and returns were "seen" by comparing the present constantly to the next instant of time in the "watched" area. This is a form of machine consciousness because it involves the logical realization when some new object is noticed, which is in effect; cognition. To us, it *appears* that the machine is conscious and therefore we can say it has the *attribution* of consciousness. We can call what those machines accomplished as cognition and that is indeed a mode of thinking. As the target is tracked with a second internal automatic "click" we could call that process "recognition" and that is also a mode of thinking. I reiterate that it should be apparent that the computer was by no means conscious in the human or animal sense but it did have the attribution of consciousness which is what all intelligent machines will ever possess, unless humans start playing around with biological forms of computers.

Emotional

I leave this mode for the science fiction writers to tell their stories of a dystopian future in which the machines rise up and kill all the useless humans. It ain't gonna happen unless a great amount of effort was put into doing that and that would be a stupid endeavor. As I alluded to, there are many cheaper and straightforward ways to commit suicide. I can predict that there will be detractors to my assertion who will say that without emotions, a machine can be instructed to commit murder with no remorse or feelings involved. Yes, it is possible to program a machine to kill but an autonomous weapon would be of no use if it did not have the same decision capabilities as humans. If humans ever do decide to use RAI machines as weapons it would be a good idea to program in some fail safe features to prevent friendly fire incidents. As far as "losing control" is concerned, machines will be way more reliable in that respect than are humans. It will all depend on how correctly they are programmed. The possibility of machines simply deciding they don't need us is non-existent provided negative human emotions are not programmed into them and I reiterate that would be difficult and stupid.

Conceptual

It is my hope that the reader has accepted the notion that cognition and recognition are in fact modes of thinking and these modes would be relatively easy to emulate in a machine. In fact what I have described so far would be very useful in things like surveillance systems where it would not be necessary to have a human operator watching a monitor screen constantly. This technology could also be used for things like driverless cars and other control systems. I believe I have presented enough background to have established all of these things.

The primitive modes of cognition, recognition and emotional thinking are present in many lower order animals such as dogs and if the reader has ever wondered if dogs can think, I believe the answer is yes, at some primitive level, anyway. Humans also still make use of these fundamental modes on a constant basis. Dogs may even have some ability at primitive conceptual thinking but I leave that for the research of animal behavioral scientists. Being cognizant and recognizant of heat is not the same thing as thinking about the concept of heat as electromagnetic radiation.

Conceptual thinking is actually the next higher mode of thinking following cognition, recognition and emotional. It is somewhat of a paradox that a basically primitive mode of thinking such as conceptual is what has enabled humans to develop all of the innovations that have given us our technological advances.

In the early developmental stages of humans, we had the same basic abilities to conceptualize things like heat as dogs do today. The difference between a dog and a human brain is the human brain has much more storage capacity and the structures necessary to use that capacity. Humans have higher abilities to *learn* information. There are many people walking the earth today who do not have the slightest idea of the concept of heat being a type of radio wave. They only know that if something is hot, they can get burned. The only difference between those people and individuals versed in some basic physics theory is the latter group has had what we call *training*. Training involves the transfer of information which has been accumulated by other humans going back in time towards the beginning of recorded history. Conceptual training would not be possible without a storehouse of historical information to train people with. The point is: Understanding complex concepts just doesn't happen by itself, it takes lots of training.

In order for a machine to "think" conceptually, it will have to be trained with the same information human students are trained with. It should be readily apparent that it would be impossible to train human students in any concept other that the very basic concept of "this hot; you get burned!" without the use of a natural language (English, etc.). Natural language was humanity's best invention for the advancement of human intelligence. It is the great enabler for learning and without it humans would probably not have survived, let alone become successful at the technology we know today. Primitive concept thinking has evolved into language/concept thinking and is a logical progression from the primitive to the advanced.

To that extent, I believe the use of natural language will be absolutely necessary to explain things to machines and of course the machines will need to be taught the basics of the natural language we choose first. I will attempt to provide some viable methods for doing just that when I cover language thinking below. But first we need to take a look at the term "concept" and what that's related to.

We need to begin by defining concepts. What are concepts exactly? It may surprise many people to realize that concepts are always related to physical objects or human emotions. Concepts always describe a physical object or some action that describes, has an effect on, or can affect in some way, a physical object. Humans also attach emotional associations in building concepts simply because emotions are a basic human thinking mode. Some examples of concepts are: velocity, acceleration, heat, cold, distance (includes length, width, height, altitude, depth, circumference and all geometric shapes), flow (originally related to wind and water but now represents many other physical objects), gravity (weight) and a plethora of others that I am not immediately aware of. We also attach value and worth to concepts with our emotionally driven thought. These were the primitive concepts first used by humans.

At this point, if the reader has doubts about what concepts are, I invite you to perform a little mind experiment and attempt to think of a concept that *is not* related to a physical object or some human emotional trait. The reader might say, "OK how about ESP (extra sensory perception)?" It may not actually exist but it is a concept. This phenomenon relates to how people (physical objects) could possibly communicate without having some known method of thought transmission such as speech. How about thought as a concept? We know thought exists because we do it and the key here is "we" and we are "us" and us is people and people are physical objects. I do not believe that there is a single conceptual idea that does not relate to a physical object in some way. What about light? Light is the medium I chose for my optical memory and it is not physical, or is it? The reader has probably heard of the term "photon". A photon has been theorized as being a "massless particle" and is very much a component of light. Even radio waves are part of our physical world because they interact with physical objects in various ways.

The ability to think conceptually was necessary for early humans to survive. Our survival still depends on this basic fundamental mechanism. To understand how humans think in concepts it is only necessary to observe how we learn those concepts in the first place. There is also the possibility that some concepts are inborn but I do not believe that to be the case. One reason is because kids have to learn about being afraid of heights and there are numerous examples of kids just walking off roofs to their death. We have to learn the concept of height and the understanding of height comes from trial and error experiences that we store as information. We have to experience falls from non-lethal distances to learn that the greater the distance, the more injury we might sustain.

We also learn about things like spatial characteristics in nature. We learn that nature is abundant in shapes and sizes of physical objects like mountains, trees, rocks, hills, lakes, streams, rivers and last but not least; weather. Early man was exposed to all the weather we as humans are mostly shielded from on a daily basis. Thunderstorms, snowstorms and extremes of heat and cold were common to early humans and there was a need to have a basic concept of all these things to realize how dangerous they were to survival. The important aspect of the ability of humans to have concepts of all the threats; is that it is a survival tool.

We could train a RAI machine in basic concepts much as early humans knew what basic things like heat and cold were. However, that would not be of much use for the infusion of intelligence in that machine. It would be much more convenient to attach descriptors like words to aid in the storage and retrieval of information which is what intelligence is all about.

Internal visualization

This mode enables and enhances all other modes of thought by adding physical depth to our view of the world around us. In my example of the Automatic target acquisition and tracking system, the machine internally visualized radar target returns and performed calculations on them which could be thought of as a machine version of this mode. This will aid in survey thinking by comparing vast amounts of visual data to locate possible contextual similarities in similar looking objects. It should be obvious that the look-through optical memory system will streamline any search operations for images.

Language thinking

"Natural language processing" is a main concentration in computer science and many PhD students choose this as their dissertation subject. It is involved with machine interpretation and generation of human languages. The term natural language is used in computer science to differentiate from the many programming languages such as C++, Java and many others. Natural language processing techniques are used in an attempt to assist humans in writing, searching and categorization of natural languages such as English.

The word processing program I am using to type this book has some abilities that are very helpful to me. It has a spell checker which I find invaluable, because I am not so good at spelling. It informs me of grammatical errors as well and tells me if I have omitted a space between words or if I have too many spaces. I could not get along without it and for me, writing a book like this with a contraption we used to call a "typewriter" would be impossible.

One of the big features lacking in natural language checking features in word processing programs to date is the lack of contextual checking. This has been a topic of research in the

Chapter 5 – Computer Science and AI

natural language processing field for many years but to the best of my knowledge and not been accomplished by anyone. To illustrate what a context checker would do, I type words that are not misspelled but simply do not fit in or make sense in contextual way in this sentence:

Weal AI researchers do not consider how the brawn is able to "understand" our natural language and therefore are unable to write programs that do the same thin.

The spelling and grammar checker missed the words "weak", "brain" and "thing". Since the checking program only has spell check no grammatical contextual (the meaning as used) capabilities, it simply cannot "read" the way a human can. It also drives me crazy by underlining some words that are correct but it notifies me nonetheless.

So, just from this simple example we can glean some insight to the level of performance natural language processing has achieved to date. The failure of this concentration to develop a working context driven grammar and spell checker has to do with a failure to understand how the brain does this seemingly formidable task. Recall Mr. Searle's "Chinese Room" and that he postulated that his proposed system of cards with Chinese symbols written on them and a paper with rules would pass the Turing test but would not constitute what we call "understanding".

Humans instantly understand the meaning of words in their own native language because they have stored concepts which are a physical or emotional trait or some association to a physical trait stored in close proximity (or linked through MLF) to every word in their own vocabulary. This is what I call storing words as concepts. It literally takes years of use for a native language speaker to get to some level of contextual expertise. People who speak Chinese as their native language have a very difficult time in assigning contextual constructs to English if it is relatively new to them. A big problem a non-native English speaker will have in learning English is the fact that many words have entirely different meanings dependent on the present usage.

So in addition to the problem of assigning an "instant meaning" to every word in the lexicon established for a "context checker" program, we also have the added problem of multiple meanings (stored as concepts) we call "senses" for each word that are dependent on the current usage and place in the thought train. In humans, a native tongue speaker, listener and reader will literally take years of absorbing sample thought trains to build a knowledge base that will be adequate to be proficient at that language. The stored recorded knowledge base is utilized every time a subsequent thought train (a sentence) is constructed by comparing historical usages to the usage under construction. I believe that this aspect of language thinking is the big hurdle in designing a thinking machine. It is a hurdle but not so big of a hurdle that it cannot be jumped. My mother used to, say, "if there's a will, there's a way." I believe that statement and having a positive attitude helps us to find answers that may never have been considered. I now turn my attention to another weak AI category.

I'm talking about a category of natural language processing systems known as "question answering systems". To date, these question answering systems are the best effort computer science has made in emulating the human transfer of a natural language in machines. There are several versions and all were developed by professors at well-known institutions of higher learning. During its development stage, the most promising system was available for free access and use by the public. As an AI student, I was privy to the URL of this system and I used it extensively in my research. It was pretty amazing to say the least. The user enters a question in the same manner as one would enter a search term in a search engine such as "WebCrawler". The system uses grammatical constructs as well as a large lexicon of words with the various sense definitions associated to each and information from the internet to gather what usually turns out to be a close semantically correct answer for the question asked.

From what I have been able to gather in the way of technical design of this system (and a few others which attempt to perform the same function) is that in the first operation, the words of the question are "parsed" and each word is placed in a grammatical category, every elementary student is aware of, such as nouns, pronouns, adjectives and verbs. The term "sense" is an important factor in English as many words do have multiple meanings or senses. This all has to be taken into account and the definitions of the words and their various senses is compared and treated like a concept by placing a value on that word through a ranking system. The value or rank that is placed on each word could be considered a computer science equivalent for how humans attach concepts to words and it is what allows us to instantly understand meaning. Using this strategy gives the system a better probability of matching the actual question to an appropriately worded answer because the system has used semantics in a similar fashion to the way humans do.

The ranking system I have just described is closely related to the basic way humans understand the meaning of words without reading a dictionary explanation of each word as we go. Think about this. We automatically and instantly understand every word we are presented with provided it is part of our learned vocabulary, no extra thinking or effort needed. Once we have used a word a number of times (we were told as elementary students this number is 5 times) it then becomes part of our vocabulary. How do we do this? If we can answer this question, we can also describe how we can perform this function in a machine.

I believe the answer to this important question has already been answered by a group of people that never intended to describe the human attribute of word understanding for emulation in a machine. I am referring to the people who first categorized our words into grammatical constructs such as nouns, pronouns, verbs and adjectives. These terms describe something other than what is apparently visible to humans; they describe *concepts*. We as a species have inadvertently described the logical structure of our invented language and in doing so; we have laid out a plan for a mechanism that could be built in to a machine. The reader is probably asking, "How would this possibly work in a machine?" I'm glad you asked! I will try to explain.

We are physical objects and so it is easy for us to relate to everything in our physical world. As I alluded to, all concepts are related in some way to the physical. Even God is related to the physical because he is supposed to be the creator of it all. If we and the world didn't exist then there would be no need for a god would there? What about time? Is time related to the physical? To us, it actually is and to a group of people known as physicists, it definitely is. We think of time as the process of day and night and that is a result of the earth moving around its axis in a 24 hour period. The point is, humans are physical beings and as such we automatically assign concepts to everything, including words. We also relate many things in emotional terms and many of the human generated concepts we attach to words do contain an emotional element.

Chapter 5 – Computer Science and AI

However, I don't believe the emotional element will be a problem in designing machines to perform language thinking. I will elaborate on this shortly.

When we recognize a word, the recognition of that word is very much like recognizing a physical object such as a large rock that we have been exposed to at some prior time. When we see the rock, we understand whatever it was we originally learned about the rock. If we tried to pick it up we know how heavy it is, what the color is and the coarseness of its surface. All of these characteristics are concepts. The meaning of words is also stored as concepts which are related to the grammatical constructs we have defined for our invention of our natural language.

The reader should also note that when we think of concepts, we get an internal picture or "feeling" about that concept that describes to us the meaning associated with that concept. When we read or listen to speech, each word causes a determinate acceptor to trigger an accept signal to the brain. In the case of words, the "language" of the accepter is satisfied by an externally supplied natural language word if it matches the stored version. The defining acceptor language is the stored version of that word that we have stored with an attached concept. When the external and internal words are a match, we get the recognition signal and in the case of word / concept pairs the recognition signal is the concept part of the pair which gets played back to the conscious mind. If the reader is paying attention, the understanding of that word did not happen at the time of recognition but it happened at the time of *learning*. Of course the problem is complicated with the notion of multiple meanings per word (senses) but that could be solved by comparing the past uses of each word with a contextual comparison of leading and following words in a set of examples. The memory structure I have suggested makes operations like what I have just described relatively easy.

When it comes to machine understanding of words, the most difficult problem would be designing a synthetic concept generator algorithm. I believe this could be accomplished using many different strategies and it follows that research into the various methods would prove the merit of the most promising design. One way to do this (I'm not suggesting this is the only way) would be to use a pre-planned, word loaded system that used a matrix of words that had been stored in a specific method relating to the category and rank the words were placed in. Once the words had been ranked and categorized and placed in a lexicon, the algorithm could use this ranking and category to assign a unique synthetic concept that the machine in essence would "understand". I alluded to the possibility of the first RAI machines being trained solely by plugging them into another computer. In that case the synthetic concepts could be generated before being stored as word / concept pairs on the RAI machine's memory system.

Another possible design for the concept generator would involve research into codes similar to cryptographic systems but not for the same purpose. Our purpose is not to secure our conceptual constructs but to enable them. This would involve a complex algorithm to enable a machine to assign a specific code which is derived ad hoc for each word presented to it just as humans learn words for their vocabulary. The code generated by the algorithm would then be attached to each word and is basically a concept the machine can understand, because it was programmed in those concepts. In the future, when our RAI machines become self-learning, an algorithm such as this might serve to process new words that are presented to them.

Chapter 5 – Computer Science and AI

The synthetic concept applied to words could be generated by placing each word in categories such as people, places or things. Things would be further ranked as other animals, plants, scientific terms, mathematical terms and even medical terms if we wanted our RAI machine to be a doctor. There would also need to be connections or action categories and ranks for words describing the actions and interactions between those people, places or things. I don't intend this proposal to be an exact design specification. This is just a proposal so many bugs will need to be worked out, there is no doubt. However, I believe I have provided a good debarkation point for the research and development of synthetic concepts which I believe are the key to language thinking in machines.

If the reader has been paying attention, then it should be clear where I am going with all of this: Memory. Every aspect of human intelligence can be explained by the use of a very large and properly structured memory system. In the case of contextual "understanding", that understanding comes from the ability to place a physical connotation or concept to the word in question and refers to that word being used in every possible correct way that the "thinker" has ever used it. Of course the learning or training has to be correct because if it is not, that will result in the word being used incorrectly. The optical memory system I proposed will lend itself to all search operations needed for word understanding. It should be obvious that if in fact we can design, build and program a machine to understand individual words, assembling words into a thought train or reading from a thought train should be a relatively easy prospect and all of that is in essence language thinking.

Summary

Computer science or computer engineering are the fields of study most likely to design and build a real artificial intelligent machine that not only equals human capability but far surpasses it. The only roadblock to achieving this monumental step in the progress of humanity may be the attitude that humans have about their own intelligence being the result of some insurmountable obstacle that could never be duplicated by machines. This is narcissism and arrogance at its finest.

Once we have gotten past our own egos, we can begin to solve the most important problem humans have ever faced. I say this because I believe we may not survive as a species if we don't create a super intelligent machine. Intelligence has always been a survival tool and it is needed more than ever as threats loom on the horizon in increasing numbers. In the game of survival, if we don't advance, we fail.

If I make any point in the book, it is that human traits such as thinking and understanding are easily explained and really not that big of a deal. We assign importance and complexity to these things because it is a reflection of our own ego.

If we put as much money and effort into real AI research as we do elementary physics study with "super colliders", we would be at our goal in less than 20 years, tops. The big obstacle is a memory system with as I alluded to would be difficult but nowhere as difficult as the Large Hadron Collider at Cern, Switzerland. Billions of dollars have been spent on that with no discernable benefit for the advancement of humanity. Of course we don't know what the benefits will be until we get there but would it not be advisable to have a super intelligence guiding us with that as we go?

My final point is that using RAI machines as survival tools is just a natural progression of the use of natural intelligence for the very same purpose: Survival.

Reader's Notes

Chapter 6 - Social Implications of Stupidity

"The police are not here to create disorder – they're here to preserve it!" – Chicago Mayor, Richard J. Daley, 1968 Democratic Convention

"Could you see everyone having guns in their home?" - Chicago Mayor, Richard M. Daley, 2009 Press conference on gun violence in the City of Chicago

"Yes, I would love it!!" – Frank Scurio, 2016

"If democrats had any brains, they'd be republicans" – Ann Coulter

"I don't give people hell, I give them the truth, and they think it's hell" - President Harry S. Truman, 1951

Intelligence Recognition Desire and Intelligence Comparison Phenomenon

Of all the possessions human beings can acquire, none are as highly prized by humans as intelligence. This can be empirically proven by simply observing people. Once people are viewed through the lens of *Intelligence Recognition Desire* (IRD) and *Intelligence Comparison Phenomenon* (ICP) anyone will come to the same conclusion. The only requirement is to be observant of people's actions and then attempt to determine what the impetus of that action was. Anyone can do this. When you begin to observe people in this manner, you will be a believer.

One of the main hypotheses in this book is my belief that intelligence is the driving force of all our actions. Psychologists have attempted to identify the significant driving forces behind human actions. The top contenders end up being power, sex and money. My belief is this is totally incorrect. Allow me to explain. Again, the main driving force behind man's actions is without a doubt; intelligence. The main reason for this is: It is perceived that one needs intelligence to obtain any of the proposed drivers, such as power, sex and money. What is more, people have a natural built-in desire to possess the attribute of being intelligent. In other words, people very much *want* other people to believe they are smart. They also want the moniker of being smart for themselves.

People have a natural built-in "intelligence judging mechanism" for other people and I labeled this as ICP. In other words, people assess and analyze the intelligence of other people and they compare that to their own intelligence on an ongoing, continual basis. They do this on all social levels and at every stage of life. How can anyone who has ever dealt with another human being deny these statements? The desire to be thought of as being smart and the desire to judge other's intelligence with respect for one's own *is* the driver of all of human actions. In other words, intelligence *is* the primal driving force for humans. I believe this will become obvious as I provide many historical examples of this ultimate driver of humanity.

Chapter 6 – Social Implications of Stupidity

From the time we are old enough to start communicating with other humans, we begin to access the intelligence of every one we come in contact with. Some of us also attempt to display our own intelligence as a measure of worth. This plays out noticeably in any sort of communal activity such as what is known as school. This continues throughout life in and after school, and then in workplace environments and any other social activity where people interact, including modern day social media.

The worst possible insult you can bestow on another human is to call them stupid. Why is this? My belief is that we are programmed to value intelligence. We are machines and we therefore must obey the programming we have inherited. The reason this makes sense, is because intelligence had to be considered the most important asset for a human in hunter-gatherer societies. An individual who couldn't solve day to day problems was a burden to the rest of the group. This could also have life threatening implications for the others in the group. This is a matter of survival. The smartest individuals were also able to solve survival related problems and predict future threats with a higher probability than were their stupid counterparts. Humans instinctively know that intelligence is important. It is this instinct that pushes the individual to prove that they are at the top level of smarts. People are constantly attempting to prove that they are not only smart, but the smartest.

This is evident in every walk of life and in every profession. This is true whether the profession requires no skill to one that requires years of training and experience. For example, automotive mechanics will attempt to prove that they have a more complete knowledge of what could only be considered mundane subjects and will get into arguments about who knows the most about it. When challenged about their knowledge, they will even become angry or agitated. My professional background has always been electronics but I have been an automotive enthusiast since the age of 15. During a conversation I had with a mechanic friend, I casually mentioned I thought that cylinder head design was the single most important factor of the entire engine when it comes to performance.

He responded to this by losing his temper! I was befuddled. When people become angry because of an issue of knowledge that is the time to sit up and take notice. This is akin to holding up a big sign that says, "I want to display my smartness, but you are getting in the way!" This guy might have said, "How dare an electronics geek such as the likes of you, lecture me on the finer aspects of racing engines!" He didn't actually say that, but he didn't have to. I knew exactly what he meant by the expression (anger and disgust) on his face and when he said in a very condescending manner, "No, heads are not the most important thing!" I know for a fact that my statement is and was 100% true. He didn't know as much about engines as he thought he did, or he didn't want to admit someone else (especially someone not in that field) knew something that maybe he didn't.

I believe the words, "You didn't know that?" are probably the most utilized phrase in the English language when technical people are conversing. I have heard that phrase so many times that I cannot even begin to guess the approximate number. In my personal experience, it has been used by technical people to promote the concept of their own smarts, while simultaneously making their intellectual opponent appear stupid. I referred to this as "glibness" in chapter 2. This kind of thing happens way too frequently, for my liking. It is a big negativity promoter in the work place

Chapter 6 – Social Implications of Stupidity

or anywhere. It seems that the primal desire to be accepted as smart and to assess others' smartness is not easily controlled and some people not only have no desire to control it, but seem hell bent on using it as frequently as they can.

During my career in military electronics I worked with communications security projects. One of many government printed-out guidelines in security practices for personnel using standard communications channels made it clear that good security practice was *not* to engage in knowledge battles. The reason for this edict was that two technical people privy to sensitive classified technical specifications could and did invariably end up revealing secrets to God knows who simply because they were attempting to prove to each other how smart they were! This is about two people compromising classified information for the sole purpose of trying to prove that they were smarter than the other guy! This is a glaring example of the desire to be recognized as being smart. I'm 100% sure that this sort of thing continues to this day, and at this very moment! Does this make you feel safer?

My personal experience has shown me that this kind of thing happens on every social and occupational level. Even professionals like medical doctors are keen on retaining a positive image with the medical community at large. The worst thing that can happen to an MD from their own point of view is that any notion of incompetence be attached to them. Incompetence is perceived by humans (especially MDs) as relating to some level of intelligence, whether this relationship is valid or not.

What I have just alluded to could be interpreted as being "competitive" but this is a misconception. The underlying impetus for the actions of others when they attempt to discredit someone while giving credit to them-selves is not competition! The understandable human assessment of "competition" is that these described actions are normal for people to do, when they want to advance. The fly in the ointment for this view is the fact that much of this "competition" occurs in places where there is absolutely no material advantage whatsoever for doing that. This happens between friends (as in my mechanic friend), and at all levels of social interaction, where no monetary benefit of any kind can be realized. My mechanic friend did not become monetarily richer because of his supposed superior knowledge of engines, displayed to me. This is IRD.

What follows is what I consider to be the best possible proof for my theory of intellectual impetus, i.e. IRD and ICP are the primal driving force behind all human action: There is an ideology that is responsible for more human death and misery than any other in human history. It is called communism, socialism, state socialism, fascism, state capitalism and here in the U.S.; progressivism. Progressivism is a form of communism in which the framers of the ideology realized they cannot get to communism overnight, so they take the slow, gradual approach. The end result will be full blown communism; it is just a matter of when. This slow approach has been likened to putting a frog in boiling water. The frog will jump out because of the abrupt change. However if a frog is placed in cold water and the heat is turned up, by the time the frog realizes he is being cooked, it's too late! Progressives like Hillary Clinton know this and she willingly admitted that she is a progressive! Many of the stupid electorate supporting her believes her admonition is completely benign because after all, everyone wants progress! Hillary knows that the American public would not stand for being submersed into the boiling water of communism so she and others of the same ilk take the slow; cold water and turn up the heat method. She knows this because the world history record of communism is clear.

Joe Stalin was responsible for killing 20 plus million of his own people. Adolf Hitler killed a total of 10 million Jews and other nationalities. Mao Tsai Tung killed an estimated 60 million of his own people. All these deaths occurred because of totalitarian governments and their desire for total control of their people. The excuse that was given by all of these leaders, for all the death and misery, was that the collective was the most important issue. It didn't matter if a few million people had to be sacrificed, because, in the communist mantra; the ends justify the means. The ends being a utopia in which the collective had no wants, no needs and was basically; heaven on earth!

Communism, socialism and fascism have been tried over and over and over but have never worked. In fact, the historical records are clear; these ideologies always end in disaster with millions of people dying. It is really not difficult to understand why these forms of government do not work. One big reason is simply because they take the incentive away from anyone wanting to accomplish more than their contemporaries. That's it; it is really no more complicated than that. The author, Ayn Rand described this perfectly with her book, "Atlas Shrugged". Technical people such as engineers realized that they were expending a lot of effort to become proficient at their trade but were forced to share the fruits of their labor with people who had nothing but apathy for learning. So as it is told in the book, all the highly professional people started disappearing to leave the lazy masses to fend for themselves. Unfortunately that probably would not work in the real world. Keeping the hiding place a secret would be a formidable task.

The fact is; centrally controlled economies do not work! The one big reason for this is that when a country's economic system and system of government are intertwined to the point where the government controls how business operates on every level, gridlock is always just one mistake away. Recall that all humans make mistakes. The communist leaders believe that they cannot make mistakes and that is the problem. You don't have to be smart to understand why this system won't function properly. You do have to be informed though. This is one of the fundamental concepts of ideologies such as communism; propaganda. If you want to control the populace, you must lie to them on a regular basis. Wait a minute! Isn't lying a glaring indicator of stupidity? Beginning to see the picture? This is just a sample of how stupid communists are. Another big reason communists are stupid is that they actually believe it is possible to squeeze blood out of a turnip. How else could we explain the way communists will suck all the profits out of businesses (and individuals) and then expect those businesses to survive?

Contrary to the hyperbole that says the U.S. won the cold war and communism has been defeated, it is very evident that communists have not given up on their dream of world domination. They have only recently changed tactics because they understand that they need money to make their dreams a reality. Communist China is now what could be described as a government of "State Capitalism". They need money to build their military machine and their influence in Asia and throughout the world. The paradox here is that they turned to capitalism to obtain that money! They are admitting in a very direct and unambiguous way that capitalism works. What they don't seem to understand is that the system they have set up will not endure the test of time like true capitalism has.

Chapter 6 – Social Implications of Stupidity

Although capitalism is responsible for getting more people out of poverty than any other form of government, the proponents of socialism and communism remain stuck to their guns (even though they want to take guns away from the citizens). Albert Einstein said that the true measure of insanity was doing the same thing over and over and expecting different results. I believe Albert was trying to be kind to stupid people and he transposed insanity for stupidity.

The big mystery is: Why do the proponents of communism continue to adhere to ideas that are proven to not work and what is more they are ideas that have resulted in more death and misery than any other form of government? Not only do communists adhere to their concepts but they actively conspire in every way imaginable to make these ideas a reality. In the United States, they lie, cheat and steal to push their antiquated ideas on the American people who for the most part (for the time being anyway) want no part of it. Another aspect of this should be obvious. If being dishonest, lying, cheating and stealing is required for your ideas to be adopted by the people, then how can you possibly say your ideas have any merit? If Hillary were honest and told her followers what a progressive really means, they would probably not support her (I hope, but at the same time I am reluctant to give intelligence credit to the electorate).

If progressive ideas are so great, they should stand up on their own merit. Tell the truth. Tell the American people that a government run single payer health care system is your ultimate goal. Tell the people that this will result in death panels, higher costs and fewer doctors entering the medical profession. It should also be obvious that if they told the truth they would have not gotten into office to begin with. The necessity to use all of the negative emotional traits is indicative of a super stupid group of people, attempting to take control away from smart people who have no need to lie, cheat and steal because their ideas don't require that sort of behavior.

The big question is, why? Why do people like Barack Obama and Hillary Clinton and Bernie Sanders (a self-proclaimed socialist) want to impose communism on the American people? Make no mistake. I am talking about full-fledged communism in the worst possible form. The "Affordable Health Care Act" otherwise known as "Obamacare", is the road to communism. It gives more power and information about citizens to the Federal Government than it has ever had in the history of this country. If communism is a camel, Obamacare is the head of the camel under the tent of government. Get the head into the tent and the rest of the body is soon to follow.

The psychology of communists

Communists see themselves as "ranchers" and "creators" and they see the people as cattle. Cattle need to be taken cared of because, after all, cattle are way too stupid to take care of themselves! They see some kind of government role in every aspect of the cattle's lives. Cattle need to be fed, they need to be checked for disease and given the proper shots. They need a lot of medical attention and the sickly ones need to be "weeded out"; you know, like as in "death panels". Do people like Barack Obama actually believe that the government can be an engine of prosperity and make utopia a reality? In other words, does he really believe that his ideas will create a "heaven on earth"? My view is that he probably believes that; but that is an oversimplification of a complex idea, which is: He believes that these convoluted ideas will work because *he* is the one now doing it! In other words, *he* is *so* smart that if *he* turns the country into a communist state it will work *this time* because *now* Barack the great is in control! I'm being unfair to Mr. Obama because in reality, all progressives believe that, not just him.

What is important to him (and his followers and others like him) is that by making *his* beliefs a reality by turning the United States of America into the Socialist States of America, he is attempting to prove to the whole world how smart he is. It is simply IRD on steroids. In the case of people like Barack Obama, he doesn't just want you to know he is smart, but he wants the rest of the world to know that he is the smartest!

That is the only logical reason why any politician would want to turn a successful country like the USA into a second rate, also-ran nation. Why else would anyone push old ideas that don't work? In case you are wondering, the people that I am talking about here are the stupidest of the stupid! They represent the apex of stupidity; no matter how they are portrayed by their loving media (who suffer from IRD also) or what manner of degrees have been bestowed upon them. Think about it; this is the only explanation that makes any sense. I'm not only talking about every member of the Democratic Party that has been completely taken over by progressives. It is also at least fifty percent of the Republican Party who believes in the same worn out, big government hype that has ruined many other nations throughout history.

In the case of President Obama, he uses the IRS to harass and intimidate his political opponents (such as the TEA party); he uses the Justice Dept. to attempt to drum up support for a weakening of the second Amendment (Fast and Furious). He used the Labor Dept. to go after companies like Boeing because they opened a plant in a state with a "right to work" law (this is an unconscionable act in a communist state which he wants us to be). He uses the EPA to go after Coal fired power plants because his idea of a world free of CO_2 is just a regulation away. Progressives don't care about the environment. They say they do but that is just another ruse. Their true agenda is to inexorably link government to private business by controlling every aspect of business. A carbon tax would accomplish that and would in effect establish a communist government in the U.S.

In a side note, many people believe that communism was invented by some guy by the name of Karl Marx in the mid 1800's. This could not be further from the truth. Communism was invented by a bunch of stupid people in the very early stages of human banding. This is when hunter gatherers began to assemble in little groups and some kind of pecking or social order began to take shape. The very moment that happened, I would wager that there was always at least one individual who wanted to prove how smart he was to the rest of the group and in doing so, invented ways to control them. If you are control of the rest of your group, you must be smarter than them; at least that is the illusion created. This was the beginning of the war between the smart and the stupid and it has been raging ever since. During the many skirmishes and major battles that occurred over centuries between these two groups, the notion of "good" and "evil" was attached to the actions of the smart and the stupid.

No matter how stupid our elected officials may be, it is the stupid segment of the voting public that is responsible for putting them into office. I impose the stupid label on progressives simply because they believe in things that are not based in fact. This is a glaring indicator of stupidity. Another reason I bestow this title on them is their underhandedness: They lie, cheat and use their

Chapter 6 – Social Implications of Stupidity

power to eliminate detractors in ways reminiscent of a dictator. The predominant problem in electing stupid officials is the fact that they actually do get elected! It is the stupid electorate that believes everything their party tells them. To them, belonging to a political party such as the Democratic Party is very much akin to being chosen on a team in a game of street stick ball. They feel as though belonging to their party gives them relevance and it gives them comfort because stupidity supports and protects itself.

Communists may be stupid but if it were not for stupid people voting them into office, they wouldn't be much of a problem. They would be like bugs that can't get in the house. They are only a pain if they get in. It is said that it takes "Two to Tango" so in this case I will rightfully blame the "low information voter". This is a person who has been brainwashed, usually for a very long time. They are easily deceived and easily brainwashed and because stupidity reinforces itself; they support each other. They support each other for several reasons.

One reason is that stupidity breeds stupidity. Stupidity also sticks together, protects itself, and propagates itself through society. People with stupid ideas deceive themselves into believing they are smart, so they will cling to anything that enforces their beliefs. They usually hang around the same social circles, live in the same geographic areas and even attend the same churches. One of the sad realities about the low information voter is that they believe that to admit that they are wrong or that they were ever wrong about anything; is an admission of stupidity. Being afraid of looking stupid will actually make you stupid in this case. The individuals who will never admit that they were wrong at some point in their life, are the truly stupid because all humans make mistakes and smart people will not only admit when they err but are constantly asking themselves if everything they do is correct.

What I just described is actually a part of the intelligence algorithm. Do, then check for correctness, then and only then proceed. Stupid people don't do that. These are often people who find it too taxing to actually find out facts on their own. They find it easier to immerse themselves in one political party's propaganda and trust whatever the leaders happen to tell them at the moment. It's much more labor intensive to be smart but it pays off in the long run. It's easy to be stupid and that can be a result of just being lazy.

People who live in large cities fall for the lie that the government can provide every need you may develop in your life. This is because they are way more likely to depend on government for their needs. Add to that, the indoctrination that has been going on for about 100 years by progressives. People have been taught a number of things that can be taken right out of the communist party play book. One of the big things that go virtually unnoticed by even the brainwashed themselves is the mantra that guns are bad.

If you want to control people, one of the first things you must do is render them helpless and defenseless. So, communists create a school system in which guns are portrayed as evil and only owned by bad, bad people. The amazing thing is, a majority of educators have the same ideology and they really don't need marching orders because they are able and willing to promote this garbage autonomously with no outside pressure. This is evident by school districts that have called the police and have had children arrested for offenses that I find laughable, such as:

Chapter 6 – Social Implications of Stupidity

having a pop tart chewed into the shape of a gun; a little scrap of paper that was torn into a "rough" shape of a gun; having a "hello kitty" squirt gun that was intended for toddlers.

This is only a small sample of the kind of nonsense that is being inflicted on the children of this country in order to promote the ideology of demonizing guns. Why is this done? To create a generation of zombies who think the way the communists want them to think, that's why. Why is it that the vast majority of educators at every level seem to embrace this mantra? I am talking about everything from elementary to graduate school. In order to answer this question we need to observe the main groups of people that lean towards socialism because they all have one thing in common besides being procommunist. They all have professions that put them in front of large numbers of people where they have exposure and are seen and heard as part of the job.

The groups I am talking about are: Educators, news media and the film industry (mostly actors). They are all well known to be predominately left leaning. This fits in nicely with the point I am attempting to make here and that is they all see themselves as creators of a better world, a utopia or a heaven on earth if you will. This is caused by IRD and it is the only logical reason why these people believe in the garbage that they believe in. They probably chose their profession for the same reason they choose communism, they want others to judge them as being smart. I cover each group in depth later in this chapter.

When the issue of an "assault weapons ban" comes up again in the near future, the zombies that have been brainwashed beyond reprise will willingly vote for the politician who wants to pass this legislation, "for the safety of the children". That's the way things work and the progressives know it. They need to resort to propaganda and brainwashing because if they told the truth, they would lose and the smart side would win. If their ideas were worth anything, they would not have to resort to these tactics.

There is a multi-billionaire who by all accounts is one of the wealthiest people in the world. He is also into control which is a glaring indicator of stupidity. He constantly meddles with the internal affairs of the U.S. One example is what was known as the "Secretary of State Project". This was an attempt to ensure that the secretaries of state in all states would be left leaning and his organization provided funding and propped candidates he supported. If the reader is not aware, the secretaries of state are responsible for making decisions in elections where the votes are close to ties. This is a classic example of how stupid people can and do become very successful; people like this multibillionaire. There are many people like this who have attempted to control vast numbers of people in the name of an ideology that claims it is just looking out for the poor person. Another fact about communism that the majority of zombies don't know about is that there are always a few uber rich at the top who influence the leaders of the party and insure that their assets are protected. This is the big fat lie about communism. It's supposed to be about protecting the common person but it is the common person who always ends up in poverty and turmoil.

In past communist dictatorships, the populace didn't have much of a say so, one way or the other about the way they were treated by the ruling class, mainly because they had been disarmed at the very beginning of the dictator's rise to power. In present day America, the same forces that were responsible for millions of deaths and misery for the living over the past 60 years are now

Chapter 6 – Social Implications of Stupidity

trying to establish the same kind of totalitarian system. This is what they want; do not doubt me on this. My rational for this belief is what I have been presenting here so far: These people are out to show the rest of the world how smart they are. If they were truly smart they wouldn't need to transform a country that didn't need transformation in the first place. They have a need to prove something, that fact should be obvious. The need is IRD.

Smart people don't need to prove how smart they are to the world; they already have a reasonable assessment of their own intelligence. Smart people always question everything that is presented to them, just as they don't think of themselves as smart. If they are smart, then they know that no one is perfect and there is always the possibility that anyone can be wrong about anything! If they know that about themselves, it is not difficult for them to convey that attribute to everyone else in the universe. This is an element of empathy and it could be one of the most important attributes of intelligence.

There is a segment of the population that can be labeled as sociopaths. Sociopaths usually have a complete lack of empathy. I think it is safe to say, that people who lack empathy completely are probably very stupid people. This is mainly because if you have no emotional bonds with fellow humans you are then also narcissistic and you will never admit you are wrong. Bingo! I believe empathy is another in-born emotion that probably has purpose in strengthening bonds and relationships in a group.

If intelligence is indeed the result of an algorithm, and I believe it is, that algorithm should deliberately guide us all by a methodology that checks, and rechecks every concept we are presented with as the "given information". Recall that the first foundation stone is assessment and analysis of the givens. People that summarily accept anything without additional thought (analysis), necessarily need to be defined as stupid as well.

Since the probability is very high that intelligence is directly proportional to brain architecture it stands to reason that brain structure is responsible for any differences in inherent intelligence. Therefore we can hypothesize that the underlying brain structure responsible for intelligence also conforms to what is known as the bell shaped curve, normal distribution concept. We can then also theorize that we can interpolate any level of intelligence with some underlying brain structure characteristic.

There will always be stupid people. That's just nature's way of doing things. The normal distribution or the bell shaped curve is a description of how everything in nature follows the laws of probability. A graph shaped like a bell, is a plot for the number of things on the horizontal plotted against how true they are to their design on the vertical. The exact center of the bell should be where the average number of things (in this case human brains) are true to their design resides. To the left of the center are the things that don't quite live up to the design specification and the things to the right make up the number of things that exceed design specs. You can see (even if you don't look at a bell shape curve illustration) that approximately half of all things will always be less than specification with respect to how well they follow the original design. This means that about 50% of all humans have the propensity for stupidity or at least the construction of their brain could be less than optimum for the production of intelligence.

Chapter 6 – Social Implications of Stupidity

Don't believe this? Was not Barack Obama elected for a second time? Was not the country in dire economic straits? Obama care was just beginning to be implemented and many people watched as their healthcare premiums skyrocketed. Things like fast and furious and Benghazi were still fresh in the populace mind. What the heck happened? Stupid people, that's what happened. Recall that truly stupid people will never admit that they were wrong, because in doing so, admitting fault is an admission of stupidity because they don't have the smarts to know that all humans make mistakes. These are the same people who will get jealous of others' intellectual abilities because they believe those abilities were just somehow bestowed on them. The stupid mind believes that success didn't have anything to do with hard work because the truly stupid are inherently lazy people. Of course there is a category of stupid people who will work very hard to promote their own IRD. This includes people like the billionaire I alluded to.

One large factor in perpetuating the low information voter is the liberal media. If there is any hope at reversing the media bias in the United States, it must be done by the public not following them any longer. In order to sway public sentiment to that degree requires that the truth be disseminated to the public in other ways such as social media. If the government ever succeeds in controlling the internet, freedom loving people are screwed. The big question about the liberal media is how they got to be that way and how they remain that way over long periods of time. It's got everything to do with hiring practices and it turns out this is a big problem not only in news media but organizations of all types, both governmental and private.

First of all, stupid people will never hire smart people unless entirely by mistake. The stupid; being lost in a jungle of self-awareness, believe that anyone who disagrees with them must be stupid but in reality the people they judge to be stupid are probably smarter than they are. This is a self-perpetuating phenomenon that is like the preverbal non-existing perpetual motion machine and will run until the energy source is removed. The energy source in this case is public support. If people stopped watching the liberal media altogether, they would all disappear into oblivion in a microsecond.

Another problem is that there are very powerful influences in the world with big pockets full of money, who also suffer from stupid bias. People like the billionaire I love to talk about so much will continue to prop up and support the liberal media's ideology through his many organizations. My estimate is that the media will continue to be a problem for conservatives for as far as the eye can see (which is pretty far). I would very much like to say I have a solution for the problem of the "low information voter" but I would be lying if I said so. There will always be a certain percentage of the population that will be easily deceived and brainwashed by the communists in public office and their propaganda arm; the media.

Humanity may survive as a species no matter how stupid we become (maybe not). Being free is another matter altogether. If there are enough people in the United States who buy the lie that communism is the way of the future, we are all lost. The stupid will have won the last battle in the smart, stupid war that is thousands of years old. There are two big targets the left must destroy in order to win more battles in the war of the smart against the stupid. They are called the first and the second amendment of the Constitution of The United States. I will cover the second amendment in more detail because it is more complicated than the first. The first will be undermined by passing legislation that makes "global warming" denial into hate speech and puts

Chapter 6 – Social Implications of Stupidity

people in jail for voicing their views that global warming is nonsense. That's pretty simple and of course we cannot allow that to happen because if we do, we are screwed also. Socialist leaning government officials could attempt to put people in jail for the "hate speech" of global warming denial but they will have a hard time doing that if the people are armed and can protect themselves.

Gun control

The reason gun control is in this book is because it plays a major role in determining whether humanity will remain smart, and free. It is just another big step communists need to take, on their journey to world domination. The one big obstacle they have in their journey is The United States of America. It is imperative for them to get guns out of the hands of private citizens in the USA. They will take every opportunity that presents itself to further their agenda of their self-aggrandizing ideology. Just as sharks live to eat, they live to promote their smarts, which is paradoxical since they don't have any smarts to begin with. This demonstrates how stupid people at the top can manipulate and greatly influence stupid people at the bottom.

Recall I talked about the "garbage in, garbage out" paradigm. A perfect example of how this can be applied to human behavior is the use of the "false premise". A false premise is simply an incorrect or an incomplete concept which has been accepted as indisputable fact. This is akin to attempting to solve an equation that requires "plugging in" five variables but omitting one. The results will be wildly incorrect, this should be immediately apparent. Anyone with a basic knowledge of arithmetic can recognize how leaving just one variable out of an equation will corrupt the result. Some people will accept concepts presented to them, with large amounts of omitted information and they will accept those concepts as fact, never batting an eye. What I am talking about here is how communists and progressives will twist the details of information, and tell complete lies, in order to promote their agenda. People on the receiving end of these lies and innuendos, accept it as gospel, again; no eye batting involved.

One of the lies that are routinely thrown around in anti-gun circles is that the leading cause of death in children is gunshot wounds. Just the conjured up images most people have of poor little kids being slaughtered by firearms every year, brings up emotions of disgust and anger. The problem with this is: This is a big fat lie! What the anti-gun pundits don't reveal is that "a child" is defined as anyone under the age of eighteen! Yes that's right; eighteen! These are gang members killing each other in every corner of the country. Of course guns are the leading cause of death for teenagers, because "children" get recruited by gangs at the age of twelve and possibly younger. Recall that stupid people lie because they have no real, valid points to argue about. If they want to eliminate guns or anything they believe will hamper their cause; they must lie, cheat or steal to get that done. In communism, the ends always justify the means because the collective will supposedly benefit, somehow. In reality, the collective is worse off without guns.

The real fact of the matter is that thousands of lives (the masses, i.e. the collective) are saved every year because of guns. Why is it you never hear these stories on the news? It's because it doesn't fit in with the agenda the news media is promoting and pushing, that's why. The stupid people in the media have to prove their smarts and they have become invested in an ideology with all the other stupid people who are also invested in the same lies. Recall that stupidity loves company and stupidity supports and protects itself.

The biggest threat to humanity's freedom is ultimately whether guns will be banned and confiscated or not. The simple reason for this is: If a government is successful in disarming its people, it can impose whatever it wants on those people. It doesn't need to be *this* present government, doing the imposing. It could very well be some future government that is even worse than the one we have right now. Stupidity is always nearsighted and intelligence is farsighted.

The present government we have right now would attempt banning guns when and if the opportunity presents itself. Stupid people are opportunistic and will use any trumped up reason that comes along to impose their will on everyone else. The only thing stopping the current administration from banning everything in Obama's first term was a few democratic senators and representatives who were afraid of harming their reelection chances with a gun ban. In the future we may not be so lucky.

Gun control laws get passed because of two groups. One group is the government; the other group is the voting public. The government may want gun control so they can control the people. The people's root impetus for the desire to have gun control is fear. The second statement should be fairly obvious when dwelled upon. It's all a matter of fear. Some people (all liberals) have a natural fear of weapons. Liberals are no longer acting like "classic liberals" of days gone by. They now generally act like full-fledged progressives and that is time-release communism, no doubt about it. The stupid voter is probably not consciously aware of that, but it is entirely true.

Fear plays right into the hands of the communist politico who wants to exaggerate any firearm feature the fearful may find to be offensive and invoke additional fear. The term "assault weapon" is an example of the use of terms to play upon the fears of the uninformed. The sentence; "These are weapons that belong on the battlefield, not on our streets!" has been used more times than I have been able to keep track of. Statements like this are used for one purpose; to invoke fear in the populace.

Fear is the mother of cowardice. Cowardice is an indicator of stupidly. Don't believe that? Allow me to explain: A coward conjures up multiple sets of scenarios in which they pre-pose all of the possible negative things that can possibly happen to them. This means they are operating on a bunch of false premises and just like the example above, will invariably lead to incorrect assessments and corresponding defective decisions. Cowards imagine things that will never happen, or at the very least, have a very low probability of happening. "A coward dies a thousand times, a brave man only once." I have heard some gun-ban proponents flip this around and claim that pro-gun people are cowards because we are afraid to be without guns! If being aware of all the bad things that can actually happen to you made you a coward, then that logic could apply to every man and woman in the Armed Forces and every police officer that carries a firearm. This is flawed logic and is typical with stupid people. It is also interesting to note how nasty stupid people can become when they make attempts at promoting their stupid ideas.

Chapter 6 – Social Implications of Stupidity

Does this mean the people who want all guns banned are stupid? Yes and for a vast variety of reasons. Stupid people will accept the false premise of the fabricated demonizing factor for guns, in other words; "guns are bad, evil, things!" How can anyone come to a correct conclusion about anything that they have no real firsthand knowledge of? It is impossible, but the reasons they have for demonizing guns are based on emotions (fear) rather than facts (logic). That would be bad enough but there are other things the stupid do on a regular basis that contributes to their incorrect assessment.

The stupid routinely buy the argument that the Second Amendment only guarantees the right that the *militia* "keep and bear" arms. These are some biblically sized false premises to counter with this particular argument but it is not difficult. First of all, anyone making that statement is praying that whoever is listening to these donkey feces is totally ignorant of the history behind the Second Amendment. This is making a decision based on something you really have no firsthand knowledge of and in a logical sense is the kiss of death for intelligence.

The stupid people that the stupid politician is attempting to deceive will accept the above statement as fact, instead of the requisite questioning smart people do. Questions like, "What exactly was the militia in those days, long ago?" Or perhaps, "Is the current National Guard a direct equivalent to the militia mentioned in the Second Amendment?" Or maybe even, "Why would the current National Guard need a guarantee to have weapons, isn't that more or less understood that they automatically are issued guns, which are bought and paid for by the U.S. Federal government just like the Army, Navy, Marines or Air Force?"

The original meaning of "militia" meant "people" and it was used interchangeably between the folks who wanted arms for self-defense (militia who were only ordinary people and volunteers) and ordinary folks (people who were not volunteers in the militia) who could decide to have them or not to have them if they wanted. The Second Amendment DOES NOT bestow that right to anyone. It merely guarantees that the government cannot take that right away. A government cannot take something away from you that was given to you by God, or Nature, if you have a problem referring to a God. Beings, including human beings have an inherent right to protect themselves. No one, no government can take that right away from you. That is what the Second Amendment is all about. This brings up another false premise:

This false premise is the notion that you don't need a gun that uses 30 round detachable magazines to protect yourself. I can tell you that this is complete lie. We do need 30 round capabilities (and bigger) just like the police, the National Guard and the other military branches need. The simple reason for this is because we have to contend with the same threats as they do. Allow me to explain:

I first would like to present my personal opinion of some of the people I have met, that were staunchly anti-gun. In every case, they were not only just anti-gun but all had very strong emotional feelings about so-called "assault weapons". I can assure the reader that merely meeting with these people was a super unpleasant experience. The *emotional* anger and hatred that was expressed directly at me in no uncertain terms cannot be overstated. These were not nice people. In fact I think I can say they were the worst example of human crap on the face of the earth. One reason I feel that way is because of the total dishonesty and immaturity displayed by them all.

They acted like a certain group of people we are all familiar with. They acted like little kids. They treated me like I was a complete idiot for believing what I believed in and for no other reason. They didn't want to listen to my side of the story; it didn't matter to them because after all; they couldn't have possibly been wrong. They were narcissistic, arrogant and dishonest to name a few of the negative traits. These people were stupid. That is the only conclusion I can arrive at. Allow me to perform an analysis of these idiot's viewpoints and the counter points I would have liked to counter their argument with if I had been given a chance. Perhaps the main reason I was not given a chance to present my side is that they had no facts to back up their argument, but only emotional, feel-good crap.

In order to adequately explain my position, I need to talk about the main topic of interest here: Assault weapons. What is an "assault weapon"? There may be other definitions but I think the one that serves both side of this debate would be: A service rifle which is; a rifle that is of direct design inheritance of a rifle that was or is currently in military service. It is an important distinction to say that the civilian version is a service rifle that is only capable of semi-automatic fire. A true assault weapon would have full automatic fire capability, but this is how these weapons are described today.

A good example of this type of weapon would be the military M-16 and its civilian counterpart; the AR-15. The firearms novice would probably not be able to tell one from the other just by looking at the two. The big difference between the two is that the M-16 has three positions that the "select fire" lever can be turned to: "safe", "fire" and "auto". The AR-15 only has two positions that lever can point to: "safe" and "fire". There is no "auto" position on an AR-15 hence that rifle is not capable of full automatic fire.

Now, what is the difference between full "auto" fire and just "fire"? The difference is: On full "auto" the rifle will fire every round that is available in the detachable magazine, one after the other until there are no more rounds left just by holding the trigger. In other words, it's fully automatic. On the "fire" position (also known as "semi-auto" or semi-automatic) the shooter has to pull the trigger every time a round is fired. In other words, semi-auto is not fully automatic, it is just "self-loading".

Self-loading means that when a round is fired, the spent round (brass case) gets pulled from the rear of the barrel (known as the chamber), it gets thrown out of the rifle to the side, then a new complete round; bullet and case, is stripped from the top of the magazine and placed in the chamber, ready for the shooter to pull the trigger for the next shot. So again, semi-automatic rifles are actually "self-loaders".

So when you hear and subsequently believe that it is very easy to obtain a fully automatic weapon: anywhere in this country; by anyone with a driver's license; you now know *it is a bold face lie!* In fact, it is a lie to state that it is easy for anyone to get a gun anywhere in the country. Everyone is checked out via the FBI instant background check database. If and only if there are no negative aspects which would preclude you from owning a firearm, then you are allowed to

Chapter 6 – Social Implications of Stupidity

take possession. It is not easy, by any stretch of the imagination. There are a few, very small numbers of firearms transfers that take place at gun shows with no background check but that has not been proven to produce large numbers of purchases that have resulted in crimes.

Many hard core anti-gun people will always object to the "high capacity" magazine capability. They don't like big magazines because they have been told that this feature, "allows the shooter to spray hundreds of bullets in a few seconds". A semi-automatic does not "spray" bullets and a "few seconds" is an over exaggeration of how fast anyone can pull a trigger. Even if the anti-gun nut were to concede that point, they will still claim that a large number of "bullets" in these large capacity magazines poses a public safety threat because it allows the shooter to fire off 30, 40 or even 100 (currently the highest capacity magazine available for the AR-15) bullets in seconds without reloading.

This is just another false premise and this is why: High capacity magazines only convey an advantage to any shooter and in any situation that involves the opponent having some capacity to *shoot back*! If you take away the element of getting shot back at there *is no* real advantage at having a large capacity magazine. Unarmed people, especially children, are totally at the mercy of any armed screwball and it does not amount to a hill of beans what kind of firearm is used against helpless kids in those cases! This means that part of the stupid's assessment about high capacity magazines may actually be true when an opponent is shooting back but that does not amount to any sort of advantage when used against others who are helpless and not armed. What horrifies the stupid anti-gun zombie is the thought of a mentally deranged miscreant holding an assault rifle with 30 round magazines and having his way with a bunch of unarmed people, especially children.

This is totally illogical. This entire scenario has initial conditions that should never be allowed to exist anywhere, anytime, especially in a school where kids are. There should be a responsible armed adult everywhere kids need to be such as school. Let us not forget, that every time this sort of thing has happened, it was in a "gun free zone". The term: "gun free zone" was conceived, developed and promoted by progressives to promote the warm and fuzzy, feel good, non-self-reliant attitude they love to preach so much. You know; in the tradition of a true utopia *everything* is nice and warm and fuzzy! Where do you suppose the concept of "gun free zones" came from? In other words, what was the underlying root cause impetus that created these wonders of progressivism? Of course it was cowardice; there is no question about it. Progressives are cowards, and cowards are stupid. You don't need to be a genius to come to that conclusion. Just the thought of a firearm is sufficient to cause a progressive's sphincter muscle to wink!

The real issue here is that *unarmed* adults or children; don't have a snowball's chance in hell against somebody with a gun. *It really doesn't matter what type of gun.* A bunch of grade school kids trapped in a locked classroom would be easy prey for an amateur armed with a 12 gauge shotgun, designed primarily for hunting waterfowl. At the distances in a classroom, number 7 birdshot in a three round magazine, with one in the chamber would be adequate to do exactly what the AR-15 did at Sandy Hook Elementary School. This assertion can be easily tested by doing a mockup of the conditions with a gun that I just suggested. I am positive that I am correct.

Chapter 6 – Social Implications of Stupidity

Anti-gun progressives were quick to blame the type of gun used, when in fact the type was not a big factor. They wanted it to appear that the gun was to blame; they always do that because that is part of their agenda; to disarm the American people. If progressives succeed in banning rifles like the AR15; this will amount to banning approximately half of all rifles in the U.S. This is because the AR15 is by far the most popular rifle in the history of this great country. They are used for hunting, target shooting and numerous shooting sports competition. Just the casual mention of the phrase "shooting sports" makes progressives lose their lunch.

The Second Amendment's real purpose

The Second Amendment was written by some very smart people. They knew human nature and they understood that there will always be some stupid people who want to impose their ideas on everyone else. I often wonder if they were aware of the smart / stupid war I am defining here. They did know about the possibility of an overbearing central government and that the only solution to that was an armed populace. This is the true reason that progressives want guns gone. They want to "have their way" with us if the need arises. I know what many low information voters will say as an automatic, knee jerk reaction to this statement. "That can't happen here!! This is the United States of America!" This is just another false premise. Just because something has not happened before does not mean it will never happen! But wait just a gosh-darn minute! It already has happened here! Don't think so? Think again.

Waco

There are actually several instances of the government, "having their way" with the citizenry. The biggest and most covered up case was the Waco Texas encounter between Janet Reno's "Justice" Department and a religious group called "The Branch Davidians". Oh wait, I forgot about the Japanese internment camps of World War Two. That is an excellent example of our own government having its way with us but I won't comment much on that because there is really not much to say. It happened, case closed. The story of Waco however, is one that really needs to be told because it was swept under the rug by the propaganda arm of the U.S. government; the media.

This is the only time I personally remember hearing about the Federal Government using an U.S. Army tank against civilians. Although the liberal friendly media didn't tell the whole story I will attempt to provide a little insight to what actually took place. Initially, the ATF and FBI agents armed with automatic weapons and full battle gear, attempted a full blown frontal assault on the "Davidians" building which was a very large structure, similar to a small factory building. The occupants of the main compound building decided to fight back. The reason they had for the opposition is not known. It could be that they felt that there were no valid reasons for the government to be attacking them in this manner and that their religious freedom was at stake. The details on their validity in resisting are not clear and the government never really made an attempt to clarify exactly what happened.

It was originally reported that the reason for the cordon and subsequent assault was because David Koresh, the leader, had several alleged illegally converted AR15 rifles. This means that the semi-automatic rifles were converted to fire on fully automatic. This can be easily done with

136

Chapter 6 – Social Implications of Stupidity

a few "fire control" parts which interchange directly with the semi-automatic parts such as the hammer, trigger and a part called the "sear". While that would have been a violation of federal firearms law, the type of raid conducted by the ATF was an over the top extreme, to say the least, response to a perceived and not proven violation. This is equivalent to hunting mosquitoes with a machine gun. My opinion is that this given reason was just an excuse. They wanted to take down this group. It was a show of authority, nothing more.

In the initial assault, the government suffered many casualties. They had to pull back. The Branch Davidians were not giving up without a fight. From the government's point of view, this group was nothing but a bunch of criminals. The question is: What crimes did they break, other than the illegal conversion charge? The charge of the illegal conversion was never actually proven as all the evidence in the way of the so-claimed converted rifles was destroyed in the eventual fire that consumed the building.

After a recovery from the initial assault loses, the government then stepped up the pace of the action and employed the use of an M60 battle tank, the same tank that was used in combat operations in Viet Nam, ramming it into the walls if the Davidian's compound building. This is a very disturbing development that seems to have gone completely unnoticed by the media and the public at the time. This amounts to the media shirking responsibility because reporting acts of abuse by the government to citizens is actually their job. When a government of the people can use military main battle tanks against those people, then all bets are off, they can do anything they want to anyone they want to do it to.

Why did everyone in the country just accept the government's explanation of all this? Because we are already brainwashed into thinking the government would never do anything to hurt us, that's why. There is also a phenomenon called the "normalcy bias". This is the false feeling of security many people need to have that tells them everything is fine, even if there is a battle tank pointing its 105 millimeter gun tube at their front door!

The last major nasty thing the government did was they used what is known in the military as "CS gas" on the people inside that building. CS gas is a riot control gas that was used against the enemy in Vietnam. I personally had to go through CS training chambers three different times in my stint in the Army. The Army dropped 55 gallon drums of that stuff in high foot traffic areas where I was in Viet Nam in an attempt at harassing enemy movement. There were times when my unit walked through this stuff and kicked up a large plume before we were able to don our gas masks. It is really nasty stuff. During training, they make you take your gas mask off while you are in a room filled with the gas. This is to give you an idea of how bad it is. If you were locked in a room filled with this stuff, you would literally kill yourself in a frantic attempt to get out. It was never meant to be used indoors.

CS is not really a gas at all, but very small jagged shaped particles that irritate the skin, eyes, nose and particularly, the lungs. It was actually called cough gas at its invention. I can tell you going through a chamber filled with this is no picnic. If concentrated enough (which it was in the chamber) it causes immediate non-voluntary violent reactions from every part of the body. Your skin, eyes and nostrils feel like they are on fire and you can't breathe due to all the coughing. If I were locked in a room with this stuff, there is no doubt in my mind that I would kill myself trying to get out. That didn't stop Janet Reno's ATF and FBI from using it inside a building that 11 children happened to be in. Eleven children were subsequently burned alive and in my opinion it was OUR government at fault because as I said, they used an army tank against civilians for some unknown and unproven accusation.

The bombing of the Mira Federal building in Oklahoma City was by all accounts; pay back for Waco. This fact has largely been downplayed by the media but if you dig into what Timothy McVeigh said about the motivation it is pretty clear. It is also thought that he and his cousin Terry Nicols probably did not act alone but were part of a group; the size of which we can only guess at. We feel bad about the kids and adults that were killed in Oklahoma City, but we should not forget that our own government also did the same thing at Waco. Terrorism is terrorism; it matters not who does it. Dead kids are dead kids.

It is the undeserved, illogical trust in the government that is responsible for the attitude of anti-gun liberals. They want the rest of us to believe that citizens don't need high capacity magazines and "assault rifles" because our wonderful benevolent government would never ever do anything bad to us. Yeah right. No government is worth of that level of trust. Since we have had whole groups of people placed in concentration camps by our own government and also had an Army tank used against civilians in the recent past, we can expect things as bad or even worse done to us by some future tyrants. Remember; stupidity is always nearsighted. If we can make any observation about this incident it is that liberals were in charge of the White House.

Ruby Ridge

The next "incident" took place at Ruby Ridge, Wyoming. This time two FBI snipers shot and killed a father and his son simply because they were suspects! Can you imagine how many people would make it to trial if every time the FBI was after a suspect; they just got out the old sniper rifles and had at it? This was also covered up and played down by the media. We cannot allow things like this to continue happening and still consider ourselves free.

LA Riots

The Los Angeles riots are well known to most people but on the other hand, most people did not get an accurate account of how severe it really was. This is in large part due to the fact that just like the police; the media scrammed! There are only eyewitness accounts from the people that were lucky enough to live through it.

The area of LA affected by the "war" (that's what it really was), was about 46 square miles. A total of 55 people died during the riots and as many as 2,000 people were reported injured. Estimates of the material losses were as high as $1 billion. Approximately 3,600 fires were set, destroying 1,100 buildings, with fire calls coming once every minute at some times. When the cops realized just how bad it was; they just decided to make like a tree and leave. The poor souls unlucky enough to be there when the "crap hit the fan" had to defend themselves or die!

This was like a Hollywood movie only real people were dying instead of stunt people just acting like they were dying. Store owners that were lucky enough to have weapons barricaded themselves in makeshift defensive positions. Firefights were a common occurrence between gang members and merchants. All of the store owners say that if they did not have weapons to protect themselves; they would not have made it out alive.

Katrina

Hurricane Katrina in New Orleans is a prime example of what can happen to law abiding citizens during a natural disaster. It only takes some stupid politician to decide that people will be a threat to everyone if they are allowed to have weapons. Methodically, one by one, citizens were approached by the police and asked if they had guns of any kind. This was usually done with an M16 leveled at the gun owners and came as a complete surprise. They took those peoples' firearms away so that they could become prey for the looters, rapists and murderers that roamed with immunity. That is not very smart, is it?

If all the above does not convince you that it can and has already happened here, than you must be one of the stupid people or politicians I was talking about! We have all heard this phrase many times over: "what do you need an assault rifle for"? This is easy to answer:

We need assault rifles with 30 round magazines (and bigger) because riots, gangs, civil unrest and natural disasters can happen anywhere and at any time. There are an estimated 20 million gang members in the United States. If we consider that most of them have some type of weapon, probably a firearm, it doesn't require a lofty imagination to dream up what the country will be like in any kind of emergency. The chances of something like this happening in your locality are much, much greater, with the new threats of terrorism we face today.

Will banning all guns reduce crime, and make our world a safer place to live? Can we actually create that utopia, that "heaven on earth" which sounds so warm and fuzzy? The short answer is: No, hell no! People that buy into that lie have been effectively brainwashed and are effectively stupid for allowing that.

Once an idea is implanted in the brain it is very hard to remove. The gun control advocate's manifesto is that, in order to stop gun violence, we must just simply the get rid of all guns, everywhere. This mimics the long held belief by Communists that in order for their system to work, the whole world would necessarily need to be operating under the same type of government; theirs. Even if the monumental task of ridding the world of all guns were possible (it is not), would it actually work or in other words would it end violence? No, absolutely not. Instead of guns, people would die from knives, swords, clubs and baseball bats.

I want to make it perfectly clear that pro-gun people like me are not thrilled at the thought of little boys and girls, mothers, fathers being caught in the crossfire from gang members on a daily basis. In fact it sickens us to the extreme. The various anti-gun groups would have you believe otherwise; that we are uncaring, egotistical, self-centered and mean spirited with no regard for life, much less the human kind. This is all a huge pile of bull-crap. Nothing could be further from the truth.

Chapter 6 – Social Implications of Stupidity

The fact that we have a huge amount of empathy for the innocent victims of gun violence should not equate to us willingly giving up our right to keep and bear arms. This is a false and unfair comparison. It is totally illogical for us to become unarmed and defenseless in order to satisfy some unknown and unproven "feel good" solution to a complex problem. There is a much bigger picture to be viewed here and there are more important aspects to this story. Communists always use the importance of the collective over the individual *except* when it comes to guns. That's a different story! We would be truly stupid to risk the ultimate freedom of the collective and relegate ourselves to a future of slavery by giving up our weapons because guns were used inappropriately in a few instances by the individual.

We have been portrayed in the media as "the guns for fun crowd". This was how one venomously anti-gun journalist who has a daily editorial column in a nationally known newspaper put it. The guy that wrote that is an idiot and he demonstrated his stupidity to the whole world. This statement reeks of arrogance, glibness, deceitfulness and narcissism which are all stupidity indicators. Yes we have fun with guns and there a quite a few of us that do, millions in fact. Just because you are stuck in an ocean of self-indulgence does not make the people who believe in recreational activities with guns idiots. The idiot is you; mister journalist. You are also a coward and that is evident because your fear is controlling your decisions. This is all about fear and you prove it.

We are portrayed and ultimately perceived as a group of self-indulgent, self-promoting sociopaths who only care about their fascination with "killing machines" that have no other practical purpose in the world other than to kill or maim innocent victims. I have also read some anti-gun journalists use the theory rooted in what the "great" Sigmund Freud labeled as phallic symbols. The gun barrel is the penis. The bullet is the seminal fluid "shot" from the end of the penis in the act of procreation. Stupid people say anything to disparage their opponents in any way that presents itself. I could counter the above argument by stating that anyone with a "the gun barrel is a penis" hypothesis may be thinking about penises way too much! Is this unfair and cruel? No more than what was dished out towards me. Anti-gun people can be nasty. We have to fight fire with fire, or in this case, penises with penises, aimed at the big penis that "disseminated" that idea in the first place! This is the only way to deal with stupid people.

By the way, guns *are* deadly. Yes, I agree with that wholeheartedly. Guns would not have any value or practical purpose if they were not deadly! Being deadly is what gives them value. Their primary purpose and practicality is not a valid reason why we should rid the world of them. In fact, those attributes are reasons we should embrace them and use them wisely.

It is no coincidence that the localities with the strictest gun control laws are areas with the highest murder and overall crime rates. Many people have died in inner cities because they were denied the basic nature's law of self-protection and preservation. People have truly become cattle in the big cities with progressive politicians like Mayor Richard M. Daley acting as the arrogant rancher. Just like Joe Lenin and Chairman Mao, they sit back in their comfy leather chair, and review the reports of all the carnage with no remorse. Guns don't kill people; gun free zones such as Chicago kill people!

Chapter 6 – Social Implications of Stupidity

The above are examples of how a bunch of very stupid elected officials make stupid decisions that can ultimately cost someone their life. The homeowner may die because the most effective weapon for home defense is by far; the handgun. If you only have a shotgun to defend yourself and your family, you are at a great disadvantage. A shotgun is way too cumbersome to be wielding inside a home. Another consideration is the damage that can be done by ricochet inside the home with a shotgun and the distance this ammunition can be lethal at. You may end up killing yourself along with the intruder (along with a neighbor or two). The criminal may die (no big loss though) because instead of a relatively puny pistol round, he is shot with hunting ammunition designed for deer.

As far as a complete ban on so-called assault rifles is concerned, would a total ban actually decrease the number of firearms related deaths? In many large municipalities and states that ban these weapons the data shows over and over resounding answer is no! The reason for this is gang bangers and others hell-bent on separating you from your belongings do not obey the law and the weapon of choice is the handgun, not a semi-automatic rifle. Why? A semi-automatic rifle is much more difficult to conceal and it is just not as handy.

Gang bangers do most of what they do on foot. It is easy to carry handguns and not easy to carry a rifle. What about drive by shootings? Yes, that happens but not as much and even in that case it is much more difficult to shoot a rifle of any type from a car and of course that happens but we are talking about the usual, not the exceptional. The number of times "assault weapons" are used in crimes is miniscule compared to handguns. It is simple as that. OK you say, "So, let us ban all handguns too!" Well, they are already banned in most big cities in the U.S. and the results are clear; gun bans do not reduce crime, in fact the data shows the exact opposite! The reason for this is clear and very simplistic.

Criminals by definition, DO NOT OBEY THE LAW! What part about this statement don't stupid people understand? Criminal get guns whether they are legal or not. Gun bans ONLY prohibit the poor self-defenseless homeowner for owning the very thing that may save him or her and family. How many people have to die before you realize you are wrong chairman Daley? Woops; I mean Mayor Daley? I am being unfair to Mr. Daley who is no longer the mayor of Chicago. But, I use him as a perfect example of a stupid progressive; imposing communistic views on the rest of us to prove how smart he is.

There are also the liberals who in their complete faith in government believe that it would be utterly impossible for the populace of the United States to put up an armed resistance to that government. I got into an argument with a rabid liberal about this very topic. He said that those of us who believe we could win a fight against the government are delusional since the government has F-16s, tanks, hellfire missiles and many other weapons that civilians don't. While all those things are true, the people have something the government does not have: Numbers.

The standing army which composes the people's militia in the United States outnumbers all of our official military units by at least 10,000 to one. If these patriots used guerrilla warfare tactics, it would not be long before some of those high powered weapons were in their hands also. Sure there would be many casualties but when freedom is at stake people will die willingly for the cause. Hillary Clinton and Bernie Sanders should consider this little aspect of Americana before considering any type of gun grab (which they definitely are). If Hillary does not get indicted and the American people are stupid enough to elect her president, she will appoint the most liberal Supreme Court judges she can find and that in turn will inevitably result in civil war at some time after the second amendment is deemed to be null and void. This is a 100% certainty; do not doubt me on this.

If the reader has noticed anything about the things I have just presented, is that most of the laws suggested and passed by liberals are all based on emotional thinking. Emotional thinking is a primitive mode that had purpose in early human groups and still does for family units but its use in large scale governmental law making is definitely not appropriate.

Stupidity throughout history

What the liberals of The United States are planning to do to its citizens has been done to the hapless citizens of numerous counties throughout historical record. If you don't believe my premise that there is no such thing as evil, that there is only stupidity, than the following may prove to change your mind. It is just a matter of having empathy for the smart people that were controlled by some really stupid leaders.

I reiterate that stupidity has been routinely been mistaken for something humans call "evil". To that end, there is an age old battle that is still underway and that is: The battle of good against evil but it is in reality: The battle of the smart against the stupid. I am of the belief that there is really no such thing as evil, there is only stupidity. It follows that intelligence produces good, while stupidity produces pain, suffering and catastrophe which humans perceive as evil. I follow with some examples of how stupidity guides governments to war with unwilling smart citizens dragged along for the ride.

Think about every bad thing that has happened throughout history. As an example I will pick the Second World War since that conflict is relatively recent and (for the time being anyway) is still taught in school today. The Second World War was one of humanity's worst conflagrations. It was one of the bloodiest wars ever fought and produced a huge amount of suffering. Could it have been avoided?

This is a question that could be applied to every bad thing that has happened to humans over our entire course of history. Of the things that people have some control over, were the bad things the result of stupid people or smart people being in control? I believe the answer to this question could qualify for axiom status simply because it is just common sense. But I will cast my vote and say that it is my opinion is that stupid people were to blame, even if only the leaders are considered and not how those leaders came into power.

Now, think about the people who were responsible for starting the Second World War. This includes the leaders of Germany and Japan. Do you believe that the start of World War Two was the result of a bunch of smart people making decisions or did the war occur because of a bunch of dummies making decisions? Obviously, we must conclude that the war occurred because of stupidity.

Chapter 6 – Social Implications of Stupidity

If you do not concur with this conclusion, than consider what was going on in the minds of some really smart people in Germany and Japan. Do you think there were people in both countries saying things like; "What are we doing?", "Why are we doing this?", "This will destroy our county!"? Of course there were. They were not heard. The stupid side won that argument. The stupid side won this battle in the age old war of the smart against the stupid and as a result, millions of lives were lost.

In the United States and Great Britain there was lots of stupidity to go around. In Britain, Lord Chamberlain made the determination that the Germans were not a threat. In the United States, it was believed we could stay out of any conflict. In reality, we should have seen; "The writing on the wall." We should have been ready for Pearl Harbor.

Let us take a look at some of the factors leading up to the Second World War: The First World War one was an extremely bloody war. There were many battles fought in which over thirty thousand were killed in single encounters. Evidently we didn't learn from that; the world allowed Germany to pick up where it left off in the first war. While we were watching Germany build its war machine, we also watched Japan do pretty much the same thing. It was just not smart to observe these things going on and then come to the conclusion that they couldn't possibly affect us. Was it?

We didn't see the writing on the wall because the powers that were; were mostly stupid. Remember, this is an age old war that began as soon as intelligence emerged as the imminent survival tool. It was and always has been the smart trying to keep control and the stupid trying to take control away and vice versa. If you are still not convinced that there is no such thing as evil, consider these examples of classic evil that has been depicted as such in every way imaginable, since the events were reported. The first example is Adolf Hitler.

Adolf Hitler has been portrayed as an "evil genius". I am here to set the record straight and I will prove that Hitler was neither evil nor a genius. He was just stupid. There is plenty of evidence to prove his stupidity. If we look at the war through a tactician's viewpoint, we see Hitler making numerous mistakes; in the way he managed his military throughout the war. From military tacticians' accounts of Hitler's decisions as far as deployments of troop and Armored units, it is very clear that if the Allies would have fought someone with brains, we all would be speaking German and Japanese today. Hitler had a pact with Joe Stalin and then for some unknown reason (stupidity) reneged on the pact and proceeded to attack Russia. I ask the reader to imagine what it might have been like for the Allies fighting the Axis powers of Germany, Russia and Japan. Do you think we could have won *that* war? I don't believe we would have. Hitler made nothing but mistakes in the war in Europe. Besides his faulty tactics, there are more examples of him being a dim candle.

The main example is Hitler's persecution of Jews and the result of that which was called, "the ultimate solution". This was the holocaust and it has always been associated with evil. The main impetus for Hitler's hatred for the Jewish people was that: *He actually believed that Jews were responsible for all of the world's financial problems.* It is imperative to understand that he actually, really believed that the Jewish people were a curse of mankind! He wasn't evil because there is no such thing as evil; he was stupid! As a side note, a guy by the name of Henry Ford also had a similar belief. This is more proof that some very successful people are in fact; stupid.

Hitler really believed that Jews were the ultimate cause of the financial problems Germany was going through and to insure that their influence would be eliminated for once and for all, they must at all costs, be eliminated, and for good! The resulting attempted genocide appeared to be evil but that's the way stupidity propagates misery and that misery is incorrectly identified as evil. The false concept of evil is actually the product of stupidity.

I could write a complete book on this topic alone but I will present the reader with just one more example. The last example is the serial killer, Jeffrey Dahlmer. He really believed that in order to have some young boys love him, the way for him to possess their love, was to consume them, literally. He resorted to cannibalism in order to fulfill his desire to be loved and to love. Jeffery was not only stupid; he was insane which is; the sibling of stupidity.

Insanity is just an extreme form of stupidity because they both have the same underlying root cause. They are both caused from faulty processing of information by the brain. I think we might say Hitler had similar problems. Stupidity along with its extreme form, insanity, is always the precursor to the phenomenon we call "evil". I do not believe it is necessary to have a large quantity of insanity to produce large amounts of evil. Stupidity does the job quite nicely. There is also the well-known accepted legal fact that truly insane people are not responsible for their actions. So that is a proxy proof that there really is no such thing as evil.

I now present some perfect examples of my hypotheses of IRD and ICP being the driving impetus to all of humanity's actions. The following are all professions which the practitioners take pride in the promotion of their own intelligence as a daily work routine. These said professions are academics, the media and Hollywood.

The academics

Who are the most powerful people in the world? Is it Politicians, Presidents, Senators, Representatives, Prime Ministers, Dictators, Despots, Corporate CEOs or Billionaires? If you answered yes to any of the above; you are wrong! The most powerful people in the world are the wonderful people employed as the purveyors of the "correct". They are; the educators. Don't think so? Think again. They control what gets taught, who it gets taught to and who is fortunate enough to get bestowed upon them the "canonization" that occurs when they graduate.

They are partly responsible for all of humanity's problems, large and small. They promote and preach ideas and ideology from a grand pulpit in the churches of "Educational Institutions". The students that pass though these churches accept whatever is taught to them, and buy it, "lock, stock and barrel". This is the way it has always been. The educators decide what is to be taught and the correctness of the content of whatever the subject matter might be. This is always true to some extent no matter what the subject matter. In some disciplines the effect is quite small. Some areas that do not suffer from biases in great degrees are some of the engineering occupations such as electrical, mechanical, software and chemical engineering.

Chapter 6 – Social Implications of Stupidity

Technical occupations are not so much effected by what can only be described as political bias. This is simply because the underlying fundamental principals have been around for a long time and the natural laws that govern these subjects are rock solid. That is not to say the educators do not have a hand in screwing something up in these fields; they usually do. The big thing that can be screwed up is textbooks. They can give conservative students a hard time but they usually don't preach socialism or communism because it would be obviously inappropriate.

I have no doubt that many people who during the process of deciding whether they will enter a technical field or not, decide against it simply because the textbooks are difficult, if not impossible to read. For example, many people do not believe they are candidates for mathematics; engineering and other technical fields because the books they are forced to begin with are simply impossible to read.

If quality textbooks were not enough of a problem, many professors and teachers are very poor in the selection of books. I have had more classes with sub-standard textbooks than not. I also came to accept the fact that the books that were selected by the instructor were selected by a hap-hazard method. There are obviously two culprits here. One culprit is the writer of the textbook and the other is the instructor. What causes this?

In my opinion, textbooks get published solely on the credentials of the author, which has no real bearing on whether the author is qualified or not. Just because someone completes a set of required courses at some "institution of higher learning"; that *is not a guarantee of competency*. It is obvious that very little vetting or review is accomplished to verify the efficacy of textbooks. Textbooks get picked because of a process similar to the court system in America. They get picked because many other instructors have picked them before. It is similar the use of precedence in the court system. An educational degree or any other title that has been bestowed on anyone is no guarantee of intelligence. The educational system needs to recognize this fact and make adjustments accordingly.

Since a degree is no assurance of intelligence that means the instructor should be subjected to the same scrutiny that the students are. That is the way it is done in a corporate environment. Corporate instructors are expected to pass the same examinations as the students. The way public school systems are set up; the instructor is looked upon as some kind of God-like entity. They are deemed to be competent solely on the fact that they have been hired and have tenure.

The one thing that throws a big monkey wrench in any possible fix for this problem is a result of progressivism. The monkey wrench is called "the teachers union". Communists love to control things including wages and benefits provided to employees of even private companies. When the employees are in the public sector such as public grade schools, high schools, colleges and universities, progressive union bosses begin salivating at the thought of all the union dues they can skim to fatten up their war chests for campaigning for their compadres in the politico.

There is no doubt, public grade schools, high schools, colleges and universities would be infinitely better schools if they could rid themselves of teachers unions. Teachers unions insure that teachers will become incompetent if employed long enough. There is no way to get rid of a teacher or instructor once they have tenure. They are there to do irreparable damage until they decide to quit or die. Another diabolical aspect of this is that public service unions are usually "all in" for nothing but democratic candidates and they do a lot of donating to the democratic national committee. This amounts to a taxpayer funded political party and this must end or our country will not survive.

It is a well-known fact that the majority of universities in The United States are left leaning in the way they promote ideas and more importantly how they hire instructors. Nearly all college level instructors are progressive leaning and they eagerly promote communism in some form at every opportunity. Why is this? This is a very easy question to answer if you adhere to the concepts I have set forward in this book. We must remember that we are talking about a profession that relies entirely on the concept of owning intelligence. Intelligence is to a professor as drawing skills are to an artist.

Recall that I said that communists have a belief in communism because they believe it will be a demonstration of their intelligence. Why else would anyone believe in an ideology that has been proven to be 100% faulty? The paradox is: Believing in communism, they are in essence; proving how stupid they are. They really are too stupid to understand how stupid they are.

This realization should make us all feel uncomfortable about the status of the educational system in this country. We have a bunch of schools that promote ideas that will result in the loss of humanity's freedom. We have professors at those schools who will teach communism as if it were the only viable form of government for the future. We have teachers unions who will ensure that the professors teaching this crap will have jobs until the day they die and no matter what they do or how incompetent they are. This is not a pretty picture for the freedom of humanity.

The future freedom of humanity may depend entirely on the success of progressive educational influence. If they are successful in the indoctrination of children before the age of 12, you can pretty much kiss freedom goodbye. That was alluded to in a communist manual that was printed in the late 1950s. It said, "If we can control what children learn to age 12, we have them for life". Nice people, huh?

Besides demonizing guns, they have worked hard to re-write history into something that fits their agenda, which is to discourage capitalism and promote socialism. They teach garbage like America is an unfair country. America got wealthy by stealing resources from the rest of the world. Anyone with any wealth doesn't deserve it because they got it by treachery. You poor people are poor because the rich stole it from you!

The only hope for the United States and the free world is a campaign for the hearts and minds of the people that have been drinking the communist laced soft drink for 100 years. We must take back our school systems from communist promoting progressive teachers. We must rid universities of progressive professors. The problem is: teachers unions at both the elementary and the college level. Teachers unions are way too powerful and need to be broken up. There is no other way. We must do this if we want our country to survive. We must do this if we want to be smart and we want the smart side to win this battle!

Chapter 6 – Social Implications of Stupidity

There are a category of academics who by their actions effectively control the prevailing thought on what's important and what isn't to the whole of their chosen field. I'm talking about the medical academics who ultimately decide what gets taught and what doesn't to the doctors who go out to the world and spread these ideas whether they have merit or not. It does not require a lot of thought to realize that what I'm suggesting here is true. The academics responsible for the research and subsequent teaching of all others in the medical profession can either be right or wrong. There is no common ground here and no room for in-between interpretations of the things they disseminate. We all hope they are right but what if they aren't? This places too much power in the hands of a chosen few, doesn't it? I believe it does and this lonely aspect of the medical profession is one reason I have the skepticism that I do about these people. I delve into the medical profession as a whole in the next chapter. There are also academics who have become invested in scientific theories which are not only related to technical principles but have serious socio-political ramifications as well. One such group is known as "climatologists".

Global warming

Oh wait; there has been no warming for the past 18 years so instead of calling it "global warming" let us just refer to it as "climate change". Is the climate changing? Sure it always is and always has changed since humans have begun recording climatic events. By the way; this little switch of terms is right out of the left's rules for radicals' cookbook. When you are confronted with a buzzword term that doesn't quite add to the narrative you are pushing, you simply change to a different buzzword. The left is heavily invested in the global warming issue because if they are successful in demonizing fossil fuels, they will turn out to be the sole controllers of energy, fossil or otherwise.

The current leftist administration in the United States is shutting down coal fired power plants at a frightening rate. This could ultimately do irreparable harm to the nation's power grid in times of emergencies that can be imagined by smart people but never considered by the stupid. These emergencies could be: Terrorist attacks, natural disasters or even an increase in economic activity which places larger demands on power due to manufacturing. The sole reason they are closing these coal fired plants is the carbon emissions are deemed to be unacceptably large.

In other words, we are risking economic breakdown and possible loss of life, possibly in the millions, because of a deficient power grid that has been intentionally reduced to counter what is basically an unproven theory. The theory of "global warming" is based on what is known as a "computer model". A computer model is nothing more than a program that was written by a human and in this case is supposed to predict what the temperature changes will be with varying levels of carbon dioxide in the earth's atmosphere. You don't need a degree in computer science to realize that if the fundamental premises the program was written on are false, then there cannot be any hope for that program to make any sort of accurate predictions.

I could write a program in C++ which is the most popular language for technical applications such as weather patterns. In my program I could pull an idea out of my posterior; let's say one that predicts house fly procreation in urban areas such as Chicago. IL. In my initial model I need to make some assumptions of the things I am attempting to prove and in this case I want to prove that global warming will increase the number of house flies in a big city. I start out by writing some conditions into the program that describe my idea of the things that house flies really like when it comes to "getting it on". I code in a temperature versus house fly penis limpness comparison curve and I *guess* that the hotter it gets, the less limp a housefly's penis will become. This should work as a prediction tool, right? Well, it might accurately predict house fly numbers, if and only if my initial assumption was correct to begin with.

The curve will strictly follow whatever parameters I have programmed into it and it just may show that if the city of Chicago experiences more hot days we can expect house fly numbers to increase. That does not mean the described results will ever happen in the real world and in fact it could very well be the exact opposite will happen because my original guess could very well be "full of hot air". That's why engineers do something we call "bread boarding", prototyping or in the software world "beta" programs. Every hypothesis has to be proven with real world test results because as in my example, I only *guessed* at the relationship between heat and house fly population. The "climatologists" who did the global warming theory, did exactly the same thing when they guessed that the amount of CO2 in the atmosphere would be directly proportional to an increase in the earth's temperature.

In other words, in the atmospheric carbon versus temperature models that global warming theories are based on, it is very obvious that the relationship between atmospheric carbon and global temperatures are not valid. In other words, the people that wrote these programs *guessed* wrong to begin with, that is a proven fact by virtue of the stability of the earth's temperature. There is also the fact that some of the main proponents of this theory have been caught in a big fat lie about the proof they claimed to have. The so-called "hockey stick" curve was a fake and that is a well-known fact at this time. It was supposed to show a marked increase in world temperatures denoted by the shape of the temperature graph being shaped like a hockey stick. This was entirely fabricated and it is proof that the stupid will lie, cheat and steal to promote the ideas they are invested in. The one factor that really has an impact on global temperature but is never mentioned by the left is a little celestial body we call "the sun". The energy output of the sun has orders of magnitude (in this case, thousands and millions of times) more impact on the earth's temperature than do humans.

The little known fact of liberal supporters of people such as Barack Obama, Hillary Clinton and others of the same ilk is that the real purpose of the promotion of climate change is the distribution of wealth from the industrialized, economically successful countries to third world countries. The communists pushing this garbage claim the wealthy countries are doing all the damage to the environment and the poor countries suffer because of it. If this were really the case, then why not just say so, promote the real intentions and drop all the climate change crap? Because that's the way stupid people operate. They need to be deceitful because if they told the truth, their argument would quickly be invalidated.

The really sad aspect of all of this is the fact that close to 50% of the voting population buys this lie; hook, line and sinker. The Democratic Party routinely calls climate change a bigger threat to the country than is terrorism. Bernie Sanders even says climate change is not only a bigger threat than terrorism but is the *cause* of terrorism!! If this idiot becomes president, all hope is lost and humanity will be plunged into darkness for a thousand years. Wake up people! You don't have to be stupid! Our freedom depends on you admitting you are wrong!

Chapter 6 – Social Implications of Stupidity

Academia's biggest threat to humanity

The biggest threat academia poses to the freedom of the world is the way communism is promoted as the government of the future in institutions of higher learning across the U.S. It is bad enough that centralized education such as common core is being unleashed on the children of this country, but selling communism continues at the college and graduate levels of education at alarming levels. Professors get hired and retain tenure because they are liberal and they then preach liberalism to the skulls full of mush who will go out and vote for nut-jobs like Bernie sanders. The point I want to make here is, why? I believe it should be obvious at this point and if the reader has been paying attention, it should be crystal clear as to why professors are liberal. They want to display to the rest of the world how smart they are. That's pretty much it. This is a classic example of IRD and ICP.

The liberal media

With the exception of Fox News, the media in the U.S. is what could be characterized as state run media. There is no question about the fact that all of the news organizations with the one mentioned exception basically cover for, promote and report positively on everything the current administration does and without apology. This fact may not be recognized by the people I have labeled as "low information voters" but that is because the brainwashing these dim-wits have been indoctrinated with continues in an ongoing basis. One of the mantras of the communist playbook is that telling lies often enough make the lies truth for the "useful idiots" who want to believe the things that they are invested in because otherwise would be an admission of being stupid. So we have two groups of stupid people here: The media itself and the people who watch them and believe every word because to doubt the content would be an admission of stupidity.

The main point here and the reason I include the media in my "trifecta of stupidity" is that the true reason the media is liberal is because of IRD. They, just like communists and the current administration want to prove to the whole world how smart they are by promoting an ideology they believe will aid them in accomplishing just that.

Hollywood

Some of the dumbest people in the world are in Hollywood producing, directing and acting in movies. One big reason I say that is because of the way they portray certain groups which they simply abhor. Show me someone that hates the military and I will show you a liberal dumb-ass who suffers from a severe case of IRD. The military is one of the groups that liberals hate and I have an excellent example I can share with the reader. The very first film about the Anti-Christ was entitled "The Omen". In this film the main character, "Damien" was supposed to be the son of Satan. When Damien was growing up, strange things would happen to him but at that point he didn't yet know who he was. The one person who set him on the right track in understanding who he was and what he would be doing was a highly decorated Vietnam veteran US Army sergeant. Yes, that's right. The one person who would automatically know who the Anti-Christ was would be a decorated war hero!

Chapter 6 – Social Implications of Stupidity

The juxtaposition here would be that a US Army Vietnam War veteran would be assumed to be the type of person who is so evil that they would be able to pick the Anti-Christ out of a lineup any day of the week. Who is more qualified to identify the devil's son than an evil Vietnam Veteran? I mean, after all, come on, we all know how close to the devil those Army infantry guys are, don't we? Well, I happen to be an ex-Infantryman and Vietnam combat veteran and I take this as a supreme insult. This is how the communist rationalizes the moral aptitude of any fighting force that was in opposition to the beloved ideology that they are committed to which is of course; communism.

There are also other reasons Hollywood and other communists in the U.S. do not like the military. I believe one reason is because stupid people are also cowards. They cannot fathom putting on combat gear and carrying a rifle into a combat zone where they could be killed or maimed. It makes their sphincter muscle pucker just thinking about that! They observe the brave young people going off to fight for their country and instead of praising them, they display nothing but contempt. This is also because of jealousy, spawned by the realization that they could never do what they watch others doing because they are in fact cowards. Another reason is that the communists (including Hollywood) in this country see the military as mostly an unnecessary expenditure that could be used for more social programs. These people also belong to the normalcy bias crowd (I cover this in chapter 8) so that supplies them with further motivation to deem the military as a waste of money. The current administration in the U.S. also may see the military as a force which invokes conflict, rather than mitigate the advent of it; "the military is not there to create conflict, but to preserve it!" That is an appropriate transposition from good old Mayor R.J. Daily's statement back in 1968. The unfortunate aspect of this is that this is not a mistake with the anti-military crowd, they really believe this crap!

The left especially didn't like the war in Vietnam in which the military was fighting against their dearly held ideology. It infuriated them to think that the "unfair" and "unjust" and "arrogant" Americans were yet again imposing their will upon a helpless and downtrodden people. Many of the stupid people in this country didn't realize the fact that it was American communist groups who were active in organizing all the protests, marches and barrage of misinformation and propaganda aimed directly at the war effort and the "injustice" being done to the Vietnamese people. These groups were instrumental at swaying the public opinion and shutting down the war effort which was a clear military victory by the time we started pulling out large numbers of troops. We just handed our victory back to the enemy and gave up on the whole affair largely because of this one group of IRD sufferers.

There have been many movies that have portrayed the American military is a negative light. This began during the Vietnam War and it continues to this day. I have seen many movies of all budget ranges that cast the ex-military as killers and sociopaths. At the same time, the movie industry acts as propaganda agents for the current administration in promotion of the horrors of global warming, pollution by evil corporations and the general raping of the earth by evil capitalists. There have been many movies that make the large corporation look like the work of the devil himself. The people that perpetrate these lies are responsible for some of the economic decline of this country as the damage propaganda is capable of is great.

Chapter 6 – Social Implications of Stupidity

Summary

It is intelligence that is the primal driving force behind all human acts. We constantly compare our own level of smarts to everyone we meet and I call that Intelligence Comparison Phenomenon (ICP). I label the desire to be deemed intelligent as: Intelligence Recognition Desire (IRD) and is the utmost prime mover in humans. This is likely due to programming inherited because of an advantage of intelligence in past social environments of our ancestors. The desire to be accepted as a viable contributor to the group would make the difference between being in the security of the group and being an outcast, lessening chances of survival.

Unfortunately, our inherited programs push people way beyond what they would have been useful for in times past. Some people intend to prove their intelligence even at the cost of millions of their fellow human's lives. IRD is responsible for the promotion of communism all over the world. Communists will kill half of their own people in order to provide an imagined utopia for the other half solely to prove their own intelligence.

The three main groups which embrace and promote socialism and communism as a result of IRD are academics, news media and Hollywood. This is because of the nature of the tasks being similar in each profession as a given platform to profess ideas to a populace and is a perfect place to demonstrate their intelligence to the rest of the world.

The average number of stupid people in the electorate will govern whether humans remain free. This could be entirely due to differences in brain structure fidelity to specification. It could also be due to an unwillingness to admit past flaws and mistakes which could be a result of not inheriting emotions as designed. I believe this is the main reason why people retain stupidity. They do not receive a compete version of emotions but get bastardized versions instead. It is difficult to be smart if one cannot ever admit fault because of self-love. It is impossible to predict if these people can be swayed to a logical way of thinking and therefore it is also impossible to predict humanity's freedom continuation.

Reader's Notes

Chapter 7 -The Medical Profession

Caution: This chapter contains incompetent medical doctor content. If you are a medical professional and you have doubts about your own abilities, read this at your own peril. The medical profession is one of the few that I am personally aware of that interprets any sort of blanket criticism as a personal affront to their own intelligence. This is partly what is wrong with medicine. Humans can never be smart if they do not admit fault. Heal thyself, physician.

"If you sit by the river long enough, you will see the bodies of all your enemies float by" – Ancient Chinese Proverb

The lesson to be learned from the above proverb is, to win the game of life; all we need to do is outlive our contemporaries. Our contemporaries include all the stupid people we were forced to endure because they somehow gained the upper hand on us. This includes: Bosses, co-workers, business people who took advantage of us, salespeople and service people we were screwed by and lastly and most important; doctors who misdiagnosed us and wouldn't admit they didn't know what they were doing.

Unfortunately, the odds of us outliving our contemporaries are not with us. Even if we do manage to live past the "average life span" age, there are no guarantees that we will actually be aware that we are still alive. If we are aware of what's going on; that may not be a great advantage due to the amount of suffering we may be forced to endure every day.

In addition to the big three (heart disease, cancer and diabetes); we are confronted with many quality of life diseases, some of which can remove the desire to live from our personality. The world is currently in full blown epidemics of sleep disorders, stomach / bowel disorders and mental / cognitive decline disorders. All types of arthritis on also on the rise. The worst problem we face by far is: The human inability to solve any of these problems.

There are more prescriptions written for cholesterol lowering drugs / blood thinners, insulin / blood sugar drugs and more cancer treatments than ever in human history. There are also now more prescriptions written for acid reducers, sleep aids, tranquilizers, anti-depressants than ever before in the history of medicine. Medicine is not actually solving any of these problems; it is only treating these problems and not very effectively at that.

Why do you suppose that is? There are several possibilities and in order to solve any problem the best first step is to create an outline of the obvious possibilities and perhaps in the process of doing that we may notice something else along the way. I start by suggesting major categories of individual underlying causes all the way to a single underlying cause. OK, here we go:

The first possibility is that there are fundamentally different, separate underlying causes for all of the human major maladies; the ones I have listed here. This is the view held by the medical

Chapter 7 – The Medical Profession

establishment as a whole and it is also supposedly the most common sense belief; widely accepted by the general population. It just makes sense, right? Maybe, for people who have no real common sense to begin with! Conversely, for the intelligence savvy, we know that what seems to "make sense" means nothing without some evidence to back up the claim.

For the sake of argument; let's say we have 6 major threats to contend with. They are: Heart disease, cancer, diabetes, sleep disorders, digestive problems and mental disorders (I will only consider cognitive decline for my argument). The notion that all of the major diseases are fundamentally different with corresponding different underlying causes makes the whole situation way more complex; than say, if there were just three common causes to all six diseases. Of course the scenario holding the most simplistic explanation would be that there is only one underlying cause for all six diseases.

Let's take a look at the two major diseases, heart disease and cancer as examples. These two diseases are currently the biggest killers and so we can logically expect any external body influences that may be responsible, to be readily noticeable or perhaps somehow distinguishable, given the sheer number of patients. Food is an external influence because if there is something wrong with food, that defect did not occur after being consumed, but at some prior time. The other obvious external influences are air and water.

If there are external forces at work in the increase of these diseases, it might be easier to make the connection to those forces simply because of the large number of people being affected by these killers. This is another way of stating that the fact that large numbers of cases occur each year should lend itself to making connections to the possible external forces at play. This makes sense because it should be easy to make note of what large groups of people are exposed to as opposed to small groups, which cannot be surveyed as well.

We have two possibilities to consider:

1. One is that all six diseases are caused by six underlying causes.
2. Another is that the underlying causes may be less than six; from five all the way to just one underlying cause.

The best way to perform an analysis for the types of causes is to make some attempt at finding similarities in cause influence. Heart disease and cancers of all types are the number one killers in the United States at the time of this writing. The medical establishment watched these diseases immerge from a sprinkling of cases nationwide to the full blown epidemics we have today. The time frame for this increase could be debated but let's (for the sake of argument) say it started about sixty years ago; at the end of World War Two. You have to ask yourself, whether you hold some kind of medical degree or not, what have we been doing as a species in the last sixty years that we weren't doing before? Is it the food? Is it the water? Is it the air? What is it? Since we are compiling an outline of possibilities we should try to come up with some logical reasons why or why not it is the food, water or the air we are living with. I begin with what may be the least likely cause and end with the most likely cause.

Chapter 7 – The Medical Profession

Is the air the problem?

It is possible that where you live pre-conditions you to becoming sick. There is a lot of evidence that uses geographical mapping coupled with the number of heart disease, cancer and other illness cases. When the criteria of heart related deaths are plotted over geographical data (as in maps) it is very clear that there is a correlation to illness and locality. In addition, we can postulate that when all environmental factors are taken into account, the most likely culprit is air quality. This is because large cities such as Chicago, IL have much higher incidences of things like heart disease, but Chicago has the same water source as smaller cities that lie around the periphery of Lake Michigan. The drinking water comes from the same source but illness (heart disease) is greater in Chicago than it is in Michigan City, IN for example.

There is supporting evidence of this claim in the studies that have been done linking Diesel fumes to heart attack. People running in marathons have had heart attacks after being exposed to Diesel fumes. A few alert doctors noticed this and decided to do a study. The results were conclusive: Diesel fumes are not good for your heart. So if Diesel fumes cause problems it does not require much of a leap of faith to conclude that other forms of air pollution may also contribute to heart disease. The geographical plotting of heart disease patients tends to back up the notion that it is indeed the air we breathe that causes problems.

The grand total numbers of heart disease and cancer deaths do not appear to be caused by only air pollution however. Although air can make us sick, we can also get sick without living in a highly air polluted area. In other words, these diseases occur regardless of the air quality.

Is water the problem?

It may be, but probably only in very small localities like around nuclear power plants. It is claimed that there are routine leaks of radioactive water into the ground water systems in a number of nuclear power plants, nationwide. There have been accusations that the number of people contracting different types of cancers is way above the normal rates documented in other locations. I believe we all can agree that no amount of additional radiation is likely beneficial to organic life.

Chemical leaks from chemical plants can also be a problem for anyone residing in proximity to those areas. It has been claimed that people who lived close to the southernmost section of the Mississippi River had higher rates of cancers and other disease. This is an area that has more chemical plants per mile than anywhere else in the United States. We are all subjected to chemicals in the "modern world" we are forced to live in.

I believe anyone that microwaves food in a plastic container is playing with fire. I don't care what the manufacturer says; I personally would not take that chance. If people really understood how cancers get started, there would be much less reliance of newly introduced cookware and similar gadgets that come in contact with our food. Cancers happen on the genetic level. This means that only one small link in the DNA molecule need be damaged for a cancer to get started. Radiation and some chemicals are known to do just that.

Chapter 7 – The Medical Profession

I always attempt to obtain something good from everything that is bad news. In this case what I get out of the information of localities that have large concentrations of radioactive isotopes in the drinking water is this: Why didn't everyone get cancer? Everyone was drinking radioactive contaminated water but the incidence of cancer was only at most one per household for the majority of households. It could have been everyone in a single household but it was not. Why is this?

One of the most ignored topics in medicine is the topic of the ability of the immune system to repair damaged DNA. I have read many articles in which research doctors have alluded to the possibility and that probability this phenomenon was indeed taking place. However, it does not appear that this paradigm has been largely accepted by the medical establishment and for the most part is totally ignored. I always wondered, why? Is this just more stupidity at work or is there a reason why this idea is not embraced. If it were embraced, it would place more of an emphasis on prevention and natural cures and less value on things like chemotherapy and other extreme curative methods.

This small but super important concept of DNA self-healing places the burden of a cure on the patient's own immune system. Perhaps the medical elite don't like that because it suggests a non-intervention approach to a cure. This idea may also expose the entire medical establishment as what they already know they are in: A state of denial. They may actually suspect but don't want to admit that the people that are unlucky enough to contract terminal cancer got that way because of some invisible, unknown adversary of that person's immune system.

Stating this differently, the medical establishment suffers from a form of arrogance and egotism sprinkled with a large amount of narcissism. They don't want to admit that there might be something that they can't categorize, put in a container, measure, evaluate and identify. They don't want to admit there are things they simply don't understand and what is more, they don't act to enact any type of understanding. They are not even attempting to see the forest through the trees.

If I were a medical researcher involved in cancer research, the first thing I would be looking at would be foods. Foods are the common denominator for every person in the world. If people have been consuming the same types of foods for decades, what has changed in the processing of those foods? What are the characteristics of some foods that have possibly changed over the last sixty years? These are the types of questions I would ask. Oh, I forgot the most important question: What foods are implicated in immune system function?

Is food the problem?

What has changed in the food supply in the last sixty years? Well, processed food has taken over. Added in many processed foods are things called hydrogenated oils. They are produced by bubbling hydrogen gas though the liquid oil (peanut oil for example) and the result is the oil becomes solid and takes on a "saturated fat feel" to the palate.

In chemistry terms, the hydrogen "saturates" the hydro-carbon molecule. We all have heard of hydro-carbons. They are basically nature's way of storing energy from the sun. The hydrocarbon

Chapter 7 – The Medical Profession

we are all familiar with is petroleum. Another type of hydro-carbon is: peanut oil! All of the oils found in nature are actually hydro-carbons. There are a number of places for hydrogen atoms to attach to in a naturally made hydro-carbon molecule, such as the peanut oil molecule.

When peanut oil is in its natural state, it is said to be "mono-unsaturated". That is; there is only one hydrogen atom attached to the hydro-carbon molecule. Monounsaturated oils are known to be the most beneficial to humans. Other monounsaturated oils include olive oil, canola, safflower and sesame. When hydrogen is bubbled through liquid oil the hydrogen atoms attach to all or some of the available hydrogen "docking stations" on the hydro-carbon molecule and the oil becomes saturated; in essence, a human made saturated fat.

When hydrogenated oil is added to peanut butter; it does two things. The now solid oil is sticky and so it sticks to the fibers of the peanut and prevents separation. The other thing it does is it promotes a "creamy, luxurious" feel to the mouth as it is consumed. In other words; it makes it really yummy! Unfortunately, things that are really yummy aren't necessarily good for us and in this case; the yummy food may be a killer! What we are doing is playing around with fundamental laws of nature and producing something that does not ever; occur naturally. It is not nice to play around with Mother Nature and when we do; we can expect Mother Nature to "play around" with us big time! There is a lot of medical evidence that eating hydrogenated oils promotes clogged arteries. The FDA finally admitted this simple fact and under pressure from the findings of several studies that backed up the feelings of a few foresighted doctors passed some regulations concerning "Trans-Fats".

Trans Fats are the medical term used to describe hydrogenated oils. The FDA now requires food manufacturers to list Trans Fats on food labels. Food processors have much political clout in Washington. It is said that most of the doctors working at the FDA were at one time working for food processors and vice versa. So when it comes to your well-being; don't depend on the medical profession to protect you because they have a different agenda. The food processors lobbied Washington and the FDA agreed to some half-measure terms to pacify them. The rules now state that a product can list the Trans Fat content of a product as Zero provided that the "per serving" amount of Trans Fat is below a certain level.

In the case of peanut butter; the serving size is usually one tablespoon. Most people will eat three and four tablespoons at one time. The amount allowed by the government is multiplied by the number of tablespoons eaten and it will not take much to put you over the danger level. Consumers are tricked into thinking that what they are eating is safe; when nothing could be further from the truth! As of this writing it has been announced that trans-fats have been officially banned by the FDA but many products containing trans fats remain on store shelves so anyone's guess as to the status of this topic is as good as mine. I wonder how many people have been harmed by the delaying tactics employed by food processors in this one matter.

Instead of demonizing trans-fats, fats of all types have been demonized by the medical elite: The medical educators pass decrees down from their pulpit-on-high to the rest of us commoners and the misguided doctors who accept without question whatever they are told. Fat is bad! Fat is bad! Fat is bad! We have all been bombarded with this mantra for the past 50 years. A trip to the

Chapter 7 – The Medical Profession

supermarket will present us proof of this campaign with a myriad of food products which are touted as either "low fat" or "fat free".

Cholesterol is also used as a marketing tool to play on the fears of consumers; who being brainwashed by the medical elite, are naturally drawn towards anything they perceive as life extending. We have been taught that high blood cholesterol levels are a one way ticket to the cemetery. Cholesterol levels came upon the scene in the early or mid-1970s. The whole phenomenon began with some herbivore bunny rabbits used in a base line experiment to determine how cholesterol clogged the arteries. The bunnies were fed animal fats and what should be no surprise to anyone; the bunnies developed plaques on the linings of their little bunny arteries. The reason I say it should come as no surprise, it that rabbits don't eat meat and therefore don't consume cholesterol, ever. This is what started the cholesterol scare that is pervasive to this day.

When these studies were originally concluded, the total acceptable lowest cholesterol level was over 320. I am not clear on how the original level was arrived at, because at that point, very few human studies had been done. My guess is that the original level was in itself, a guess. As time went on and the number of heart attacks increased even in people who had the minimum level, the number was necessarily lowered. It went down to 300, 260, 240, 200 and down to today's present "safe" level of 160. This doesn't stop people from having heart attacks though. They continue to have problems, even when they religiously take their statin drugs to keep the levels below the new "standard". I have just been informed that the new "safe" level of total cholesterol is now 100. Yes that's right, 100.

What will the medical establishment do when people continue to have heart attacks when the total level is 10? How in the world will they explain that away? My personal belief is that the total cholesterol level is meaningless without accounting for the deposit rate of all lipids on the walls of arteries and veins. Even if you had total cholesterol level of 600, and the deposit rate was zero, you would have nothing to worry about, would you? On the other hand, if you have a level of 100 but the deposit rate is 100% then you might not make it home from wherever you got blood drawn! This is a concept that is never even considered except for a few very smart cardiologists who have admitted total levels mean little.

If you are a man and you take statins to keep your blood lipid (fat) levels low, you have an approx. 10% better chance of surviving a heart attack (if you have one). That's it, that's all the benefit you will receive from a lifelong adherence to popping pills every day for the rest of your life. With women, it's not much better. You only increase your chance of surviving by 13%. If you have arrived at the conclusion that this is enough of a benefit to outweigh the hassle of being dependent on a daily consumed drug than you should definitely do what your doctor says. On the other hand if you are like me, and are skeptical of much of what the medical establishment says, then you should think twice before taking anything.

One of the rarely mentioned side effects of cholesterol lowering drugs is supposed to be a dramatic increase in cognitive disorders such as Alzheimer's disease. The theory of the connection between the two is thought to be the fact that the brain is almost totally made of fat

158

and it needs fats and cholesterol to maintain and repair itself. A low fat diet, coupled with a daily dose of statins may be just what the doctor didn't order for brain function.

I personally do not believe in the supposed safety of statin drugs, and that the risks involved far outweigh any perceived benefits. However this is a decision you have to make for you. Do whatever makes you feel safe, it's your life. I also have a tough time with doctors pushing things like statins on people who just have risk factors like a high blood cholesterol level. I don't believe cholesterol lowering drugs should be given unless there is proof that plaque deposits are actually being made. We are a society who sees no problem in giving massive doses of drugs with dubious benefits and possible unknown hazards just because the patient has one risk factor. This is dubious at best.

In summary, the environment (air and water) may contribute to heart disease and cancers, mostly effecting people living in large population areas with significant industrial activity. This doesn't say much for the effectiveness of government agencies like the EPA. Cancers can be connected to the water supplies of communities located close to nuclear or chemical plants. However for the vast majority of these diseases, it is obvious that there is some other bigger cause. The role of food in disease is the big unknown, basically because of the number of factors that could be in a cause and effect relationship.

Foods that modulate the immune system are very good candidates for a cause of heart disease, cancer and type one diabetes. In heart disease, the weakened immune system does not repair damage to the inside of the arteries and veins and any amount of cholesterol present will likely get stuck on the rough walls. In cancers, the weakened immune system fails to repair the damaged DNA. It is just that simple. While the underlying mechanisms may be simple this is overall perceived as a complicated subject. The medical establishment constantly blames lifestyle factors such as physical inactivity and just a plain lack of self-control as the many facets that contribute to the whole picture. This complicates the whole problem and may be masking the underlying problem by adding perceived complexity where there is actually simplicity. In the case of type one diabetes, it is an autoimmune disease in which the victim's immune system attacks the pancreas. Medical science seems to be at a complete loss to explain why this occurs. It appears to me to be very similar to another disease that I will cover shortly.

The human animal is a machine, no more no less; I say this throughout this writing. If we continue to believe people actually have a total amount of "free will" and they really don't, then we are giving the problem complexity it does not deserve. If we look at the patient as a machine, that needs repair, the process of affecting that repair will be much simpler. What I am suggesting, is that some of the foods we eat may actually be "skewing" our programmed control systems to the point where the mechanical systems cannot function the way they were designed. This includes the body becoming lazy, overweight and contracting a multitude of diseases such as arthritis, diabetes, cancer and heart disease. It could be that being overweight is only a symptom of a more serious underlying problem and not a cause or "risk factor" for more serious disease.

It is my belief that most of the ailments suffered by humanity today have just one underlying cause, not two, three, four, etc. It just makes sense and I believe I can provide enough evidence in the form of a logical analysis of the entire situation. I will concede that I cannot provide proof for my hypothesis; how in the world would I do that? This is not something that can be proven mathematically, because proof would require a massive study with thousands of people involved as test subjects. This is a scenario that I can only dream of because this is best left to a university that attempts to prove something they have no interest in proving. Since I do not believe a proof will ever happen, I try to provide the reader with the gleaning of already known facts and knowledge. This makes use of what we already know to shed light on what we don't know, which in this case could also involve seeing the forest through the trees.

The case for food as a single underlying cause

As a kid, I was always lethargic. I didn't like to play as much as the other kids. I was always falling asleep in school. I was not interested in sports at all. I was pretty much a couch potato and TV was my best friend. I was always overweight and eating sweets and candy was my favorite thing to do while watching superman on our 16 inch black and white television after school. I was slow at learning and I was nearly put back a grade in about the 4th or 5th grade. I didn't care much about anything. I was apathetic about nearly everything except my precious television. I was told that I was stupid because I could not memorize multiplication tables and other tasks that required memorization. My "working memory" was foggy, to say the least.

At the age of eight I contracted a rupture appendix and I ended up in the hospital for about a month. I nearly died and the attending doctor said I had about six hours to live, had I not been operated on. I recovered from the appendicitis, only to have additional digestive problems along with arthritic problems and routine migraine headaches from that time onward. I also had bouts with what I now know was spastic colon which laid me up for weeks at a time. I continually had arthritic problems with my neck from the age of seven and on. This came in the form of cramps and muscle spasms in the neck that my mother contributed to "growing pains". I was laid up with what she called a "stiff neck" for several days at a time for at least ten times from seven until I was in my twenties.

During my teen years I continued to be listless and fatigued and I slept a lot in the daytime for which I was criticized constantly by friends in high school. I started smoking cigarettes at the age of 16 and I became addicted almost instantly. I continued smoking until the age of 40, which ended a nearly 25 year habit. At the age of fifteen I started getting very thick dandruff that wouldn't go away no matter how many time I shampooed. I lost all of my hair by the age of twenty five. The arthritic problems that began at age seven became acute by age twenty seven. The migraines I suffered from as a child continued and became worse in my early twenties. I went through a period of over three years in which I suffered a migraine every day starting at the age of twenty three.

If all the problems I just described were not enough, I also had a problem with sexual dysfunction as a late teenager and young adult in my twenties. If you want to completely destroy a young man's ego and self-esteem, just take his hair away and make him impotent in the bedroom! That was my life, and I struggled through many trials and tribulations because of my health. I also suffered from mental problems that were either directly caused by medical conditions or as a result of having to deal with them.

Chapter 7 – The Medical Profession

At the age of thirty six the continual problem I was enduring with my neck came to be an unbearable daily burden. I had my first neck operation, a cervical fusion. Since then, I have had an additional three operations on my neck, a three and a half level laminectomy on my lumbar spine, a lumbar fusion and I have had my right shoulder joint replaced. My left knee underwent a total replacement and the right is bone on bone and I will need a surgery on it in the future. My left shoulder and both hips bother me continuously. Every joint in my body has been damaged from arthritis. During a period in my late thirties, I contracted every cold virus I came in contact with. I got a cold about every six weeks. This continued to my fifty six birthday. Migraines were also a constant problem up to that time. What happened on my fifty sixth birthday? Read on and I will explain shortly.

If the reader is wondering where I am going with the details of all my personal mayhem, I will now explain. At the beginning of this section I presented the possibility of several illnesses having the same underlying cause. I am of the belief that many common illnesses have common causes, sometimes causes that the medical establishment is totally unaware of, or perhaps knows about but ignores. In fact, the medical establishment makes no effort whatsoever to link diseases by common causes, with a few exceptions. Doing this would be an effort to: "See the forest through the trees" i.e. to solve problems by looking at what is already known and related in some way to other seemingly unrelated subjects.

The medical system accepted paradigm is to look at risk factors and in my opinion; they make way too much importance of them. Risk factors are very different from common causes. Being overweight may contribute to heart disease AND diabetes but it does not cause either. If being overweight caused heart disease, every overweight person would have heart disease and that is clearly not the case. If being overweight caused diabetes, then every overweight person would have diabetes, etc. My opinion is that being overweight is a symptom of some underlying cause rather than the cause itself.

I have a difficult time in understanding why the medical establishment does not put more of an effort to identifying common causes for the major diseases. I can understand that perhaps it has just not occurred to anyone, but why? It is crystal clear to me that all of the major illnesses may have common causes, or perhaps just one common cause. This logic follows the paradigm of what is known as Occam's razor; in which complex problems can be solved, by looking at the simplest of causes. It is usually the simplest cause that is the answer.

I am one hundred percent sure that all of *my* problems do have a common cause. The rest of the population may get sick from other foods because human genetic makeup varies vastly even in individuals of the same family tree. However I need to present a real world example of what the accepted foods we all take for granted can do to us. So in my instance, the problem was:

Celiac Disease

Celiac disease is the most understated and at the same time one of the nastiest diseases humanity has ever been threatened with. I discovered that I am a Celiac at the age of fifty six. All of the problems I just described were caused by a disease I have had the entire time, but I had no clue even existed! This is due to the way the disease has been downplayed and marginalized by the

Chapter 7 – The Medical Profession

people who screw up lots of things: Medical academics. The information has been out there for over a hundred years. But, the medical establishment, in their infinite stupidity, decided that the common people and other doctors didn't need to know about it! That's right; we didn't need to know about it!

That is correct! They knew about this for over a hundred years but they have not been educating the myriad number of doctors that have passed through a system that is entrusted with the health and wellbeing of the rest of humanity. This disease literally destroyed my whole life. I can only guess what my life would have been like had I known about this early in life. The immediate question that I had upon the revelation that Celiac disease was what was wrong with me, "I wonder how many other people have this?" The answer to that question is the answer most people would not believe possible. The answer is: No one knows! That's right; nobody knows how many people suffer from this disease. Who would have imagined, that in this day and age, we would have a serious disease that is rarely talked about and what is more; no one knows how many people have it!

I could be wrong but it appears that the powers that be in medical academia felt that the people affected by this will eventually find out! Yes they will eventually find out; albeit the hard way! Too bad that they just might contract some very serious illnesses along the way; like cancer! Then, they can get help and stay away from gluten! This is closing the barn door after the horse runs away. If someone has a problem with wheat gluten (what Celiac disease is supposed to be), they may have a number of serious life changing illnesses way, way, before they ever discover (sometimes on their own) they have it. Is it only me, or is there something drastically wrong with this approach? It seems the presumed protectors of health and well-being don't really have the public's interests at heart. It seems to me that they have let the rest of us down, big time!

What follows is what I understand about Celiac disease from the information available. Keep in mind that a lot of what the medical community says they know about disease (Celiac disease included); is basically all theory. They have not proven much of anything when it comes to Celiac disease. That said; Celiac disease is supposed to be sensitivity or "intolerance" to the gluten molecule that is native to the species of the wheat plant. This means that the relatives of wheat such as barley and rye also have the same gluten molecule and can cause the same problems in the person deemed to be "a Celiac".

The theory says the way it causes problems in some people that are supposedly intolerant of the gluten molecule is that the immune system in these people "misidentifies" gluten to be a pathogen. The immune system then attacks the gluten and in the process the small hair like villi in small intestine gets in the way and gets damaged. This is sort of a "collateral damage" in what could be thought of as a "battle zone". The term "pathogen" can be utilized to mean a microorganism like a bacterium or perhaps a virus. As I said, this is just a theory. Personally, I don't buy this lock, stock and barrel. There is something drastically wrong with this theory. One of the many things that bother me about this is that it requires us to believe that the immune system doesn't know what it is doing.

The big difference between Celiac and other auto-immune disorders is that in celiac disease, when gluten is eliminated from the diet, the disease disappears. In other words, without gluten,

Chapter 7 – The Medical Profession

there is no disease! You cannot say that for other diseases like multiple sclerosis, or at least that's what the medical "gurus" tell us, anyway. To the best of my knowledge other auto-immune diseases do not have known causes like Celiac does. For all anyone knows, gluten causes MS! The medical elite don't know what causes MS; they only know what it does to the patient. I often wonder if anyone has treated their MS by just eliminating gluten. I try not to talk about things I know nothing about so that is the extent of my discussion on other auto-immune diseases. If at some later date it is discovered that gluten is not good for people with MS, then that will only serve to bolster my point of view.

My point of argument remains a valid one. If the immune system doesn't know what it is doing, what is it exactly about the gluten molecule that makes the immune system of the "Celiac" into a big fool? Does the gluten molecule bear any resemblance to a pathogen of any kind? To the best of my knowledge, it does not. I have yet to read an explanation of why gluten gets misidentified as a pathogen by the "celiac" immune system. I believe no one (research doctor or otherwise) knows why the misidentification takes place, if in fact this is what's happening.

Another thing that bothers me about the theory is that no one has been able to distinguish the differences in a celiac immune system and a non-celiac immune system. If we take the theory that the celiac immune system is defective as gospel, then why doesn't the Celiac get sick from other illnesses that occur with a defective immune system? It doesn't make sense. In fact, when gluten is eliminated, the Celiac is usually a way healthier person in every way possible than a supposed non-celiac. If I successfully eliminate gluten (that is a formidable task), I do not get sick, AT ALL! The logical explanation is that people who have celiac disease may just have stronger immune systems than the people who appear to be symptom free! That's right; a celiac may have the strongest immune system in comparison to the rest of the population!

The fact that a celiac immune system cannot be categorized and labeled as somehow different; tells me that something more than meets the eye is going on here. There are no reliable tests to diagnose celiac disease. The gold standard test generally accepted by medicine is a biopsy of the villi of the small intestine. This is done as a sort of "post mortem" in which it is assumed that if the patient has sustained damage of the small intestine then he must have the disease. It is not really a diagnosis but more like secondary circumstantial evidence. The rational is that if the patient has villi damage AND we think that patient might have celiac disease; then the combination of these two factors should prove the existence of the disease. The big problem with this is sometimes there are false negatives and positives because of the mechanism of the test. The test is a pathology test.

We are relying on someone's expertise at reading a language that very few people in the world are really familiar with. This is the language of microscopic damage to cells from the immune system. The "someone" I am talking about is called a pathologist. These doctors are asked to make a determination by simply observation of a small sample of villi cells. This is not a reliable teat by any means. Your life and the quality of life you will enjoy are dependent on someone's opinion! There is also the locality factor or where the sample was gathered from. The small intestine is some 30 feet long, with only the first few inches being accessible. You could have damage somewhere in the last 20 feet and the test might from the first few inches might come up negative.

Chapter 7 – The Medical Profession

There is a genetic test that supposedly will tell the patient if there is likelihood that they are "sensitive" to gluten. It only tells the patient if they are "likely" to have the disease, it is not a definite indicator. This test does nothing to confirm celiac disease and is also not reliable. From the information I have been able to uncover, there are no reliable tests that will either prove or disprove whether anyone, no matter what the age, sex, ethnicity or race has the disease. The only real test is to simply eliminate gluten from the diet and observe the results. This is called an "elimination diet" and can be used to identify anything any person might have a problem with in their biological makeup.

Logic, like truth, has no agenda. We have no control over what the actual causes for diseases are or if those causes suit the likes or dislikes of anyone. If we come up with the solution to a problem, we have no control over whether that solution will be liked or will be popular with the public. In this case, logic should tell us all that it is way more likely that gluten is not good for anyone, rather than a small select group. If you give this concept some thought you will see my rational.

I know, without much pondering, that a public announcement that wheat (and possibly all grain and legume) products may be doing damage to every segment of the population, would be taken by scorn, disbelief and outright hostility. One of the reasons that would be so is that wheat and other main food stuff products are addictive. If you don't believe that, then try going without bread, pancakes, cookies, cake, pie, pasta and fried chicken breading for a few days. Consider this a challenge that if you won't accept, you provide credence to my hypothesis. It won't kill you doing without it, and it is by no means essential to anyone's health so it should be easy to cut it from the diet. It should be easy to stop eating it but it is not. The fact that it is addictive is further proof that it may not be good for you. We become addicted to things that hurt us physically, this is a well-known fact. It has to do with a cycle of damage, recovery and craving when the addictive substance begins reducing in strength in the body by some elimination mechanism.

I believe Celiac disease does something to the immune system. Actually it is the gluten molecule doing something to the immune system, not the name of the disease which is only a label. Since I have not had the training that would make me an expert in immunology, I can only speculate that the immune system expends energy fighting the gluten molecule and therefore the body is more vulnerable to other threats such as bacteria and viruses. In the case of damage from radiation and chemicals, DNA does not get repaired because the immune system is "maxed out" fight another threat.

The immune system has an upper limit to the number of threats it deals with at any time. Any machine (engine in this case) has a limit on its capacity to do work. The immune system can be thought of as an engine. An engine uses fuel and converts that fuel into usable energy or in other words: Work. In this case, work happens to be repair work in fighting off intruders that pass through the digestive system as the small intestine attempts to extract the needed nutrients. It is claimed that a full seventy percent of the human immune system is in the gut; being everything from the stomach down. Why would this be so? It is because that is where seventy percent of the threats come from; the things we ingest, like food, and water. The other thirty percent of the threats are external, from ultraviolet rays from the sun and chemicals and poisons that come in

Chapter 7 – The Medical Profession

contact with the skin and pollutants in the air we breathe. If the immune system becomes weakened from internal threats then it should be less able to deal with the external ones. This is just common sense.

If eating gluten weakens the immune system through a mechanism of fighting off an internal intrusion that it perceives gluten to be, then it stands to reason that the same immune system will be less efficient in repairing DNA that has been damaged by the sun, for example.

If we look at foods that are well known and documented as being immune system modulators, wheat is right on the top of that list. It doesn't take much of a stretch of the imagination (for me anyway because I lived this), to make the connection between wheat and every disease suffered by man. I know what happens to me if I ingest wheat over a period of more than a few days. I usually get a severe cold or sometimes influenza. This has happened to me so many times that I have no doubt that this is what happens. It usually begins with some food that I thought was gluten free, only to find out later (usually after getting sick) that I was wrong. This has happened with candy bars and other food items that were deceptively labeled.

I also know it causes problems in the entire digestive system, including "heart burn", "acid stomach" and general discomfort in the gut. I have had problems with eye infections only to find out the soap I was using had gluten in it. A few molecules must have been getting in the eyes, even when rinsed off very well. I have often wondered how many cases of heartburn that were treated with acid reducers and acid absorbers were actually caused by gluten reactions. As I have alluded to, there are millions of prescriptions written for acid blockers every year and many more bottles of the same, sold as over the counter meds. This evidence although purely anecdotal also tells me that the entire theory of what happens in the small intestine with gluten is wrong. The reaction starts anywhere and everywhere the gluten molecule touches the body tissue of the Celiac. I will concede that this could be due to some Celiacs being fully allergic to gluten as well as being "intolerant".

There is also documented evidence of immune system dysfunction in a person who has "intolerance" to gluten and therefore can be labeled as a Celiac. What follows is supposed to be a fairly common complaint among Celiac patients and is used as a diagnostic tool by some doctors. I get blister-like sores in areas "where the sun don't shine" every time I unknowingly eat gluten. This used to happen to me regularly every time I drank beer, towards the later days before my epiphany of being a celiac. I thought I had herpes or some other social disease but as usual consulting a physician was to no avail. The skin rash caused from Celiac disease is called, "dermatitis herpetiformis" which gets the name from the similar appearance to the herpes virus blister. It looks very similar to herpes but is caused from an immune reaction. I get acid reflux when gluten is eaten and my eyes react with soap immediately which to me tells me that the whole notion of the body mistaking gluten for a pathogen in just one place (the small intestine) and that's where the reaction starts is categorically wrong. The acid reflux symptom started in the last ten years of my ignorance about celiac disease; I believe my immune system was getting weaker as I got older.

This all tells me that the immune system is being "modulated" (for lack of a better term), by gluten. I can say with certainty that it weakens the immune system. Anything that weakens the immune system, even in minute amounts that are unnoticed and undetectable, cannot be good for any biological life form that has an immune system.

Anyone who has had tonsillitis or appendix problems, people who get an overabundance of colds or flu and anyone who gets recurring problems that cannot be readily identified or do not respond to treatment should be considered as possible candidates for a gluten elimination diet (this includes all types of gluten such as corn and rice). If you have any kind of arthritic problem, it would be worth your while to try an elimination diet. Migraine headaches are also a common problem connected to gluten. Since I have personal experience and have done much research; I have theories on how gluten may contribute to arthritis and migraine headaches:

Besides possibly inducing a direct immune system reaction upon ingestion, Celiac disease is claimed to be a mal-absorption disease. It interferes with assimilation of nutrients because of the damage that it does to the villi in the small intestine. It may cause arthritis by interfering with the absorption of minerals such as calcium or the compounds that allow calcium to be absorbed. There is also the topic of what are called "micro-nutrients" which little is known about. This is just another example of the general population believing that medical science is some all-knowing God like entity when they are definitely not.

The loss of essential micro-nutrients could very well be the underlying mechanism cause for osteoarthritis and even some if not all inflammatory arthritis. My explanation is just as good as any other, which by the way, is non-existent. Medical science has no explanation for osteoarthritis. They call it the disease of "wear and tear", mainly because they have no clue as to the mechanism behind it. Calling osteoarthritis the wear and tear disease is just an excuse for not being able to explain the underlying cause. Believe that, because it's true.

Migraine headaches are also an illness that may be directly tied to a mal-absorption syndrome. The mechanism here is very clear and direct. The essential nutrients for neurotransmitters don't get absorbed or they get absorbed in inadequate amounts. I believe the essential nutrients for neurotransmitters are amino acids. I believe this because one of the known triggers for migraine is consumption of compounds known as "Tyramines". Tyramines are decayed amino acids that are in things like aged cheese and wines. In the case of cheese, the amino acids present when the milk was fresh, have now decayed by losing electrons and what remains is a degraded version of the original molecule. My hypothesis is that when consumed, the brain expects to get the full fresh version of the amino acid it wants to produce the required neurotransmitter. Instead it receives a "watered down" version it cannot use readily.

The resulting produced neurotransmitter is defective because the components used to manufacture it were also defective. This results in brain stimulation rates that are out of timing, either longer or shorter in duration than the optimum neuron firing rate. This results in module deadlock in which one brain module does not receive the stimulation it requires from intercommunicating modules and stimulation depression occurs. This is a migraine headache in a nutshell.

The fact that wheat (and other food stuffs) has been accepted as a food source for generations and is consumed on a daily basis worldwide is no proof that it is not the culprit I believe it can

Chapter 7 – The Medical Profession

be. There are many examples of poisonous plants worldwide with thousands of variations in ways to be harmful. Many plants will kill instantly while others will take a considerable amount of time to do their job. The fact that wheat (probably the largest cultivated crop) is so "engrained" in society does not mean that it is safe. It is as simple as that. The idea that wheat may be a poisonous plant is not so far-fetched! I want to be fair and point out that wheat may not be the only culprit, so read on.

I have my own hypothesis of why gluten (all types, not just wheat) is bad for animals, including humans. My simplistic Occam's razor explanation for the celiac phenomenon (for example) is that anything "sticky" is probably not good for biological entities digestive tracts which mammals (like us) employ. My guess is that gluten tries to stick to everything and the immune system interprets this as an attack. Since anything sticking to the villi of the small intestine would affect the absorption of nutrients, it just makes sense that the immune system would object to this behavior. The recent popularity of gluten free (and now grain and legume free) dog food presents an interesting dilemma for the medical establishment. So far the question has not been raised by the people who should be raising these types of questions; the news media. Until I hear an explanation from the medical gurus, I stick to my own conclusion about this: It's OK for you to eat gluten of all types (all grains) and legumes, but never give it to your dog!!

If this hypothesis is correct, that would mean that anything sticky is bad for us, including rice and corn gluten. It is probably not a good idea to eat things like glue either! So it is not necessarily only wheat gluten, but any sticky food item that may be bad for us. There is also the theory outlined in the "Paleo Diet" which says that all grains are bad for us. Livestock who are fed grains are also supposed to be unhealthy because of the types of fat produced from eating grains, just as we can also become unhealthy by eating grains. The consumption of grains by humans and livestock is supposed to produce the types of fat that can easily stick inside of the arteries. Grass fed livestock and wild game meats will have yellow colored fat whereas supermarket grain fed meat fat is white. The color difference is supposed to be an indicator of the fat's ability to get stuck in arteries in livestock and humans. Humans can be subjected to artery clogging fats simply by eating grain fed livestock instead of grass fed animals.

There are also many other plants that are thought to have negative effects such as legumes. Many people are allergic to peanuts but could that be an indication of a broader more pervasive problem with the population at large? All types of legumes are supposedly not good and the Paleo Diet theory behind this indictment of a major food source is a culprit known as an "anti-nutrient". There was a recent movie titled "Into the wild" in which a young man ventures out in the backwoods of Alaska by himself. He ends up eating a plant that he mistakes in his plant guidebook for an edible one. The plant he eats is a poisonous plant that kills the consumer by blocking any further digestive action the hapless adventurer may attempt. In other words, you starve to death because you cannot absorb the nutrients or calories from anything you may subsequently eat.

I reiterate that a well-known, commonly accepted and cultivated on a grand scale, food crop are the family of plants known as "legumes". It is well known that many people suffer from "peanut allergies" which can be fatal if the sufferer does not pay close attention to what they eat. It is also a well-known fact that peanuts should never be eaten raw by anyone, allergy sufferer or not. The

Chapter 7 – The Medical Profession

reason this is so is that the peanut plant has a defense mechanism that uses the same strategy as the plant that killed the hapless victim in the Alaska movie. It works by interfering with the digestive process of the animal who consumes it. In other words it tries to prevent your digestive system from working while digesting it or any subsequent food. It is claimed that cooking destroys the compound responsible for this but I happen to know many people who cannot tolerate eating peanuts of any kind, cooked or otherwise.

What I have just described could be an indictment of all legumes in general. The fact that this characteristic shows up in peanuts is a big clue that any plant in the same family could very well have the same anti-nutrient properties. Legumes include beans of all kinds, including soy beans, peas, snow peas, green beans, etc. The really scary aspect to all of this is the fact that soybean oil is used universally as the cheap food processing oil for the vast majority of food products. So, if it is indeed bad for us, we are consuming something that may be bad for us on a grand scale. Soybeans may have added risks for women because many of the animal hormones present in human females are mimicked by plant hormones in soy products. If I were female, I would not eat any soy product (or any legume) unless my life depended on it to prevent starvation.

It could very well be that the human race has inadvertently adopted some semi-poisonous (and perhaps poisonous to some individuals) plants for our domesticated plant farming stock. In addition, we have altered many plants from their original form provided by nature and the negative effects have been increased with breeding techniques. Dairy products are also culprit perhaps because the dairy cows are fed grains. The paleo diet is said to completely reverse and sometimes cure things like rheumatoid arthritis. I have an undiagnosed type of inflammatory arthritis (the cause of my joint problems) which improved drastically with the Paleo diet. In other words, the considerable damage that was done by Celiac disease was mitigated by the paleo diet. As soon as I introduced dairy products back into my diet I noticed a definite change for the worse in all my joint pain.

The reader may be asking, " Well Frank, if you're so smart, how come the rest of the population is not hurt by eating things like wheat, rye, barley, beer, pizza crust, sticky rice, rice, corn and legumes?" My response to the reader is, "How do you know that the rest of the population is not being hurt?" We really don't know anything of the kind.

Everyone is required to take mathematics throughout the educational system, but few people can apply the principals of math in everyday life. What happens if you plug a zero as variable factor in a simple multiplication problem? The result or the product goes to zero. What happens if you plug a large number like 200,000 into the same problem? This should tell anyone that the factors of physical laws of nature can vary by anything from zero to infinity. Everything in the universe is a continuum; math wise.

This means that some people will never display any ill effect from eating sticky things or eating salad dressings made with ingredients such as soy bean oil. Some people will take years to succumb to the assault by developing cancers, heart disease, diabetes, etc. Others, such as people we call the Celiac will even die as early as infancy. There were thousands of cases of babies dying from infectious diarrhea in the early 1900s. It was discovered that the newly devised baby formula was responsible; it contained wheat. I guess this small historical medical event was completely forgotten by the medical academic gods.

For people who may be Celiacs, the fact that the vast majority of people walking the earth today are not exhibiting any outward symptoms means absolutely nothing. It may be the strongest immune system people who do show symptoms but even these people take years to show the real damage being done. The people whose immune systems are borderline weak may not show any symptoms until a major life threatening illness like cancer presents itself.

The borderline weak immune system people may be quietly developing life threatening disease like heart disease, cancer, diabetes and perhaps other auto-immune disorders like MS. The fact they have no other symptoms just says the immune system they have, does not deal with the mal-absorbent threat as violently as the so-called Celiac immune system. So, they may not have digestive symptoms like frequent diarrhea. They may not have arthritis. They may not have migraine headaches. They may not experience weight gain or loss. They may not exhibit any of the current accepted symptoms for celiac disease known about today.

They go on with their lives unaware that minute amounts of nutrients are not being absorbed because the sticky stuff they eat is interfering with that important process. This results in the inside of veins, arteries and capillaries not being constructed with premium materials. It may also prevent the immune system from repairing DNA damage and the inside of vein and artery walls because of a lack of the correct materials to do so. Medical science has no way of disproving anything I just said, because they are limited in measuring the really essential micro-nutrients in the body. There are no precise tests for measuring micro-nutrients.

What does this all mean? It means that you are responsible for your own health. Many people will eat anything, as long as they don't keel over immediately after the last bite. If I had cancer or any other serious illness; I would not eat legumes or sticky stuff like wheat, corn, rice or glue. I would go on a gluten free diet, and the Paleo diet just to play it safe!

There are many doctors who will probably laugh at all of this. Go ahead, laugh. At the end of the day (or perhaps century), everything I said here is pure logic and the only thing that will prove me wrong is time. One hundred years from now maybe I will have been proven right. Can anyone with a life threatening disease wait that long? I realize the profundity of all of this will stupefy many people. How much of your resistance to this idea is due to your addiction to bread, pizza, etc.?

"Question with boldness, even the existence of God" – Thomas Jefferson

Stupidity in the doctor office

The best gift I could get would be proof that getting an education does not necessarily make people smart. I am very happy to say that the medical profession is the gift that keeps on giving! There are enough incompetent medical doctors to compel us to ponder how it is possible that anyone gets cured in the medical system we now have in my country. Also consider that what we

Chapter 7 – The Medical Profession

have in the United States is supposed to be the world's best! That doesn't say much for the rest of the world, does it?

I would wager that the vast majority people reading this book have had what could be called "encounters of the incompetent kind" with medical doctors. The medical profession should be a highly technical field based on logic. The fact that it does not follow that paradigm will affect us all at some point in our lifetime. I will attempt to provide an appropriate example that is demonstrative of the medical profession as a whole. This will provide great insight to how humans use knowledge and intelligence as well as exposing exactly what intelligence is, as opposed to what we believe it is.

Recall from chapter two that problems with stupidity begin to emerge when we start believing we are smart. This is a result of arrogance and narcissism. If any one group of people really has a deep rooted belief of self-aggrandizing intelligence it has to be people with Medical Degrees. I want to stress that there are many doctors that are actually very smart, but recall that really smart people don't consider themselves smart. That is an indicator of a correct algorithm in use, the algorithm that questions everything, including one's own capabilities. Apparently many carpenters are smarter than many doctors because they have the useful occupational habit of measuring twice and cutting once. This is an admission that we are only human and as such will invariably make mistakes. It is unfortunate that many doctors cannot lower themselves to think this way. I now want to present the reader with my own personal experience of some not-so-smart doctors:

As I have alluded to, I have had many problems with my neck and back spine for over thirty years. I consulted with at least twenty neurosurgeons in that time span and I have had four neck and two back operations. Of the twenty doctors, there was only one who was what I consider to be honest. He was also the best doctor of the previous nineteen. Do you think this is a coincidence? I can testify that this is most definitely NOT a coincidence. His competence and intelligence were apparent by the complete lack of arrogance. If you are competent; there is no logical need for arrogance. The main purpose of arrogance is to cover up some unsightly aspect of one's capabilities.

It seems to me, many doctors come from the same family or at least the same school. I say that because of the apparent similarities in personality they display. Of course, in truth they come from all ethnic backgrounds and from a myriad of schools located in every part of the world. So, if they are not related genetically and they most certainly are not graduates of the same medical school, why is it they act so damn similar? Could it be that attitudes in the medical profession are so well engrained that it doesn't matter much what their ethnic background is, what part of the world they come from or where they were educated? There is a "medical culture" that permeates society on every level. Let's face it; doctors have their own way of looking at things.

Doctors are logical when it suits them and illogical when it doesn't. They are skeptical of things that don't support their own egotistical views and supportive of things that do. It doesn't matter much if solid data points to a contrary viewpoint. Sometimes they will adhere to a belief if that belief is the accepted norm of the day. Doctors are so afraid of looking stupid in the eyes of their peers (or anyone) that the vast majority of the time they will not take a chance and make a

Chapter 7 – The Medical Profession

diagnosis based on what is biologically possible but instead take a statistical analysis viewpoint on just about every conceivable problem. They are stubborn creatures who are not easily swayed once they have made up their minds. This is a form of brainwashing. Since the early 1970's or so the medical establishment has been disseminating the propaganda that fat is bad for us. I label this as propaganda because that's basically what it is. We could define propaganda as any information published or otherwise spread through a population to promote a point of view without establishing that point of view as fact.

That is precisely what happened in the case of the "fats are bad" campaign. This idea spread like wildfire through the medical community and was universally accepted for the next 50 years. It was OK to stuff yourself with any food item that claimed to be low fat (usually the low fat or no fat items get all their calories from simple sugars). Things like butter, cheese, bacon and my personal favorite; eggs were condemned as the killers of humanity.

Never mind that humans have been consuming these items for thousands of years with no ill effects. A common pro-medical establishment response to the above would be, "we can't depend on records from hundreds of years ago to determine the causes of death in the past." This is what I call "biased denial". It becomes convenient to dismiss any argument that doesn't conform to what you are pushing.

The standard operating procedure for most MDs is to try to place cases of complaints in categories. If they have not heard of a specific complaint they just don't know what to do because they have no idea of which category to place the puzzling case. In other words; if you happen to be unfortunate enough to have a problem that is even slightly rare; you sir or madam, are in deep crap! I say this from personal experience and I am sure that many people reading this have had similar experiences and understand completely. Many doctors fall way short when it comes to "thinking out of the box". Why do you suppose this is so? Medical Schools concentrate way too much on "Case Histories", that's why. They actually teach doctors to diagnose their patients this way.

If aircraft mechanics used the same troubleshooting methods most medical doctors use, airplanes would be falling from the sky like leaves on an autumn day. Consider a scenario such as this:

A pilot notices an engine oil pressure gauge showing a zero reading in a well-used passenger propeller aircraft. For the mechanically declined, oil pressure proves the engine is being lubricated and without lubrication the engine will seize and stop running. He reports this to the maintenance crew and a mechanic is assigned to troubleshoot the problem. The mechanic does a required check in the department's computerized database of mechanical problems for this aircraft. There are no history returns for low oil pressure failure and so the mechanic tells the pilot it must be a defective gauge. In this methodology of thinking, if there is no record of something happening in the past, then it is not possible! The pilot is advised to go ahead and take off and they will replace the gauge later. The plane crashes because of a failed engine due to no lubrication. Get the picture?

This is basically the way most Doctors diagnose their patients. They operate on the medical equivalent of legal "precedence law" or "case law". In other words, if something has never

Chapter 7 – The Medical Profession

happened before, it is all in the patient's head or they are just lying. I know this is true because it happened to me. What follows is my personal experience that demonstrates how Doctors will attempt to diagnose by pure "precedence" instead of troubleshooting the body and brain utilizing in-depth knowledge of brain-body mechanics:

It began during a routine day at work. I was reading and after a short time I noticed that something was wrong with the amount of light hitting the page. I looked up at the fluorescent tubes in the ceiling and was surprised to see not one light, but three stacked up on top of each other! My initial thought was, "Man, I better get my eyes checked!" I decided I was just straining my eyes too much and I quit reading for a while and went about doing other things. After about a half hour my eyes returned to normal. I tried reading again on subsequent days and incurred the same problem, every time with a corresponding recovery in about 30 minutes. This went on for about a month and I then decided this was not going away and I better get an examination. I was not prepared and was totally shocked at what happened next.

Over the course of the next two years, I saw a total of seven ophthalmologists, one ophthalmologist/neurologist and two neurologists. I never got my problem cured but the last doctor at least gave me a "suggestion" as to what the problem might have been. During the course of searching for a cure, I was treated like I was a con man, a charlatan, a liar and a scoundrel!

Every one of these doctors had an eyebrow raised during their examination. They were skeptical, to say the least. There were even two assistants of two different doctors who treated me like I was the scum of the earth for attempting to defraud their employers. I am still at a loss as to what I could possibly have gained in perpetrating a hoax over these "poor victim" doctors! Why would I do that? Why would anyone want to do that? I was trying to solve a problem that from my perspective loomed as a very formidable problem. I was an engineer who had a problem reading. I couldn't read for any more than 15 to 20 minutes before my vision became so blurred I could not make out the words on the printed page. It was very close to being legally blind in that I couldn't read long enough to accomplish anything worthwhile. The doctors I asked for help didn't see it that way.

The fact that they operate on "case law" and they personally had no experience with anything even remotely close to what I was describing were all they needed to make a decision that I was lying through my teeth. I was befuddled. I didn't know what to do next. So I went on the internet and I searched for answers myself. What I came up with was astounding. The fact that I had this condition did not surprise me, what was perplexing was that none of the doctors I had seen had even the slightest clue as to what my problem could have been! Not one of them was able to see the forest through the trees! My problem was a migraine headache! It was me, myself and I that was responsible and successful for diagnosing my problem!

The last doctor I saw confirmed my own diagnosis with a test called a brain SPECT. This is a test in which a radioactive isotope is injected in the bloodstream and the brain function is looked at for the "brain metabolism" level. This is like getting an x-ray from the inside out. The rational is that if all parts of the brain are processing everything they are intended to process (high metabolism), the blood flow in those areas will be correspondingly high, resulting in bright areas

Chapter 7 – The Medical Profession

an x-ray image. My brain SPECT showed a low processing level in the areas (modules) responsible for vision. I was now sure of the source of my problem.

Unfortunately, there is no cure for this type of problem. The only sources I was able to find were internet pages that did not detail any kind of treatment but only suggested strategies that had to do with limiting the field of vision to "avoid confusion". In this case, confusion means by the vision processing hardware of the brain, not whether or not I was confused (although at that point I really was). The doctor that confirmed my self-diagnosis was clueless as far as a cure was concerned. This doctor was also not a very nice person, in that he became agitated when the various fixes he experimented on me (drugs such as Adderall) had no effect. He even accused me of doing illegal drugs in my past which he claimed could have caused some brain damage and the problem. I got the impression that even he was skeptical about my problem and that I was not telling him the truth. This experience did more for my understanding of human stupidity than any other benefit I may have wished for, such as getting cured!

To summarize, I ended up seeing nine doctors, the first eight had no idea what my problem was and in addition they thought I was scamming them for some unknown reason. Two of the doctor assistants were totally and uncharacteristically abusive to someone they suspected of being a con man and a scum bag! I ultimately solved the problem myself.

As I said, even the doctor who confirmed what I had diagnosed had no cure. I found a partial cure myself on the internet. This employed a strategy of limiting the field of vision and avoiding confusion by applying black tape to the bottom half of my reading glasses. This allows me to read for about an hour before I begin to have problems. This works by reducing confusion; brain processing confusion. This is similar to photographic processing software such as "Photoshop" not being able to sharpen up an image because the processor primary memory was attempted to be loaded with a file that was too large to process.

This was not the end of my encounters with doctors who rely on case law to diagnose patients. Since my eye/brain diagnosis, I have reported my problem to several doctors that also had complete disbelief in my story. Even after "letting the cat out of the bag" by telling him that my problem was a migraine aura problem, a doctor at the VA would not treat me any further unless I consented to have my eyes checked! Although I nearly pleaded with him to accept what I was telling him, he would not listen. Then I went through the same routine with the non-believing eye specialist, who did the exam. I wanted to say, "You're kidding, right?"

The really amazing aspect of this story is that optometrists I saw later for eyeglass prescriptions were totally aware of migraine vision problems. Several of them told me that this is taught in school. I guess the higher up the educational ladder you go, the less information sticks to you. The optometrist that checked my eyes for my eyeglass prescription knew all about what I was telling her. The guys that actually do eye surgeries for a living did not!

This is an example of how things can get screwed up when the information is available, but not known about, or ignored completely. The information in my case was the basic workings of the mammalian vision system. In other words; the function of eye and brain vision processing. This is basic stuff and things any medical student should know after one or two years. I educated

Chapter 7 – The Medical Profession

myself about it in a matter of days on the internet. If we have problems like this with doctors and stuff that is known, what about stuff that is not known?

Let's face it; there are many things Medical Science just does not understand. In fact if we want to be realistic, we would have to say the number of things not understood far outweighs the things that are understood. You wouldn't know that by talking to a doctor though, would you? The first rule for a doctor in doctor/patient relations is, "If you can't dazzle em' with brilliance, baffle em' with bullcrap!"

Doctors will rarely if ever admit that they don't know what the problem is. If all else fails: if the tests they have ordered don't back up their original "guess" they will resort to other strategies like blaming the patient for not being completely honest. It is not beyond them to try to discredit the patient this way to avoid admitting that they just don't know what is wrong. My story is proof of that. Their attitude does not help anyone and in fact it just delays the patient in getting an accurate diagnosis. I'm sure that many lives have been lost because doctors did not want to admit they didn't know what a problem was and so the patient, believing it must be all in their head, went off somewhere to die. The above is especially true for cases in which a patient is complaining of pain. If we take a look at the garbage that medical schools teach student doctors about pain it is not difficult to understand why so many people "fall through the cracks".

Medical schools teach that pain is mostly a "perceived" phenomenon and that the ethnic background of the patient should be taken into account! Furthermore, people from places like China typically put up with more pain than does someone from Italy, for example! So, they are told if a Chinese person comes in the emergency room complaining of pain you had better listen to them. On the other hand if it is a person from Italy, they can be largely ignored because these people tend to be emotional and over exaggerate! What a crock of crap! Think about it; these are the people that we entrust with our lives!

It is not hard to understand the medical community's ignorance of how pain is perceived (and by the way; yes it is perceived) because the medical community has a very, very superficial, perfunctory understanding of the brain. Pain is only one of many things about brain function that they don't understand because everything our conscious (and non-conscious) mind encounters about our surrounding world is perceived.

The fact that everything is perceived doesn't mean it is not real. The fact is that someone may be more sensitive to pain than someone else, and that may be in itself a symptom; not an excuse to belittle the individual who has more sensitivity to pain. That's another thing that annoys me about some doctors. They use logic to bolster their point of view when it suits them but in reality, they themselves don't act very logically most of the time. The above example about how pain is taught in medical schools backs this point of view.

My assessment on the whole mess described so far is that the medical profession could do themselves and all of humanity a big favor by just being honest about what they know and what they don't know. This is just adhering to the intelligence guidelines that we all should follow. As far as what they know and don't know is concerned; let's have a quick review of the state of affairs in Medical Science today. I will talk about the good first and the bad next:

174

Chapter 7 – The Medical Profession

First, the good stuff. Medical Science has become adept at fixing injuries. If you happen to be unlucky enough to be in a car wreck or even more unlucky if you are shot, your chances of surviving are greater than they ever were in history. Medical Science is great at repairing damage. The damage could also be from years of arthritic assaults that destroy cartilage in the joint and eventually end up crippling the patient. There are many highly skilled surgeons in the world and these are the medical professionals I have the upmost respect for. That said however, this is largely repair work and what is required for the most part to do this repair is a detailed knowledge of how the body mechanically goes together. I'm sorry to say; that's it for the good stuff.

Next, the bad stuff. Now I will try to elaborate on some of the not so well understood areas of Medical Science. These are disciplines that typically require a more in depth understanding of how things actually work and tend to be the most complex areas in medicine. Some of these areas include things like cancer, arthritis, diabetes, allergies and the most misunderstood in my opinion; brain function. As we all already know, everything we know as our world is perceived and that perception is done by the brain.

If for example, if medical science really understood addiction; many of the modern social problems of today could be eliminated. When I say addiction I mean any kind of addiction including food, drink and of course drugs. I will concede that addictions like gambling and even sex may have the same basic underlying brain causes; I am concentrating on the main medical problems, the ones that kill or damage and ultimately destroy people's lives which are undeniably drug addictions.

Just as we trust the military to be on top of any threat that may do us harm, we also need to have a firm trust in the medical profession as a whole to keep us informed of medical related threats and in addition to that, actually come up with solutions to all medically related issues. The biggest medically related social issue that confronts mankind today is drug abuse and the many connected problems it brings with it. The governments of the world have failed miserably at eliminating the trafficking of illegal drugs. There are more people serving prison time for drug charges than all other crimes put together. Huge government agencies have been created and grown to enormous sizes just to slow down the flow of illegal drugs. We even have a "Drug Czar" in the United States. I don't think I need to elaborate any further on this problem. I would bet that most people reading this very likely know or have known someone with a drug problem.

My point is: The medical profession; who being charged with the duty of being the protector of every human being's health is not doing their job at all. It is just that simple. Why? Because instead of being realistic and recognizing that we all are just a bunch of biological machines, who are not entirely in control of their actions all of the time, doctors continue to operate under the assumption that people are in total control of their bodies and this is not the case. Most people at some point have had a doctor tell them point blank to just "lose weight", "quit smoking" or "quit drinking". To the patient being on the receiving end of this advice, this sounds laughable at best. Doctors routinely tell patients to do things they know the patient is incapable of doing but that doesn't stop them from giving this advice regardless. People probably use drugs simply because they don't feel good. The problem should be evaluated by working from that starting point and not some assumed notion of the way people are supposed to act.

Chapter 7 – The Medical Profession

Doctors should have a better understanding of how addiction works. That understanding would include the concept that we really have no micro control over ourselves, at least in the way we believe we do. Doctors need to start looking at the human body and brain as more of a machine and less of an "entity". We are more robotic than we would care to admit.

Obesity is one of the big contributing factors in many serious illnesses. One reason this could be so is we are all programmed to eat. Doctors should research the mechanisms of the program controlling that function. They should at least concede that there is more to all of this that readily meets the eye. Instead, doctors are fixated on the responsibility of free will that humans "are supposed" to have. This phenomenon is apparent in many aspects of medicine. The reason this is so is very apparent to me: Doctors have been brainwashed by medical educators who act as dictators who push propaganda that supports ideas they are invested in. These are ideas they believe in that will support the notion that they are smart. In this particular instance the ideas being pushed are that it's the patient's responsibility to eat less. Doctors place so much importance on the patient's responsibility of free will that they never acknowledge the 500 pound gorilla in the room. The gorilla is; that humans are a machine; nothing more, nothing less. People can no more control how much they eat any more than they can control their sexual desires. Both the desire to eat and the desire to have sex are programmed into all of us as hardware. We don't have to learn or be taught about either; we are all born with these program "routines".

Recall that I stated that free will is a required human decision making function because the alternatives to free will would not be adequate for complex situational instances. I believe that statement to be true. However, the micro-decisions on behavior such as eating and sex (both necessary for survival of the species) don't require a lot of pre-decision processing since both are essential basic survival requirements. We can control both of these with free will but it is difficult and for some people impossible. The number of overweight people in the world is proof of that as well as the number of divorces that clog the court system.

I alluded that I cannot stress how much morality plays a role in everything intelligence wise and this is yet another example. If doctors were honest, and they just admitted they didn't know why people can't control how much they eat; perhaps, just perhaps mankind will discover the true reason! I believe the true reason is the contained in the mystery of non-conscious information processing. I believe it could be the things people eat are causing them to eat more of those things and I personally believe that hypothesis to be true. Certain foods direct behavior because of the influence they have on the most important organ in the body; the brain.

Radiologists

Radiologists are the black sheep of the medical family that the other family members don't want to admit they are related to. There is a big problem in medicine with the people that are tasked to read important diagnostic test results in the form of x-rays, CT scans, MRI's and nuclear imaging tests. The problem I speak of is the miss-reading of those test results in about 75 percent of the attempts (my personal experience). Radiologists nearly always got it wrong with my tests! Why is that? I have spoken to several medical doctors about this problem and it seems to be a problem in which the entire medical community is totally aware. They are aware of it but paradoxically, nothing is done to correct it. From what I have been able to gather in the form of anecdotal and informal opinionated testimony is that radiologists are expected to know every area of medicine well enough to read radiology media tests and provide a diagnosis even though their brethren doctors are pigeon holed into one tiny aspect of what is a very diverse and complex subject. They should not be expected to know everything, but they are!

This is just another indictment of the medical academic establishment as a whole as it is they who condone the ritualistic reading and subsequent monetary charges to the patient that for the most part is unnecessary because any doctor worth their fee will go about reading the films on their own. Add to that, the fact that as I have alluded to, the diagnosis is usually wrong (that was true for me). So, we have another situation in medicine today where the public at large is worse off because of a few academics on the top that control the situation and insure the status quo remains intact. I personally have not had one correct diagnosis by a radiologist in at least 20 tests. They always miss something that the doctor who ordered the test will pick up on. Regardless of how many times they have misdiagnosed me, I always seem to get billed for their service. A service I would rather do without.

Summary

Medical academics are ultimately responsible for what gets taught as relevant subject matter to new doctors entering the field. The result of this top-down approach to medical education is that when the current thought is wrong, this wrongness will be propagated throughout the medical community as a whole. This is not good news for the public seeking help from doctors. Doctors in general are taught to practice medicine with a "case study" or "precedence" approach in which statistics of what has already happened is considered more important than actual brain / body mechanics. Humans should be treated more like the machines they are and less emphasis placed on free will for micro-decision categories such as eating, sex and pleasure gratification as with drug abuse. Not enough of an emphasis is placed on the role of food in the major diseases plaguing humans today.

Reader's Notes

Chapter 8 – UFO's

Right off the bat: Why do you suppose that there is a chapter about UFO's in a book on human intelligence? The answer to that question is very simple. It demonstrates stupidity in a large group of people who don't believe in things they should believe in: Scientists. It also demonstrates stupidity in another large group of people who believe in things they should not believe in: The "tin foil hat" crowd. This subject could very well be the most important that humanity has ever looked into and this is no joke. The possibilities of an unlimited energy source, as well as a possible understanding of all fundamental physics are just two positive benefits of embracing this as a genuine scientific research prospect. It is well worth looking into.

I reiterate there are two camps of people who could be accused of being stupid in the UFO phenomenon. The first camp is the scientists who will not take this subject seriously, no matter how many highly credible witnesses report seeing things. The second camp is the "tin foil hat" crowd who believes everything they hear about the subject including the government possessing alien bodies at some Air Force base.

The UFO phenomenon has been going on for quite some time. Let us ignore the fact that people have been seeing strange things in the sky for as long as there was a way to keep records of whatever it was that they witnessed. Let's just say that the whole phenomenon started in 1947 as many people believe. There has been enough strange goings on since 1947 to warrant serious attention by the mainstream scientific community. That has not happened at the time of this writing and will most likely not happen for the foreseeable future. The reasons mainstream science has not had interest in UFO's has several underpinnings. One reason is that scientists are human with all those human emotions that tend to drag down the intelligence of the best of us. This is in itself is a great handicap. If humans were not perpetually concerned with the consternation of how they would be viewed by their peers we would all be a lot better off in many ways. Recall that I label this as ICP for Intelligence Comparison Phenomenon.

Scientists are worse than the average person when it comes to worrying about the condemnation by their peers. The fear of looking stupid is the main impetus for skepticism about UFO's. There is nothing worse than looking stupid (crazy is not so bad) to a scientist. I listed unfounded skepticism as one of the main causes and indicators of stupidity in Chapter 2 and this is a prime example of that.

This is a situation in which thousands if not millions of *reliable* witnesses have seen things in the sky that they could not explain. Add to that, the hundreds if not thousands of *expert* witnesses that have seen things they also could not explain. The experts I speak of are people like military pilots who can tell the difference between a flock of geese and an intelligently made object. In addition to sightings, there has been hundreds of what are known as "trace evidence" cases where impressions were left on the ground and in some of these cases there were even eyewitness accounts of a craft landing and occupants walking around. The number of these cases are overwhelming to the point where any rational person, scientist or otherwise would have to admit; something (I am not saying what) is going on. The point is: there is enough evidence of epic proportions to more than just warrant serious scientific research into the subject.

The main objections mainstream scientists raise to this subject is that we do not have any physical proof. In other words, for mainstream science unless a craft lands on the White House lawn; they will not take the subject seriously.

Let's take a look at some of the objections raised by skeptic scientists:

1. There is no physical evidence.

    There may not be a craft we can touch and look at, but there *is* trace evidence. There have been numerous cases where indentations were imprinted in the ground and many other similar markers. If we are indeed witnessing something from an advanced civilization, then they probably don't make mistakes the way we are accustomed and if they don't want to make contact; then they won't! We have a difficult time understanding the level of intelligence that would be required to accomplish interplanetary or intergalactic space or perhaps interdimensional travel, if in fact that is where these craft originate. That level of intelligence does not create a machine that makes mistakes, so don't expect a sample.

2. Just because people are seeing things, it doesn't mean that the things are extra-terrestrial.

    Where else could they be from? There are only two possibilities: They are from some other world or they are from here. The people that reject the extra-terrestrial hypothesis don't usually have other alternative explanations. Making that statement is poo-pooing the entire notion of UFOs being something real. Sure, not everything qualifies for the ET label but what else and where else could something be from if it can hover without making a sound and then take off straight up at 3000 MPH? Clearly, people see machines that perform in a way that our current technology does not allow. Many prominent scientists scoff at the possibility of the earth being visited by other-worldly creatures. They cannot possibly have valid arguments for why this would be true. If something cannot be proven with physical evidence that does not mean it can be dis-proven by out of hand logic.

    Another possibility is what I call: "The Captain Nemo Hypothesis". Captain Nemo was the mythical character in Jules Verne's "20,000 Leagues Under the Sea". The very intelligent Nemo had managed to design, build and operate his very own nuclear powered submarine; in the late 1800s! I often wonder where Mr. Verne came up with this idea. I know that there were many UFO sightings in the 1800s. Did Mr. Verne see something that defied explanation? Did he see a UFO and were there people inside that UFO? I say this because this is what I personally saw at the age of 14 in Chicago, IL in 1961. I explain this is detail later.

    What if there is an independently wealthy and highly intelligent human being somewhere on this earth who has figured out anti-gravity flight and some unknown power source to make that happen? This idea is not so far-fetched. The question is not why would there be such a person; but why not? Universities are not the know-it-all entities that they profess to be. They don't even have answers for the run of the mill problems that plague humanity. If there was someone that had everything figured out, why would he or she share that information with the "academic elites"? Especially, the elites who probably laughed at her or him for the outrageous ideas in the first place?

3.   Because distances are so vast and the journey would take so long, biological entities could not live long enough to make the trip.

There are two counter points to this. One is that the craft might be controlled by intelligent machines; it wouldn't matter how long they have been on their journey. 10 million years is a walk in the park for a properly designed and constructed machine. The second point might be that the biological entities on the craft are immortal. The only requirement for this would be a complete understanding of the way genetics work which is not a problem for an advanced race. I reiterate, we have a difficult time in understanding that level of intelligence. If they can travel the universe or dimensions, then they already have a complete knowledge of their biological makeup, and probably have made design changes to achieve perfection.

4   It is impossible for extraterrestrial craft to get here because the distances are too great and nothing can go beyond the speed of light.

While we may not be able to go faster than light, there may be other ways of crossing the universe: like through a wormhole in the fabric of space. There are many things we do not know about nature in general including what dark matter and energy are and how they function. It is thought that dark energy is the force that is accelerating all the galaxies in the universe away from each other but right now we just don't know enough to come to any conclusions.

This is why unfounded skepticism is a sign of stupidity. When we make assumptions (always problematic) about things we really know nothing about; that is a sign of stupidity. To say something is impossible, when that something happens to be a subject riddled with unknowns; is truly idiotic.

One problem mainstream science has in dealing with this topic is all the charlatanism surrounding the whole UFO phenomenon. There are claims of abduction. There are claims that not one but several alien spacecraft have crashed and the wreckage along with alien dead bodies recovered. There are claims of governments covering up the real facts. There are even claims that aliens have already invaded earth and are walking among us.

It is understandable why scientists do not want to be connected to any or all of the above. It really does sound like class A bull-crap. There are many facets of the UFO phenomenon that make me furious because instead of advancing our spiritual and intellectual enlightenment, we are held in a place that brings back memories of the dark ages. I will next summarize each and give my views on why the things that many "tin foil hat" types believe; are actually nonsense.

Chapter 8 – UFOs

Alien abduction

The alien abduction phenomenon probably began its notoriety in 1961 with the Betty and Barney Hill abduction story. Before that "monumental" occurrence, there were no reported abduction stories in any news media outlet. As far as I know, there were no project blue book, project grudge, or project sign reports made of abductions prior to 1961. 1961 seems to be the seminal moment in time when the aliens finally got their act together and made the decision that we humans had spent enough free time and we needed to be abducted on a regular basis.

Since 1961 many thousands of people now claim that they have been taken from their bedrooms or where ever they happened to be when the "alien visitors" decided to take them. They also claim that they were brought to some type of craft where experiments, usually of the medical variety, have been done on them. The problems I have with this are manifold.

The first problem I have is the "professional psychiatrists" who have made the conclusion that "these people all really believe that something has actually happened to them". Wow, what a conclusion to come to! Even if the entire population of the earth believed this really happened to them; does not mean it really did! Another assertion made is that "they all have the same basic details in the accounts of their experience". Wow, another earthshattering revelation to arrive at! Could it be that they all have the same details because they have all heard, over and over, the same exact same details as many of these "abductees" attempt some sort of monetary gain by selling their ordeal in the form of magazine stories, books, etc.? Duh!

There is another major group of "abductees" that claim they have not only been abducted once, but they have been abducted since they were kids, sometimes as young as five. The abductions continued periodically over the years into adulthood. I am not a psychologist but doesn't this sound like a fundamental tenet of human nature that people use to prove that they are somehow special? I know if this were happening to me, I would either go crazy with the realization that this was actually happening, or I would do my best to prove to the world it was true. I do not believe the average human has enough mental stability to endure the knowledge that this was true. None of us could withstand the pure mental anguish that this would impose on the victim. All of us would go completely crazy and that would be *all* of us, not just a few of us.

After over 50 years of supposed abductions, why is it: No one has ever gotten a video of the abductees floating through a wall, etc.? Unless of course, this is not a true physical phenomenon and if it isn't that means it is only happening in the minds of the victims. I believe that "abduction" is in fact only in the minds of the "victims". It is some type of dream state produced by the brain. It is *not* really happening and if I thought it *was* really happening to me I would do everything in my power to either stop it or prove it was happening. My room would be bristling with cameras; I would have a copper "Faraday cage" to sleep in with a bunch of weapons (rifles, shotguns) at my disposal. I would do everything in my power to stop this from happening. Going to therapy or a support group would be the last thing I would think about doing. I believe the people that go those routes, do so to draw attention to themselves as victims, not to obtain any real help. I would feel nothing but relief in knowing that none of my experiences were actually true instead of relying on a bunch of so-called "professionals" telling me that they really believed in what I was saying and thus effectively making me feel controlled and helpless.

Chapter 8 – UFOs

The human brain is capable of doing many things that are little known about in even the neurology world. If you want a good idea of the hallucinations the brain is capable of read Oliver Sack's book, Migraine. I personally have had migraine induced hallucinations that I reported to several neurologists only to receive a look of contempt for my insolence. This is what happened to me. I was driving home from work one day and I had gotten a headache about two hours prior. I was on the toll way doing about 70 MPH when I saw what looked like a small bug swirl in front of my car. It revolved in a circular motion a few times and then it headed right for my windshield. It went through the windshield, and hit the tip of my nose. It went right through my nose and disappeared. I didn't feel anything as it entered and I wasn't shocked or afraid. I now know that I was in some kind of "dream like" state and the whole episode was a hallucination. I probably should not have been driving.

These are things that the brain is more than capable of doing to unsuspecting "brain owners" so it does not surprise me in the least that people are experiencing what they believe to be alien abductions. The amount of suggestive material that is present in the world today is astounding and it would be surprising if there were no such incidences reported. There are movies, documentaries, news reports, books, magazine articles, etc. There is no shortage of stories of this happening all over the world. This is part of the problem in that it ends up being profitable for some and destructive for others. The people that profit are all the hoaxers and the people that suffer are the ones who may just have really severe types of migraine aura and get freaked out by believing that what they hallucinate may be true. It is claimed that Lewis Carrol, the guy that wrote, "Alice in Wonderland", was a "Migrainer" and suffered from migraines all his life and this may have contributed to the visions he wrote about in the story.

I have heard some really inane explanations for why the so-called abductees can't seem to capture their alien friends on video cameras and the like. They claim cameras don't work during the "trans-dimensional" process or whatever it's supposed to be. Yeah right. Cameras don't work. OK how about a simple pressure sensing device you place under your body in the bed maybe? How about having that connected to alarms that would wake up the whole neighborhood? They don't want to do stuff like that because they probably know the whole thing is inside their head and they don't want to admit that they are just attention starved.

Hoaxers do more than just fool the book buying public into shedding some of their hard earned cash. They perpetuate the alien abduction myth and prey upon people who may be receptive into imagining this might actually be happening to them. It is a sad state of affairs but the situation today is that if anyone desires to make an enormous amount of money, the only requisite is that they claim to have had alien contact since they were five and it has continued into their sixties. They can fabricate the whole thing but if they have a creative enough imagination, people will not only believe their story but spend loads of money on ancillary things like prints of paintings the contactee has made of his alien buddies. The potential for monetary gain is stupendous and the effort required is minimal.

There is one aspect of the abduction / contact phenomenon that is never discussed. This is the concept of the super intelligence that the aliens would be required to possess in order to travel to other worlds or dimensions and develop craft that defy gravity and can perform at speeds of thousands of miles per hour and make ninety degree turns on a dime. I cannot state this enough;

Chapter 8 – UFOs

we cannot begin to understand the level of intelligence required to accomplish those things. This is intelligence so advanced in relation to us, that we have a hard time conceiving what that would entail. However, I believe we can make some basic assumptions about that level of intelligence.

Super intelligence

First of all, any entity capable of doing all the wondrous things UFOs are purported to do would be knowledgeable about everything. When I say everything, I mean everything. They would have a complete understanding of everything there is to understand. There would be no need for "experimentation" on us lowly humans. What would they want to do that for? It would be synonymous to we humans flying from Canada to somewhere in Brazil to abduct a grasshopper to do experiments for some unknown reason, on a species we already knew everything we wanted to know about. It doesn't make any sense and I do not believe they would waste their intellect on something as mundane as that.

I don't believe they come here to experiment on us, so why do I think they come here? I am using the extraterrestrial hypothesis as if it were the only explanation here just to make a point. If anything, our world and our species may be a curiosity to travelers from other worlds. They may be coming here for purely entertainment reasons. The earth really is a beautiful place and as far as inhabitable planets are concerned; may be entirely different than other worlds. It may create an interest since the odds are that it may be as strange to them as their world would probably seem to us. I believe this because of one of my personal sightings which I will describe in detail shortly.

As far as what aliens actually look like, I do not believe that they would look like reptilians, insects or any other worldly related appearance. Reptiles and insects are both purely world centric objects and the life that may have developed independently on another world could be stranger than anything we could hope to imagine. "Grays" are the big head, large eyed skinny armed and legged short characters that are as much a part of pop culture as the Beatles. Once the description of the gray was disseminated, the cat was out of the bag and everyone and their brother jumped on this bandwagon.

This brings me to point out another aspect of the entire ufology phenomenon. Most of the important points of ufology are based on dubiously accepted ideas that have no real provable historical background. Even the so-called "crash" at Roswell New Mexico is based on here-say evidence; most of which looks to me like a bunch of local folks in Roswell attempting to make some financial gain off of the story. Every one of the local residents who were interviewed on camera all looked to have an air of phoniness about them. They all looked like they were telling tall tales. The stories about some Army Air Force radar knocking the craft out of the sky are laughable at best. Can you imagine a craft that was capable of interplanetary or interdimensional travel but could not withstand one of our puny radars? If you can, I have a bridge in New York City for sale!

The big point here is that everyone in ufology and even people in all walks of life that do not even have a passing fancy towards the UFO phenomenon seem to take Roswell as a given. That is; they assume that something happened. Maybe something really did happen, albeit what that

Chapter 8 – UFOs

something was is totally unclear. Whatever the military discovered, if in fact they discovered anything, is still a mystery and this is ammunition to all the conspiracy theory freaks who want to build a mountain out of the molehill that this really is.

The fact that the military has not come clean with whatever it was that they found in the New Mexico desert, does not translate into evidence of some type of cover-up. The military still does not talk about UFOs for the simple reason that in doing so would negate the free-of-charge cover they now have for any black ops projects they may have going on right now. Just because Roswell happened a long time ago, in 1947, does not mean you just throw away your story about UFOs. If they admitted it was or it wasn't makes no difference, they would still be showing their cards to any opposition the U.S. military may have in any future conflict. We don't want the Russians or the Chinese communists to know what we have and we want to keep them guessing. It is just that simple.

The stories that everyone takes for granted, may be just stories after all. Roswell was not the only crash if you believe some of the UFO "experts". Many of the people who make a comfortable living off this subject claim that two or three craft crashed at Roswell, at two different sites. Then there are the numerous crash sites around the country and even several around the world! We have all these craft crashing in spite of the fact they were able to do one or perhaps all of three of these things: Time, dimension or interplanetary/ galactic space travel. Yes, that's right; they could accomplish all of those feats but they found flying in the earth's atmosphere to be too much for them! Am I the only one that appreciates how ludicrous this is? Perhaps the aliens that crashed were the hillbilly aliens that the other aliens don't want to admit they are related to!

These stories seem to take a life of their own as time passes. The Betty and Barney Hill abduction story, when originally told said that it required hypnosis regression for the couple to recall the events. Years later that story morphed into Barney recalling the events immediately after the event with no hypnosis required. Somebody is lying and I would bet that whoever that someone is has something to gain. That something is money. Is it not usually money?

There is another milestone UFO event that is widely known about in ufology circles and that is the Rendlesham Forest, UK UFO encounter. This happened at a NATO airbase and U.S. Air Force security police were involved as well as a Lt. Colonel who was the deputy base commander at the time. The original story mentioned a craft which was witnessed by most of the security force sent out to investigate. This story morphed into entities leaving the craft in later stories. It seems that if given enough time, some of these accounts have the ability to be morphed; affected as if by some "writer's embellishment" scheme.

I am instantly skeptical of any story that requires hypnotic regression. Hypnosis is a very inappropriate method for memory recall and it is usually only a method that that is utilized to "motivate" people to do things which is a completely different and the only appropriate use, if in fact it works at that task. The patient is put in what they call a "suggestive state" and the therapist proceeds to suggest strategies for improving. This may lend itself to many self-improvement obstacles like losing weight, quitting smoking or low self-esteem but the jury is still out as to whether this stuff actually has benefits. Hypnotism is not well suited to help people remember instances that the subject has no conscious recollection of. It might be used to help a witness to a crime remember the color of a getaway car or similar but it has no place in inducing the subject to remember *everything* about an occurrence including the occurrence itself.

The propensity to plant memories in people who might ultimately believe those memories are true is great with regressive hypnotism. Recall what I said about how the brain stores information. We remember things that happen during episodes of intense emotional stress or excitement because of the high consciousness intensity which is the brain's memory management device. Any increase in consciousness intensity causes an increase in information storage.

People have a hard time forgetting things that happened to them during periods of duress; not the other way around. The people who claim they were abducted say they were subdued by some anesthetic but they are able to recall the events nonetheless under hypnosis. This must be another case of the inbred hillbilly aliens doing things without the knowledge of their cousins again! We humans are very good at anesthetizing other humans for major surgery, but our space brothers have a tough time doing that? No amount of hypnosis will compel a patient to recall the events during an operation once put under. Apparently the hillbilly space aliens don't know how to properly anesthetize us and so we end up finding out their "alien agenda" (whatever that is).

The "Cosmic Watergate"

If you have not already done so, I suggest you read J Allen Hynek's book – The UFO experience. Dr. Hynek's qualifications are impeccable. He was a Professor of Astronomy at Ohio State University and later the Chair of Astronomy at Northwestern University. Dr. Hynek was originally a devout UFO skeptic. Only after spending years as the chief technical consultant to the U.S. Air Force's Project Blue book did he begin to change his mind about the seriousness of the situation. He was even at odds with the Air Force because he didn't think they took it seriously enough. There is the incident in Michigan where Dr. Hynek reported to the media that what people were witnessing might have been "swamp gas". Later when he was questioned about this, he said the Air Force pressured him into giving some type of explanation. This is one reason why the popular opinion about Dr. Hynek is towards him not being a believer.

The Air Force had one mantra; these things are not possible so why take them seriously? At least that was the public relations face the Air Force presented to the world. I think there was more to it than that. I believe that the Air Force was probably way more interested in this phenomenon than they publically advertised. I believe they still are interested because they really have to be interested in craft that routinely violate our airspace and the origin, purpose and threat is totally unknown otherwise.

I don't know if the military has changed their opinion about UFO's since the closing of Blue Book in 1969. They officially have no interest in the subject. Some UFO researchers say even Blue Book was just a cover to hide the real interest of the military and intelligence establishments. At this point we don't know what the actual stand of the United States Government is on UFO's. Many other countries have released their information on the subject but we can't be sure if we are getting everything because there is always the issue of national

Chapter 8 – UFOs

security. Even if the U.S. Government is interested in UFO's they may have many national security reasons for not admitting it.

In many ways; the government has used the UFO phenomenon to their advantage from the very beginning of the "modern day" (beginning in 1947) UFO craze. The part of the military responsible for maintaining new secret craft as secret; viewed UFO's as the gift that kept on giving. It was much easier to allow the public to believe that what they were observing was extraterrestrial than it was to admit that we had experimental craft that looked pretty strange in the sky.

It was also a good idea to let the Russians and Chi-Coms keep on guessing as to what it was that we actually had in our bag of goodies. It is a relatively good wager to bet that the official U.S. analysis of what UFO's actually were; had some element of the possibility that the Russians had some technology that we didn't know about. So it worked both ways. We wanted them to keep on guessing and vice versa. The crash at Roswell may have been a Russian craft and there are many possible reasons for the U.S. government not stating that publicly. We didn't want the Russians to know for sure we had their stuff and we sure didn't want the Chi-Coms to know we had a Russian craft and we didn't want the American public to know a Russian craft was violating our airspace. If you think about it, the actions performed by the government at the time at Roswell were pretty smart, if this is what happened, and I would bet that it was.

So given all of the above, it was only natural that the military and intelligence entities of the U.S. Government take the stance they did and still do, about UFO's. If the conspiracy types believe the government knows more about UFOs than what they admit to they are probably right. The question is: What is it that they know? I would wager that they have many high quality videos, photographs, radar images, possibly signals intelligence and other high quality proof that UFOs are indeed craft and they probably are not from here. The one caveat is the Captain Nemo Hypothesis and that is actually less believable and has a lower probability of being true, than the extraterrestrial hypothesis.

When someone like Gordon Cooper tells you that he witnessed a craft swoop down over his head, hover off the ground for a while, put down the landing gear and land, then lift up, pull up the gear and take off like a bat out of hell, I believe him. The interesting thing about this sighting was that Cooper was part of a film project the Air Force was doing on the base this happened at. They caught the whole thing on film which the Air Force took away and never released to anyone who did not have a need to know. That's the way security stuff works. You don't get access to stuff that does not concern you.

I do not believe the stories of captured alien bodies, reverse-engineering projects on crashed craft and all the other stories about the government's involvement in "the alien agenda". I do believe the government has no more knowledge of the origin, purpose or so-called "agenda" of UFOs than does the uninformed public. I can predict that I will be called a government dis-information agent who is just deflecting attention away from the truth in yet another attempt at a "cover-up". I can assure the reader that this is not true and I am not now nor was I ever employed by the government for this purpose. I invite anyone who wants to waste their time to prove me a liar.

Chapter 8 – UFOs

So, does the government have lots of proof of the realness of UFOs? I believe they do, without a doubt. Will they ever release the stuff they have to the public? This is not likely, unless the operators of the UFOs reveal themselves to the entire world, which is also unlikely for a variety of reasons, one of which may be that we just appear to be way too stupid to them. I explain myself below. It is unfortunate that all the nut cases interpret the actions of the government as evidence of a government cover up. This brings up one of the main reasons way mainstream science has not taken this subject seriously; charlatans out to make money.

Charlatans in Ufology

There are so many people making a living on UFO related bull-crap that it just may qualify as a class of industry in its own right. There are literally thousands of books written on hundreds of UFO related topics ranging from abductions to secret government agreements which allow those abductions to happen; in return for alien technology.

The list of books is endless and if you were to select the ones that don't speculate; that is books that just report on factual occurrences (like the UFO Experience) you are left with two or maybe three books at most. That is the extent of the bull crap surrounding this topic and the main reason why scientists don't want to get involved.

My point is and one of the talking points of this book; scientists should be able to "see the forest through the trees" and come to the correct conclusion: Just because there is a lot of nonsense promulgated about a topic; that in itself does not make the topic nonsense! Most mainstream scientists will look at all the bull-crap and correctly point out that we don't have parts of a craft to study. These two aspects are enough to convince them that no serious investigation is warranted. I will be the first to admit that most of the civilian evidence in existence for UFO's is just eyewitness accounting. However, if you happen to be one of the eyewitnesses; you know something very strange is going on. Sure, people misinterpret things they see in the sky, no doubt. The fact of the matter is: The phrase, "I know what I saw" gets an awful lot of use, doesn't it?

If you took my lead and read "The UFO Experience" you already know about some of the strange sightings that turned Dr. Hynek from skeptic to believer. I personally have had four sightings of my own and that is the main reason I am a believer. What do I believe? I believe that some UFOs are real actual physical craft which probably are not of earth origin. Could I have misinterpreted what I saw? Anything is possible but I believe I have been completely honest in the possibilities and I am satisfied that I scrutinized every possible explanation. I will tell you what I saw and then I will discuss the possibilities after each. Before I do that, I present some basic premises about UFO sightings in general.

UFO propulsion

The one aspect that I don't understand about the "mainstream science" attitude about the UFO phenomenon is that fact that these people are just not behaving like the scientists they profess to be. Scientists are supposed to be inquisitive, open minded, far-out minded and above all adventurous. The cowardly attitude most of these people adopt when it comes to the UFO topic,

Chapter 8 – UFOs

is that it is all nonsense so why even give it the time of day? You have an attitude like that and you call yourself a scientist? What a bunch of cowards! What a bunch of non-dreamers! How will science ever advance when people such as you dominate scientific research? I believe the operators of some of these craft (that's what they are; no doubt) display the performance of those machines mainly as a hint (a very big hint) to the dumbfounded human observers who have enough smarts to pay attention. In other words, in many sightings, *that* is the purpose! They are making an attempt to show us how much we don't know but we are too stupid to pay attention!

In UFO circles it is always assumed that "aliens" (if in fact that is what they are) possess a "much more advanced" or "highly advanced" intelligence and I believe that to be true. However this does not mean that we are not capable of understanding their technology. They obviously know stuff that we don't know but that kind of thing occurs here on earth between humans. The tribes in the South Pacific treated aircraft as Gods during WW2. That was because the disparity in intellectual enlightenment was too vast between the islanders and our western technological society.

Recall that intelligence also is dependent on a certain level of spiritual enlightenment and this requires being honest as well as adhering to a number moral attitudes. Truly high intelligence can't be achieved without being honest about everything. I would bet that the operators of these craft are as honest and moral as possible. I'm sorry to say I cannot make the same statement about humanity. Much of the skepticism of UFOs in scientific circles stems from the notion that we already know everything we need to know. It is this narcissistic attitude that always kills intelligence.

To that end, it is very possible that we and the aliens are not that far apart as far as "potential intelligence" goes. What I mean by "potential intelligence" is; the concepts our brains are capable of understanding, which is enabled and limited by the architecture of the human brain. This is of course, dependent that the understanding comes to us in the form of learning which as you already know, always comes from relating what we know to something we don't know. Unless we have the alien's craft propulsion system explained to us, we have no way of knowing whether or not we are capable of understanding it. It is probably very complex but if all the concepts were explained to us we just might be able to understand it. Until we try, we will never know for sure!

My point is this: we cannot assume anything when it comes to UFOs. We may be like the starving mountain climber who only has to climb another ten feet to see the shopping mall parking lot in the valley below. Everything seems complicated until it is explained adequately. The explanation could be in the form of a book that does a good job at explaining things. Of course this would be exceptionally different from human textbooks that very rarely explain anything or put anything in understandable terms. If something is explained correctly, then the only limiting factor will be the intelligence potential of the learner. We just may be smart enough to understand this stuff, if it is explained to us correctly.

My guess about UFO propulsion systems is that they have something to do with "Dark Matter" and "Dark Energy". Everything that is known in modern physics is based upon visible matter; the stuff we can see, i.e. stars, planets; everything we know about. Recent discoveries tell

Chapter 8 – UFOs

physicists that visible matter only accounts for about 40% of all matter in the universe. This means that the other 60% is an entirely different category of matter we really know nothing about and this is called "Dark Matter". This fact could mean that we only understand 40% of the physics present in the universe. Understanding only 40% of anything is not good.

The discovery that the universe is actually flying (accelerating) apart gave rise to the theory that there must be a force doing that and the term "dark energy" was born. Whatever dark energy is; it is definitely a force to be reckoned with. Any force that has the power to accelerate entire galaxies apart is a force that we can say with 100% certainty does exist. Dark energy appears to be an anti-gravity force. That is; it negates gravity and in addition adds a little kick of its own. If the universe were not accelerating apart, none of this presentation would be valid but in fact it is and so we have an interesting situation. We now have a basis for understanding how UFO propulsion could possibly work. We don't understand any of the details necessary to start working on our own propulsion systems but nevertheless we do have a basic idea to work from. The point is; it is possible. It's impossible to predict how probable it is.

Robotics researcher Hans Moravec says we will have human level intelligent machines in 50 years. I think it will be much sooner. Once that happens, it won't matter how much potential intelligence we have, our machines will explain all the complicated stuff (like UFO propulsion) to us, they will be our knowledgeable professors and they will even write our text books for us.

Why don't our space brothers talk to us?

I have had the unfortunate experience of living in close proximity to some people that I believe could be classified as genuine morons. Some of these people wanted to converse with me at every opportunity that presented itself. It did not require much in the way of interaction with these folks to compel me to avoid these people at all costs on subsequent encounters. Why do you think that would be the case? Well for one thing, they really didn't have anything to say that was the least bit interesting to me. They all had the irritating characteristic of repetition. They repeated entire sentences over and over as if I were incapable of being cognizant of the first or second iteration. It was a very frustrating and non-constructive use of time. I came to the conclusion that conversing with these people would be fruitless no matter how many times I attempted some sort of rapport with them.

Could this be why super intelligent entities would not want to make contact with humans? We are just way too stupid. Do you believe that they would have ways of monitoring our communications so that they know as much about us as we know about ourselves? I believe they would if they are real, and I believe they are real. So if that is true, then they are totally aware that we have labeled them as abductors and in some cases, evil abductors who impose their will on a helpless "earth beings" population. This may just be repugnant to them and why would it not be?

So, we have our unfair characterization of them and they are entities we have never met and have never done a single thing to us to warrant our assessment of them. We can add to that, the fact that we just don't appear to be very smart. Remember that there is no such thing as evil or good, there is just stupidity and smarts. If we look at all the evil in the world, we can glean a rough estimate of how much stupidity there is. We have a multitude of situations in the world where people are being slaughtered because of religious beliefs. In other cases, we have stupid communists and their ilk attempting to control everything. This is not a small problem, in fact two of the largest countries in the world are communist and both of them want to spread their ideas to anywhere that doesn't agree with their ideology. This is the stupid attempting to control the smart and this must be super repulsive to a super intelligence. I don't blame them for not contacting us because we are not worthy. Why would they want to talk to a bunch of morons that constantly try to control and gain power over the smart of their own species?

My own experiences

Sighting one

In the summer of 1961 I was 14 years old, a freshman in high school and I was with two high school buddies at about 9 PM in the city of Chicago, IL. We were sitting in a Chicago public school playground bench looking at Sawyer elementary school on the city's south side. One of my buddies was a classmate all through elementary school and he lived just down the block from me in our neighborhood. The other guy was a new friend we had just met in our first semester in high school. We all knew each other pretty well and none of us were known to be victims of hallucinations or any other mental maladies. Since it was summertime, it had just gotten dark but the city is lit up like a Christmas tree every night of the year so things flying in the night sky are easily visible.

We all noticed this craft nearly simultaneously. It was the typical flying saucer with portholes at intervals around the periphery of the craft. It was very sleek looking, and appeared to be like two Chinese woks stuck together, the one on top flipped over to form the top half. The periphery did not come to a sharp edge and was rounded very much like the top and bottom, only had a much smaller radius. There were no lights and it made no sound at all. The only light emitted by the craft was the light coming from the inside which was clearly visible and appeared to be a pure white, similar to the new daylight fluorescent lamps. The outside surface was a flat black color which contrasted greatly with the internal light from the portholes.

This is the really amazing aspect of this story: There was what looked like a man sitting sideways in one of the portholes, looking out and down on the city below him. We could clearly see the inside of the craft which was very bright and we could see activity in the background. The thing that caught my attention in addition to the man was what looked like a stewardess walking in the background with a tray of drinks! The craft was rotating slowly clockwise if viewed from above and when we first saw the man, the porthole he was looking out of was to our right. As the craft moved slowly from right to left (south to north) the porthole with the man slowly advanced from the rear (south) of the craft's movement to the front (north) of the craft's movement.

The craft was only about 100 meters away at the most and it was close enough to enable us to see the inside of the craft and the entire goings on there. I have attempted to estimate the size of the craft and I decided to use the man as a reference. If I accept that the man was indeed a human and of average size, than the portholes would have to be on the order of two meters high and about one and a half meters wide. This is because the man's upper body filled up the window at least by one half and the head was more or less in the center of the window. I remember about six portholes so that equates to a diameter of about 50 or 60 meters for the entire craft with the portholes spaced about the same as their height. This would make the craft about 10 meters high at the thickest point.

We observed this craft for over 5 minutes at which point it had gone far enough north so that we couldn't make out any of the details any longer. We continued to watch as it moved north and it just became a light in the sky. It then appeared to make a right turn and move east towards Lake Michigan where is disappeared. My impression was that this was some type of sightseeing tour and perhaps not all the entities in the craft were all that interested in looking at Chicago, because there was only one guy looking out! Or, maybe he was a wealthy alien and could afford his own little tour of the cities of the planet earth?

I never saw anything like this before or since this instance although I admit I wanted to afterwards. This could be why I have had three other sightings in my life. I look at the sky a lot hoping to see another craft.

What was it?

That is a very good question that I have been asking myself for years and have not been able to answer adequately. I know it was not an airplane of any kind. I grew up right next to Midway Airport in Chicago and I was accustomed to aircraft making the landing approach nearly over our house. I knew what airplanes looked like because I had seen enough of them. Through the years that have passed since this instance, I have attempted to place a worldly explanation on this with no success. The one possible scenario that would even come close to an explanation would have been a lighter than air airship of some kind, at a much higher altitude with cables or ropes suspending the craft we saw hanging underneath. That would have required the airship's engines to be heard which we did not. Remember this was 1961; there were no quiet electric motors nor were there batteries good enough to power them. In addition to that point, it was a clear night and we would have seen anything above it in the sky. This also would not account for the craft's rotation, which would have necessitated the use of a single rope or cable at the middle. This would have caused a lot of instability and we did not notice that. The craft looked very stable and moved very smoothly.

There is really no logical explanation for this except it was some type of gravity defying craft and probably not from earth. Since the beings we saw did not look alien at all, the captain Nemo hypothesis might also be an explanation. Although the entity we saw had the basic structure of a human, it's impossible to say what the features really looked like at the distance witnessed. There are speculations by mainstream science that say intelligent life evolving somewhere else just might have the same basic structure as humans because that would be the most efficient layout; two legs and feet, two arms and hands, a head and torso. While this story may sound fantastic, it is just one of many thousands and thousands of similar things being reported all over the world by credible people like me.

Chapter 8 – UFOs

I was so shook up after witnessing this object that when I got home a few hours later, I called the police to see what they would say. They already had an explanation waiting for me. They said it was an airplane towing a sign. Well, I know that was not true at all. It does prove that there were many other people in the city that saw the same thing and I would bet still remember it to this day.

Sighting two

The second sighting I had was in 1984 in Chicago. It was in the middle of summer and I was working in my backyard. I lay down under the tree to take a break and was just gazing at the sky when I noticed something shiny at a very high altitude directly overhead. It was the stereotypical cigar shaped craft and it was moving slowly from east to west. I estimate the altitude to be at least 30,000 feet simply because if it were a very large aircraft that's how high it would need to be to be for that size. Of course, I was guessing the size as if it was the size of a 747 airliner. It would need to be much bigger if it were higher than 30,000. It was a clear day with only a few scattered clouds and this craft was literally shining like a mirror in the sun. I could make out no wings or tail and it was not shaped like any airplane I ever saw. It was perfectly cigar tube shaped with the ends rounded off nicely and not pointed at all. I watched it for about 5 minutes at which it started to rotate from the horizontal to the vertical and proceeded to move straight up until it disappeared. My impression was that it was not putting on a show, nor was it some kind of sightseeing tour. It looked like it had some other purpose that it had just completed and was going back to where it came from.

What was it?

I do not believe it was any type of airplane and I say that because of its shape, the altitude it was at and the way it rotated to the vertical. I have never seen an airplane do that maneuver, especially an airplane with no wings. I believe it was either an extraterrestrial craft or that guy Captain Nemo was messing with me again!

Sighting three

The third sighting happened in St Charles, Illinois in 1996 at about 3 PM on a partly cloudy day. I was sitting in the cafeteria at work drinking a cup of coffee during my break and as usual I was staring out the picture window at the sky to the north. This object appeared out of nowhere and began dancing around the sky. I watched with amazement through the cafeteria window for a brief time of perhaps 2 minutes and I then decided to go outside to get a better look. When I got outside the object was doing even crazier things than what it did a few minutes before.

It was self-luminous and it looked like a mini sun, it was so bright. It was not very large, although it would be difficult to estimate size, distance or altitude considering there was nothing to reference to. I can just say what my impressions were and it looked to be very small perhaps the size of a small airplane, like a Piper Cub. I would estimate the altitude at no less than 5,000 feet and no more than 10,000 feet. Given the size and altitude estimates I would say that it was about 600 to 1000 meters away. It was so bright that it was lighting up the clouds as it moved in and out of them. There were patches of blue sky with about 70 % fluffy white clouds that day.

Chapter 8 – UFOs

It did all the crazy maneuvers that UFOs have become synonymous for. It did: Loop the loops, zig-zags into 90 degree turns, 60 degree turns and even 30 degree turns after stopping on a dime and reversing direction. This object did things no airplane could do or no pilot could withstand. In fact, I doubt if any unmanned airplane could withstand that kind of punishment. It appeared to defy the laws of physics that say; once an object is in motion it will resist any opposition to that motion. It was doing things that are impossible as far as we know with the physics we know of. I watched it for over 5 minutes, then suddenly; as fast as it appeared, it disappeared. My impression at the time was it was putting on a show for anyone with the common sense to notice and be impressed.

What was it?

Considering the way it was moving, the way it was illuminated and the fact that the movements it performed are impossible for anything we now know about, I would need to speculate that it was indeed some type of extraterrestrial craft or object. Since we know nothing of the physics required for such movements, I cannot say with any amount of certainty if a human (old Captain Nemo) would be able to withstand that punishment or if the craft's physics would protect him. My best guess is that this was from somewhere other than earth. It could be Captain Nemo again but it is less likely. I have considered "ball lightning" as a possibility but that seems unlikely.

Sighting four

The last strange thing I saw in the sky happened in 2004, in suburban Chicago, in the township of Alsip, IL. I was returning from a night college class at about 10 PM driving North on South Pulaski road at about 125th street. I was stopped at the traffic light when I noticed a bunch of multicolored lights in the corner of my left eye and above in the night sky. It was summer and my window was down so it was easy for me to look out sideways and up at the lights. To my amazement there was a strange looking craft moving from north to south and in parallel to the road. It made no sound at all and it had a delta wing shape. The really strange thing about it and what drew my attention in the first place, were its lights.

It had very large "gumball machine" lights under the wing. There were at least five lights under each wing and each light's diameter was about half of the wing's width. The lights were also very long and I would estimate that they were about twice as long as they were wide. They really did look like the proverbial glass dome gumball machine. They were all different colors. Instead of red and green running lights that any aircraft would have, they were yellow, blue, orange, red and green. An aircraft, like a boat, will always have the green on port and red on starboard. These lights were a multitude of colors all mixed up and in disarray.

It was moving very slowly; in fact so slow that it should not have been able to maintain altitude without going into a stall. It looked as if it was standing still and I had to watch it for about a minute to determine if it was actually moving at all. I made a left turn at the light I was stopped at and I parked on the side street to observe the craft which was now moving away from me as I was looking south. It maintained its slow flight path until it disappeared from view obscured by the buildings in the area. It was no more than 500 feet in altitude, probably less than that, depending on how large it actually was. I would estimate the size of the wings to be about that of

Chapter 8 – UFOs

a 737 jetliner. There was no fuselage, only a delta wing and there was no sound at all. My impression was one of complete bafflement. I had no idea of what it was, what it was doing or why it was there. I now guess that it might have been some type of reconnaissance craft, somewhat like the drones we are putting into use now.

What was it?

I did not observe this craft doing anything crazy, other than flying so slow it was nearly hovering. I cannot say with any amount of certainty, that it was not some type of aircraft with the caveat that it was too small to be a lighter than air craft. It made no sound but there were electric motors quiet enough to do the job when this occurred. If it was powered by electric motors it would have to be aerodynamically suited to be powered that way. My opinion is that the huge gumball machine lights would severely alter the aerodynamics of any wing and I do not understand how that particular craft could have even been flying in the normal aerodynamic sense. In this case, I will have to say that I just don't know. I cannot make a determination about this one way or another. I will say that it was very strange and I got the feeling that I was looking at something extraordinary and my gut feeling is that it was not an earthly conventional aircraft and was probably either extraterrestrial or Captain Nemo. The one clue that it was probably not an aircraft is the fact that the lights would make it totally illegal.

The current state of affairs of ufology

There is one group of stupid people who refuses to take the UFO phenomenon seriously and they confound any understanding we could have of UFOs. These are the so-called main stream scientists who are usually also the academic icons of technology. They refuse to take this subject seriously for some reason that I personally cannot fathom. The benefits outweigh the possibility of ridicule from peers or contemporaries. I would think that the prospect of knowing that we are being visited by extraterrestrials would far exceed any perceived threat of being chastised by a bunch of non-thinkers. The resultant truth may have a lot to contribute to the human cause.

With respect to charlatanism, anyone who understands human nature will have a handle on why people fabricate stories about abductions and the like. This undesirable element of the human species should not deter a serious scientifically minded person from seeking the truth. This brings us to the second group of stupid people who undermine the prospects of understanding UFOs. The other group of stupid people is the tin foil hat crowd who spend millions of dollars each year supporting the plethora of charlatans who lie to the "groupies" who religiously follow them. It seems that there is no shortage of people who are so eager to accept the notion that UFOs are extraterrestrial that they inadvertently are eager to accept any bull crap that is fed to them.

The impetus at least in part, for all of this enthusiasm is the many television shows that cheapen the genuineness of the whole phenomenon. These shows play upon the desires of the audience they cater to by "suggesting" things like government cover-ups, recovered crashed craft and videos of things that are routinely promoted as "possible" UFOs.

Chapter 8 – UFOs

The one video that comes to mind immediately is a grainy video of flashing lights sitting on the ground. The narrator espouses the views of the videographer that these craft appeared night after night "mysteriously" and the video luckily "captured" the craft as they were doing their thing. The entire video consists of a bunch of flashing lights with a tree line as a background. That's it. What came to mind when I saw this was the Cheech and Chong movie where Cheech thinks a cop is going to pull them over but then he comes up with the famous words, "Oh Man, it's only an ambulance!" I cannot believe this UFO show wasted my time by showing me crap like this but this is only a small sample of the crap that some of these shows promote.

In my opinion, one of the worst shows in this respect is the History Channel's "Ancient Aliens" series. Its name should be "Ancient False Premises and Convoluted Assumption Aliens". Just about everything presented in this show is based on a false premise of some kind. The narrator usually starts by saying something like this: "If it were possible that a bunch of monkeys were able to grow wings and fly out of my butt, would that be evidence of a family of monkey pilots? If so, is it possible that they would also be able to sing the Star Spangled Banner during flight and if so would they be considered patriotic?"

It pays to take note of the number of instances that the words, "if so" are utilized. This is the majority of what they do on Ancient Aliens. Some of the things they talk about make sense but that amounts to less than 10 % of the show's total content. This is exactly the type of thing that turns off any self-respecting scientist.

What is needed is an honest show on UFOs. A show that carefully screens videos and still photographs so that all the fakes are eliminated before they are ever considered for airing. This would require a lot of preparation and the process would be costly resulting in only a few shows a year. I estimate that there is enough quality evidence floating around to produce possibly two shows of this level each year. If this were done correctly, the ratings for a show like this would be off the charts. The public is eager and waiting for quality information about UFOs. They are weary of the nonsensical stories of abduction and "planet X's" and the giants that ride on it, who are responsible for re-programming in us our intelligence! This is the kind of crap that turns off the average person as well as the scientist.

In regards to obtaining quality photographic and video graphic evidence (you know, like the military possesses), we as civilians have the capabilities to get the evidence that would prove once and for all the UFOs not only exist but they have capabilities non-existent in any worldly produced machines. The only reason the military probably has a bunch of high quality evidence is because they have access to all of the high-tech equipment like high-resolution telephoto digital video and still photo cameras. With the advances in technology available to the public, we should be able to put together a system that will eliminate the possibility of a hoax or manipulation of a video or still photograph in any way.

First of all we need to discard the notion that infrared is the way to go to obtain evidence. This is a big misconception that has been promoted in various UFO "researchers" methods. Many of them are using it just because it has been used in the past and once this so-called evidence is presented, there is no way to discount it because it is just blobs of light and blobs of light are impossible to discount. The thing is; it is just not very useful as evidence because looking at a glob of light proves absolutely nothing. We want to see clear, high resolution photos and videos only. Globs of light in the night sky as well as globs of light on a FLIR system mean nothing, unless that glob of light is doing something really strange as in my third sighting. I have seen people presenting FLIR images flying in formation in the night sky and talking as if this were credible evidence of alien visitors. This is pure nonsense and it is very likely that the image actually was a flock of geese. This is not what is needed or helpful for an understanding of UFOs.

The system we can put together will put an end to scenarios like the above mentioned. We can put together a system using off the shelf parts and integrated into the internet so that encryption can be utilized to virtually eliminate any manipulation of the images once they are captured by the camera. A telephoto high resolution video camera can be mated with a "web cam" interface so that videos or stills are immediately uploaded to a dedicated server that cannot be accessed by any other computer or device. The server would exist solely for the purpose of uploading and storing the videos and stills taken with the specially selected cameras. The cameras would have a browser with encryption suited to ensuring that no hoaxing or faking could be promulgated. The camera could also employ a laser range finder or other optical range finding mechanism to enable the correct size estimation of any object. A GPS system could also be implemented in the system to enable accurate speed, location and direction estimation. The optics could be choreographed with the GPS for range, speed and heading information. We would not only know what the craft looked like but how big it was, how fast it was going and where it was going.

This would require somewhat of a large expenditure, money wise but it will be well worth the effort to anyone who wants a substantial answer for what is going on with UFOs. The camera systems would need to be placed strategically in locations known as "hot spots" to increase the likelihood of capturing something interesting. This may take a while but I believe it would eventually produce results. The cameras may look for years before they capture anything but if we compare this to a program like SETI which has been in operation for over 40 years with no results to speak of, the prospects look much better for this. If we consider the vast amounts of money that are spent on the SETI program each year, this will be considerably less expenditure with the prospect of much higher probability for results.

If and when we do capture a quality image of a UFO, we will know what time it was captured, what the range to the camera was, the approximate size and the speed and heading. It will be tough to explain away something we have on video that registers at 1200 feet diameter going 3000 MPH. Science will have to take this seriously, they will have no choice.

Summary

The study of UFOs is probably the single most important area of study in the history of humanity. The two groups of people that degrade the prospect of a meaningful answer are scientists and tin foil hats. One group is stupid because they refuse to simply acknowledge something because it has not been proven to them yet. The other group is stupid because they believe something because of pure conjecture with no basis of proof. They are both equally wrong in each respect. My personal belief is that this should be given the consideration it deserves because the benefits to be realized far outweigh any effort we can impart.

Chapter 8 – UFOs

I close this chapter by commenting on something that theoretical physicist Steven Hawking said about aliens being a threat to humans because they may want our resources such as water, gold, silver and other rare minerals. I could not have asked for a better example of the concepts I am trying to promote here. It is really obvious to me that professor Hawking does not believe the millions of qualified sensible people who have reported strange things in the sky. My question to him is: Why not? Why do you not believe these people? I happen to be one of the people who have witnessed things and while I will fully admit that it is entirely possible for anyone to experience hallucinations, I do not believe that mass hallucinations are possible. What he is really exposing by his statement is that he does not believe that aliens have been here before, because if they have, they possibly would have taken us over or eliminated us thousands of years ago. An additional and next logical question is: Why don't you believe aliens could have visited earth? There are no logical reasons why they would not have and many logical reasons why they would. It is a matter of odds and probability of what the universe could contain in the way if intelligent life. The odds are very much for alien visitation, not against it.

As far as needing our natural resources, that is pure hogwash. There are asteroids that contain many more rare metals and minerals and they are much easier to get to than what we have here on Earth. Water is also plentiful in the universe and a civilization advanced to the point of interplanetary/intergalactic, time or dimension travel could manufacture water. I reiterate what I have said many times in this writing, there is no such thing as evil; there is only stupidity. Evil is a label humans have placed on other humans that do stupid things. Any beings with an advanced intelligence that would be required to accomplish space, time or dimension travel would not be evil. It's impossible. That particular misunderstanding about the UFO phenomenon is entirely based on a human misperception of intelligence.

Chapter 9 – How to identify stupid people

Prior to providing a methodology for identifying the stupid who walk amongst us on a full time basis, we need to define stupidity at finer, more exacting levels. The reason for this micro assessment of the lack of intelligence is the fact that many stupid people may appear to be stupid on some level but they may also appear to be very smart on other levels. This is evidenced in many successful stupid people in all walks of life. There are many PhD holders who while driving to their professor job at the university will inadvertently tailgate the vehicle which precedes them on the road. This is not intelligent behavior by any measure. This is the kind of behavior that gets people killed, on a regular basis, all over the world.

Some supposedly very smart people can do some very stupid things. Some of the stupid things they do can result in the end of the existence of the people doing the stupid things. In my own estimation, if you do something that you knew was in fact a very dangerous thing to do, then it doesn't really matter how smart you were in all of your other life endeavors. If you are a university professor teaching brain surgery, and you get yourself killed on the way to school because you were tailgating the car in front of you, then your overall level of intelligence has to be assessed as being very low indeed. In other words, one stupid act can negate every smart thing you have ever done or will possibly do in the future. In the real world however, people who do things like tailgating are usually stupid in many other areas as well. In other words, tailgating is a stupidity indicator and as such the probability of acting stupidly in other endeavors is usually very high for those individuals.

It is in this spirit of philosophical rational that I employ my methodology of stupid identifiers. In electronics; the higher a frequency is; the class or category are delineated with "high", "very" and "ultra" with ultra being the highest (not really but it will suffice for this purpose). High frequency is; "HF". Very-high frequency is; "VHF". Ultra-high frequency is; "UHF". I will continue this convention here and categorize stupidity in these three levels. HS is highly stupid, VHS is very-highly stupid and UHS is ultra-highly stupid. I begin my journey through stupid land with the largest identifiable group of stupid people.

Stupid tailgating drivers

Tailgating is a stupid identifier for a myriad of reasons:

- Tailgating the vehicle in front of you will not compel that vehicle to go any faster but many people who tailgate obviously do it for that very reason.
- Tailgating will probably not make your trip faster even if the vehicle in front responds by increasing speed because the next car may not.
- Tailgating decreases the time the tailgater possesses to stop. The closer you are to the car in front, the less time you have to stop, if it stops.

Chapter 9 – How to ID Stupid People

- Tailgating decreases the viewing distance you have down the road. There could be cars crashing and tumbling end over end a mile ahead and you will not know this until the front of your car becomes one with the rear of the car you were tailgating.

It is my personal opinion and a rough guess on my part, that approximately 50% of all people on the earth today have less than optimal life dependent decision making capabilities. I think we can also say with a high degree of correctness that this can be proven empirically simply by direct observation in the things that humans decide to do. If you doubt my estimate, just take a ride on a freeway, toll way, expressway or any roadway where vehicles operate and observe the maintained distance between vehicles.

I'm not sure if tailgaters fall under the HS, VHS or UHS classification. Some of them may be pre-occupied with life problems, illness or crazy bosses. I give those people a HS rank because of the circumstances. The VHS tailgaters may be the young, impressionable, immature or generally misfit part of the tailgating population. The UHS element is the hard-core tailgaters who if questioned, will answer with defiance and will refuse to admit fault. They will say something like, "I have driven this way all my life and I have never been in an accident!" Yeah OK stupid, just keep it up, I look forward to seeing your car piled up someday. I just hope no one else gets hurt besides you.

Stupid communists

This is a topic I alluded to in chapter 6 but it is worthy of more consternation. People that espouse the virtues of communism as being the modern government and economic system of the future might just as well have "I'm ultra-highly stupid!" tattooed to their forehead while simultaneously chanting, "Hey, hey, hey, hey… hey, hey, hey, hey - I'm stupid!!" This consternation includes the people of the media, who unashamedly back up the current U.S. administration; who seem hell bent on installing a socialistic system in a free capitalistic country. I reiterate that these people qualify for the ultra-highly stupid classification of the stupid clan. Communists and anyone who promotes the socialistic principals in which communism is built upon qualify for the UHS moniker.

Progressives and some liberals also qualify for the dubious distinction of the UHS title. Recall that progressives are "time-release" communists who want communism as the government and socio-economic system of choice, but they know that they cannot achieve the lofty goal of pure communism overnight. The people will resist and rightly so. So the clever plan progressives undertake is to subvert the capitalist system one step at a time. They don't care if their plan takes a hundred years. The main objective is what counts and as long as they can achieve that they are happy. But why does this make them happy? Why does the fundamental transformation of a country like the United States of America from a prosperous capitalistic system to one of mediocrity and socialism make them happy? I described the reason for this in the 6th chapter and I will reiterate here: They want that to promote the illusion of their own intelligence, (IRD). That's it and that's all there is to it. These are UHS people who are engaged in an all-out attempt to reverse the label of UHS, which they want to run away from and hide from the world by putting on a mask of what they believe is an indicator of high intelligence. The mask is the outward presentation of being a modern liberal or progressive. Of course they are wrong at many levels but being stupid suppresses the truth.

The list of UHS communists and communist backers is quite lengthy but is easily compiled. In other words, it is relatively simple to identify this group of ultra-highly stupid dim-wits. Just look at most of the members of the Democratic Party as well as members of the so-called news media of CNN, NBC, CBS and ABC news. The Republican Party should not be omitted as a potential source for your UHS, dim-wit search. There are many Republicans who for a variety of reasons, seem to have lost their way. Any Republican that promotes "common core" is UHS. This is because Common Core has the potential to be morphed into an attempt at brainwashing children from the first grade on and up. Remember communists will do anything to promote their ideology including lying to and brainwashing kids about how the country was actually started and how the founding principals were actually implemented. They are lying about America and they are attempting to paint a dark shadow over the character of the U.S. They are doing this to our children so that they will be more receptive to the communist agenda in the future. This is diabolical and UHS!

Normalcy bias freaks

There is a class of dim-wits who are distinguishable usually only at times of distress or need. These are people who lack intellectual skills and because of that are usually on the wrong side of reason at any instance of importance. They will inadvertently assume that everything is fine and dandy even when all indications are that the whole world is about to explode. These are the people who always choose to believe that there is no danger, there is no problem, there is nothing to be concerned with, everything is the way it is supposed to be and that it is normal. They are cowards in essence and this is the main reason they will always decide to go with the status quo rather than taking the difficult path of resistance. Why take risks when all the envisioned things that cowards conjure up might happen? They are not smart enough to see the big picture which usually tells a different story. Smart people attempt to transcend the present and see into the future and they attempt to conjure up all the real possible scenarios that could be harmful or non-productive. Smart people differ from stupid people in that the smart person will attempt to consider *valid* scenarios and not a collection of unfounded assertions that have little probability of ever occurring which is the mark of the coward. This is a big difference.

It has been claimed that only 20% of the population participated in fighting in the American Revolution. The other 80% decided it would be better to stick out the known rather than tempt fate by going with the unknown. Of course when independence was finally won from the British, they were prompt in becoming active in deciding the future for the new country. They reaped the benefits while expending no effort to the cause. They didn't appreciate the possible benefits of independence when the war was being fought and they also didn't see the adverse conditions that were inherent to a continuing British rule. This is an indication of stupidity and in this case it involved 80% of the population of the 13 colonies! What was the level of stupidity? Was it HS, VHS or UHS? I will have to inject my opinion here and guess that the level was HS. I say that because of the obvious conditions the colonists were forced to endure and recognition of the possible benefits of independence. Some folks were just not that courageous and that may have had something to do with the ruthlessness of the British in the way they ruled. You would be

Chapter 9 – How to ID Stupid People

considered a traitor and hung which is delineated by Ben Franklin's famous quote, "We must hang together or we will surely hang separately". So, I guess we cannot blame the 80% too much as being a rebel really did take a lot of guts.

We are in a situation today where the normalcy bias plays a big part in the foreign policy of the U.S. and leaders who preach diplomacy instead of toughness are admired by the dim-wit crowd, who will vote their dim-wit brethren into political office, such as the Presidency. This is partly why stupid people vote for liberals with socialistic leanings and the voters in this case earn an UHS rating. A strong military is usually frowned upon by liberals because of the normalcy bias world view they maintain and that view is; "why worry, everything will be fine". Really, everything will be fine? How do they know that? They don't and being invested in that rhetoric is not only naïve is it dangerous. There are many UHS people in the world and some of them are leaders of very powerful countries. Recall that there really is no such thing as being "bad" or "evil" there is only stupid. The UHS leaders of the USA's adversaries want to promote their countries' imperialism as proxies for their own intelligence. It is the same old story about IRD; only entire countries freedoms are in play in this case. There are some UHS in powerful countries who would like to control the entire world and here in the United States, the normalcy bias freaks that don't believe that statement are also UHS.

The last category of normalcy bias dim-wits is the democratic voters who will actually support, cheer for and vote for politicians that have been caught red-handedly lying not once but repeatedly over and over. The present administration lied about the attack on our embassy at Benghazi, Libya. They said the attack was the result of some internet video and even had the guy responsible for that video thrown in jail. They lied about the program known as "fast and furious" where guns were sold to drug cartel members on purpose. A U.S. border patrol agent was ultimately killed with one of the government supplied guns.

The biggest and by far the most dangerous lie the UHS leaders of the U.S. has told is the nuclear deal they made with Iran. Iran's UHS leaders can be described as an "apocalyptic death cult" who really, actually believes that starting World War Three and bringing about the end of the world will re-awaken some Muslim Imam who has been in hibernation in a well or something of that nature. In this case, the normalcy bias of Democratic Party voters could just give the leaders in Iran exactly what they want; an atomic bomb. Yes that's right; these voters are so UHS that they will follow along in lock-step with every inane foreign policy screw-up their UHS political leaders concoct. Even when the end of the world is at stake, they will not falter from the loyalty of their party because to do so, in their convoluted logic would be an admission of their own stupidity. By now I hope the reader is aware that to not admit fault is a true indicator of stupidity, and in this case happens to be the UHS variety.

The next topic was also covered in Chapter 6 but it deserves a more thorough and in-depth condemnation.

Manmade global warming

The normalcy bias freaks buy this crap which is the reason I insert it here and it follows that anyone who buys this idea, lock, stock and barrel can be deemed stupid. While the UHS

Chapter 9 – How to ID Stupid People

politicians they support tell them disaster is imminent, they interpret this as the truth and refuse to believe their beloved leaders could be leading them astray. In their convoluted thinking, believing everything their leaders tell them is being normal. The leaders are UHS people that are not invested in the idea that everything is normal but on the contrary; everything is by no means normal! In fact, if we don't act and act right now, we are all doomed! The earth will shrivel, dry up and blow away if something is not done and done right now! If you listen to the news media, movies, documentaries, celebrities, etc. etc. etc. they all say the same thing: Global Warming is the most imminent danger to humanity and it is the cause of all the bad stuff going on right now. Global warming has been blamed on: The drought in the western US, polar bears drowning in the Artic, sea ice depleting in the Antarctic, super storms, tornadoes, hurricanes, typhoons, tsunamis, earthquakes and a cornucopia of other stuff that couldn't possibly be connected to climate change. What is going on? Are we all going to die? Well yes we are all probably going to die (someday anyway but probably not from global warming). This will go down in history as the biggest hoax ever perpetrated on humanity.

The earth's temperature has increased by 1.2 degrees F in the last 100 years. That's it; 1.2 degrees. Does this sound like an eminent crisis? The 1.2 degree increase may have some effect on climate processes but it is totally unclear how great of an effect that would be or if there will be any effect at all. One of the huge overbearing problems the global warming advocates have is the fact that none of their projected climate models is working. They predicted a steady increase in global temperature corresponding with an increase in atmospheric carbon dioxide. The increase in carbon dioxide is happening. However the temperature is not increasing as the models predicted but is remaining steady. There are yearly fluctuations but the overall temperature is remaining constant. In fact the temperature average has not increased at all for the past 18 years.

The global warming advocates remain undaunted in their position and remain steadfastly invested in the overall theory. In the meantime, the rhetoric continues to be used to impose harsh restrictions on "greenhouse" gasses emitted by US companies and the EPA is going after the big offenders. The fact is (global warming advocates and the US government don't seem to care about facts) is that the US could eliminate all carbon emissions and it would have zero effect on the total CO2 level of the earth. There happen to be other industrialized countries (China) in the world and they will continue to dump CO2 no matter what the US does. So with the facts as they are and the actions of the US government, what is going on? What is going on is there are three distinct groups of stupid people causing this fiasco.

The first group and the major root cause of the problem are the global warming scientists who first proposed the problem and then became invested in the idea. They are committed to a strategy of "sticking to their guns" because if they don't; they believe they will appear stupid. I do not believe there is any question about whether they are stupid or not. They are clearly in denial and that is one of the clear indicators of stupidity; dishonesty and being dishonest with one's self. The ability to admit fault and just say you are wrong is absolutely imperative to the production of intelligence. I alluded to the importance of spiritual enlightenment in the second chapter and this is a prime example of this concept. I have to bestow the UHS label on them.

Chapter 9 – How to ID Stupid People

The second group of stupid people is the US government entities who are deliberately employing the whole global warming paradigm much to their own advantage. They are stupid; not so much because they believe in the global warming mantra, but because they don't care if it is real or not. They see it as an opportunity to advance their socialist agenda. It is just another way to tax and control the populace. They even had a "carbon credit and exchange" scheme all set up and ready to be used when they were forced to abandon it due to the public getting awareness of this. The software was already developed and if this had been actually implemented it would have been the largest transfer of wealth from the private sector to the government in history. The main reason why progressives like the idea of manmade global warming is that it allows them to put the big thumb of government on American business, who they consider to be their arch-enemy. When they have power over industry, they have control over the same. This is a communist edict. Again, this is UHS.

The third group of stupid people is all the normalcy bias dopes in the populace that never see anything wrong with anything the government says or does. They don't want to believe that the entity that takes care of them in so many ways would be doing anything that is not in their best interest. If the government says manmade global warming is real, than it is and they will fight for the right to believe that. I'm not sure what level to attach to this group so I will compromise with the VHS tag.

There is some late-breaking news about the entire "climate change" fiasco but just to clarify, it is in the form of some well substantiated rumors. It is claimed that progressives are attempting to label climate change denial as hate speech. Yes that's right, you could be arrested and thrown in jail for speaking against the religion of global warming. Of course the odds that such legislation would ever pass are non-existent (for the present anyway), but this is an excellent example of UHS at its finest. This is what the smart are up against in the latest battle in the age old war of the smart and the stupid. So it seems that the Second Amendment is not the only roadblock leftists have in their crosshairs, the First Amendment has to be eliminated to clear the path for worldwide socialism.

Stupid people in the workplace

I have been on more job interviews than I would like to admit. I am being totally honest when I say that the only interviews I had in which I was not "played with" were only the interviews for which I was actually hired. I always wondered why this was so and I also felt there was more going on at these interviews than what met the eye. I finally came to the conclusion that the people that were interviewing me were not that bright. I say this for a number of reasons but the primary reason is that they were obviously playing a role in an unsuccessful, feeble attempt at acting to appear smart. I am not sure if this was the routine for all applicants or if I was singled out but my guess would be that this is standard procedure. I have also considered that the act they were putting on was conceived by someone less than knowledgeable in the field of psychology. This last thought seems to make the most sense as most of the interviewers put a great amount of confidence in standardized questions. Why would anyone use a technique that was not proven, but only someone's "wet dream"? In other words why would anyone dabble in the use of psychology when they had no firsthand knowledge of this complex and often misunderstood science?

Chapter 9 – How to ID Stupid People

The answer to the last question should be obvious by now. The interviewers were in at least, the HS category depending on how much reliance they assigned to standardized questions. Asking people things like, "What is your strong point and what is your weak point" invokes several thoughts in the candidate. One of the immediate thoughts I had was, "Is this idiot for real?" Most of my other thoughts mimicked the first thought and we were on the trail to negativity. Questions like this are only useful in the minds of the idiots that dream up this crap. The amazing thing is: Everyone uses this crap! These are people (interviewers) who cannot think for themselves. They are part of the normalcy bias crowd in that they readily accept anything some so-called expert tells them they should be doing. They accept it without question and that is dangerous. What if the "expert" is a complete idiot? That means that if every business in the U.S. used the same candidate evaluation practices in hiring and those practices were wrong, then every company in the U.S. would be hiring possibly incompetent people. This will not only have an effect on individual companies but it will affect the economy of the whole country and the world. This is the impact stupidity can have on a country and the world. Using untried and theoretical procedures as gospel gets you an UHS rating.

Instead of looking for intelligence traits, interviewers almost always attempt to pigeon hole the candidate in a small specific category. For example if the candidate has a background in electronics and your company produces "Whack a Mole" amusement park machines then it is ludicrous to expect that candidate to know anything about your product. This kind of thing happened to me over and over. The interviewer had no idea on what to look for in a candidate other than find one that had worked on the Whack a Mole somewhere in the past. Not looking for intelligence is itself not very intelligent and I bestow the honor of the VHS title on these interviewers.

I was once called in for an interview at a fire alarm system manufacturer mainly because I had listed "U.S. Navy Fire Control Systems" on my application. In military jargon, "fire control" means controlling things like guns and missiles. These dim-wits automatically associated what they are accustomed to, rather than the terms that would be used for military electronics. They were in the business of "fire alarm systems". Can you imagine being in a top floor in a high rise building that was on fire in the lower floors and you had as your protection a "fire control system"? In other words the system would not be intended to put out the fire but only control it. Would that make you feel safer? They also automatically assumed that ships such as Guided Missile Frigates would have systems which detected fires but this is not the case. They sat in disbelief as I tried to explain that there are no typical building type smoke detector systems on these ships. I knew that because I worked on or knew about everything electrical on those ships. There was even a point where I felt that they thought I was telling them a big fake story about the whole thing. I was almost not hired because of some false belief they had conjured up about the way things were supposed to be but were not.

There was another job interview in which I am 100% positive that the interviewer thought I was lying about my previous job. In this case, I was asked what the technology was of the integrated circuits for the Navy equipment I had worked on. When I told him that it was the old TTL technology, he looked at me like I was crazy. In a short side trip I should explain what the acronym TTL stands for. It stands for "transistor-transistor-logic" and it is one of the oldest technologies for fabrication of integrated circuits. Anyone who has played around with the BIOS

Chapter 9 – How to ID Stupid People

(basic input-output system) in a home computer knows about "CMOS" (complementary metal oxide semiconductor) which is another integrated circuit technology and a bit newer than TTL. Getting back to my point, the interviewer in this case was in the UHS category because he assumed everything about what he thought he knew. He passed up an opportunity to get a competent employee (me) because of his flawed logic. What do you do in a situation such as that? The person thinks you are lying to him because he has some dreamed up view of the way he "thinks" things should be. The only course of action you can ever take is to just tell the truth but that won't work with the UHS which is what this guy was.

If you are lucky enough to evade the gauntlet of HS, VHS and UHS personnel department workers, you then need to brace yourself for the onslaught of HS, VHS and UHS bosses and co-workers that you will be forced to endure. Leading the list of the brain dead is the group who has decided that it is they who are God's gift to the world of whatever the job may entail. Anyone who has the arrogance to pronounce themselves as smart is doing the exact opposite. Recall that really smart people have that built in algorithm that constantly questions whether they are correct in every aspect. As far as arrogance is concerned, it could very well be that some of the educational institutions are responsible for much of this behavioral brainwashing and it stands to reason that kind of thing probably happens much more often at "professional" jobs where the worker is required to hold some type of degree. This is the category of jobs I am familiar with but I'm sure this happens at all professions and at all levels.

I had the misfortune of working as a technician for a highly notable electronics firm as my first job right out of electronics school. The other employees in this department were all engineers and they all had gone to schools that were considered as "correct". I use the term correct because I think it describes the attitude that was prevalent throughout this department. They all thought they were God's gift to the world of electronics engineering. The smugness, arrogance and pure narcissism were overwhelming and disgusting at the same time. These people were jerks. The really amazing thing was that they weren't as smart as they portrayed themselves to be. They made lots of mistakes, some of which were in the high dollar category. I ended up solving many of their ongoing problems and they thanked me by covering up that fact and taking all the credit. To them the relationship between a technician and engineer was exactly equal to nurse and doctor! This is indicative of a grandiose delusional mind that is always associated with stupidity. This is usually the case with overinflated egos and self-appointed grander.

The reason this type of individual cannot live up to their own projected image is because when images are projected as infallible, they are bound to fail because humans are always fallible. We all make mistakes but that class of stupid refuses to believe *they* can! That also means the image maker is attempting to cover up their own inadequacies. Even people with high powered degrees from high powered schools can qualify for a title of UHS. I would have to say that my observation of this gaggle of dopes was that some of them were at the HS category while others earned the VHS and UHS tag. This is a crystal clear real world example that it doesn't matter what kind of degree you hold or what your job position is. Anyone can be stupid, it all depends on attitude.

The last group of stupid people you will encounter at work are your stupid peers or co-workers. These are people who will attempt to make you look stupid while simultaneously making themselves look smart. Some people call this "competition" but I consider competition to be a fair assessment of two or more individuals' capabilities and this is not that. These people don't want a fair competition, they want to stack the deck, dope the dies, get favoritism from the referees, etc. In other words, they *want* to play "dirty pool". Many of these people are also control freaks who will watch for the right circumstance to immerge and proceed to order their co-workers to do whatever they were going to do anyway. I have had that sort of thing happen to me so many times that I am convinced that the behavior must be a universally common trait in certain personality types (stupid sociopaths). These are typical behaviors for stupid people and so when this happens to you, be confident that they wouldn't be using those tactics if they had brains. They need to lie, cheat and steal because they are not intelligent enough to be promoted by their own merits. Don't feel sorry for them because I assure you they will not reciprocate. These people can be classified at any of the three levels because the range of underhandedness they are capable of can be found anywhere in a continuum of stupidity.

Stupid voters

The stupidest voters are the dead people who are too stupid to realize they are dead, and continue to vote (usually for the democrat candidate) for years after their demise! Wait a minute; I may be mistaken here, it's not the dead people but it all the UHS who cast votes as a proxy for dead people! People who commit voter fraud are the stupidest people in the world for a number of very simple reasons. They are prime examples of the IRD hypothesis and if we analyze their possible motives that will back up my claim. Why would anyone attempt to subvert the voting process in order to advance the candidate they are backing? The only logical reason for this behavior is that these super-dopes believe that it is *they* and their kind who own the right ideas about the way things should be. In other words they don't do it for money, although there may be someone who is getting paid to act out the desires of the true instigators. If there are any paid stooges, these people are also stupid but for different reasons. If we attempt to look into the minds of the instigators we will get an idea of how important it is to be recognized as being intelligent. In their minds, they are so smart that committing the act of fraud is not important because the ends really do justify the means. The fact that they are turning the democratic system upside-down is of little consequence to them because, after all; they are the ones that have the right ideas! This is a prime example of how stupidity can end up destroying the freedom of humanity.

Another stupid voter is the voter that votes for a candidate strictly because they believe the candidate is "good looking" or perhaps displays charisma. Other inane reasons are: The candidate is black, white, Hispanic, Asian or a woman. The ideology of the candidate is unimportant to them and they usually vote for people in the same party over and over regardless of what their party has evolved into or the performance of the members of that party in recent times. These are the voters that can qualify for at least the HS award and we all would be better off if they just stayed home on voting day. These are the people who can destroy a free country in a very short amount of time because of the fact that they have no knowledge of the important issues which may have adverse effects on everyone.

Chapter 9 – How to ID Stupid People

Stupid people in daily life

There is a sure-fire way to identify stupid people in a public arena such as work, school or basically anywhere that groups of people can hear or be within earshot of conversation. It is very simple. Merely talk about stupid people and make your conversation loud enough to ensure the other people in close proximity will hear you. Invariably the stupid people will believe you are talking about them! This also works on social media with text as the information carrier. This is more proof that stupid people will promote their ideas such as socialism to advance the notion that they are smart because they have a preconceived underlying instinctive notion of their own stupidity. They are smart enough to realize that they are not so smart, but not smart enough to admit it!

This phenomenon also presents itself when talking to medical doctors. The patient mentioning of an incompetent doctor can somehow transfer that incompetence to the doctor in the room. Some doctors don't like stories of their brethren being incompetent and of course that somehow translates and transfers to them the label of being stupid. A really smart doctor will know you are not talking about him, and that is only common sense, isn't it? How can you be properly diagnosed if you don't tell the doctor what you have already been through? Sometimes just doing that will get you in trouble because you cannot tell stupid people by just looking at them and doctors are no exception.

Miscellaneous stupid people

1. People who exhibit any of the negative emotional traits.
2. People who are control freaks.
3. People who make judgements about other people's intelligence solely based on appearance. It is impossible to judge intelligence this way but stupid people do it on an ongoing basis.
4. People who will become amused at another's accomplishments. This usually presents itself as glibness and an attempt at discrediting the mark.
5. People who make judgements about other people's intelligence based on their "station in life" i.e. the job they have, the neighborhood they live in, the car they drive, etc.
6. People who make judgements about other people's intelligence for any reason other than to hire them for a position in which there will be a monetary benefit from that judgement. There are no valid reasons otherwise with the possible exception of looking for a mate.
7. People who attempt to obtain favors from you on a regular basis. This behavior is indicative of sociopathic behavior.
8. People who attempt to make you feel guilty on a regular basis. This is also indicative of sociopathic behavior.

Chapter 9 – How to ID Stupid People

Summary

We are constantly immersed and drowning in a sea of stupidity. The simple act of observing how many drivers tailgate should be an indictment for the general intelligence level of the population. Certain behaviors indicate stupidity and it follows that it is relatively easy to identify stupid people if we merely observe. When this is accomplished on an ongoing basis, it will become clear that the hypotheses I propose here are valid.

Reader's Notes

Chapter 10 - The Future

The future holds just two possibilities for humanity. Both possibilities depend on what happens in the United States in the upcoming national presidential election. The first possibility is that the stupid side will win this battle in the age old war between the smart and the stupid. The second (and less likely) is that the smart will gain the upper hand. If the stupid side wins, the United States will become a socialist state and the freedoms now enjoyed by the population there will disappear. Guns will be taken away, there will be government run healthcare and the government will control every aspect of everyone's life. Freedom will only be a fond memory of the past. If the smart side wins, freedom will prevail. It really is as simple as this.

Another facet of the loss of freedom is that there will be no place on earth for anyone living anywhere other than the United States to run to. The earth may be plunged into perhaps centuries of darkness and misery. The reason this is so is because the United States might deteriorate into the worse possible dictatorships the world has ever known. Once socialism has taken root, it is only a matter of time and then there will be government oppression like the world has never seen. It must be this way because Americans have had a taste of freedom and those memories are long lived. There is also the very real possibility of civil war triggered by some draconian gun grab laws that are passed because of a liberal majority federal Supreme Court. Once the Supreme Court has been taken over by liberals, the second amendment will be forgotten as a relic of ancient history. If it is remembered at all it will be thought of as a small foot note in an outdated document, written by a bunch of racist white slave owners, strictly for the purpose of establishing a government-run militia.

The reason I believe the stupid side might win is because of the methods the stupid use to gain control. Recall that I said the stupid need to resort to underhanded techniques in order to maintain control simply because; the stupid own stupid ideas which are not defendable. They have to lie to their constituents and maintain a constant state of hypnosis about the true state of affairs. Voter fraud is another form of lying, cheating and stealing. Smart people do not need to resort to practices such as voter fraud and in fact they find any type of fraud repugnant. This is so because they know that if we have a system in which anyone can cheat to win, then we all lose in the end. The stupid have a hard time understanding that concept.

Stupid people always are short sighted. This is evident in every bit of legislation they attempt to pass into law. They will go to great extremes to promote their agenda including destroying the economy of an entire country. If people have to be sacrificed along the way, so be it. Nothing is more important to the stupid than is the desire to be recognized as intelligent. This is the Intelligence Recognition Desire (IRD) that I explained throughout this book. This motivates the stupid into doing things that only can be categorized as sub-human behavior. The primal desire of IRD will compel the stupid to do just about anything they deem necessary to achieve the goal of perceived intelligence.

Chapter 10 - The Future

The stupid are capable of murder, enslavement, torture, brain washing, subterfuge and just about anything they believe will help their cause. They see only what the immediate results might bring to bolster their agenda and not the human suffering that is produced as a direct result of the stupid policies they promote. They must control others in order to get into power in the first place and they don't care if a million people have to die in the process because "the ends justify the means". This is stupidity at its best (UHS).

The sad part of all of this is that the nasty tactics the stupid utilize usually work. The people in countries like the former Soviet Union had nothing to say about the conditions in their county. The leaders rule with an iron hand behind the "Iron Curtain". The "Bamboo Curtain" was used to refer to Communist China and the difficulty people living inside had in viewing what was going on in the rest of the world. The people in Communist China still do not have access to the largest social media website; Facebook. Totalitarian governments need to maintain the total control they have over all the people, all the time because they know that if people are allowed to discuss, dissent or criticize the government they just may begin to realize how much they are getting screwed over. The leaders of these countries do not want civil unrest because it threatens the complete power they have over the people and they usually crush any uprising in a prompt and brutal manner.

Two of the three most powerful countries in the world are now communist countries. Many people believe that the former Soviet Union is now a democracy but that is simply not true. The Russian Federation is about as socialist as a country can get. They only allowed some of the satellite states to become "independent" but Moscow still has a great deal of influence over many of them. A good example of this is the current situation in the Ukraine. The Ukrainian people want to be aligned to Europe economically but mother Russia does not see it that way. Is the Ukraine independent? It sure doesn't look that way from Vladimir Putin's point of view. If the Ukraine succeeded in becoming aligned to Europe that would be a major blow to Russia's influence in that part of the world and in reducing its power generally. They can't have that because if the Ukraine is economically successful it will leave "egg on the face" of "Pooty-Poot". Remember, *appearances* count for a great deal in the stupid's control over the smart. It is a constant propaganda effort that must be maintained at all costs to prop-up the illusion that everything is great.

If knowing that two of the three major powers on earth are communist (stupid) controlled counties then the harsh realization that one large remaining so-called "free" country is slowly drifting towards communism should be terrifying. This notion *is* terrifying; to the smart anyway. The county I speak of is of course; the United States of America. There is currently a movement in the U.S. that is attempting to promote communism as the model governmental structure for the "modern" 22nd Century. This is happening in a majority of universities throughout the country. Universities have for the most part been taken over by liberals who would like to see communism viewed as "the future"!

If the prospect of communism being promoted at the higher learning level is frightening, than the specter of a commonly designed and arranged curriculum that also promotes communism from the first grade and up should make us all crap in our pants! This is actually happening and it is called "Common Core". When this was first unveiled to the public it was touted as being only a

Chapter10 – The Future

"test standard" for grades one to twelve. The truth of the matter is that in order to comply to test standards; the curriculum would also need to be standardized so that "the correct" subject matter would prepare students for the eventual test. Besides changing basic subjects like the way math is taught, it turns the primary school curriculum on its head, teaching things that many parents would find objectionable if only from a moral viewpoint. Things like sex education have become standard for kids in the first and second grades. Perhaps this is a tad too young to be learning about things that mom and dad have not even talked about yet?

The Common Core folks don't care what negative effects of this might foster because after all, they are the stupid (they don't know that; if they did, they would be smart) who do not care about that sort of thing. They only care about controlling others that *they* have decided as being too stupid to look after themselves. They are ranchers and they have to prove to all us "cattle" that they will take care of us in every way! One way they plan on "taking care" of us is that the kids in common core will be monitored for things like heart rate, skin resistance (similar to a lie detector) and other biological signals. This will be part of the kids dossier that the government will keep forever that defines who your kid is, what they are capable of doing, and what they are best suited to do!

In the future, it is possible that the individual choice aspect of the human existence will be non-existent and the government will tell everyone what they will be doing as a profession; provided they will not be sent to some extermination camp. The last statement might seem extreme but what if a child didn't fit in to any of the government approved professions? The only logical next step would be elimination; which of course would be for the good of the collective! If you don't think this is possible here in the U.S. than think again because humans are capable of doing anything if they are stupid enough and it is my contention that there is enough stupidity to far exceed the necessary requirement. Where does all this stupidity come from? In other words, how do people, who otherwise are capable of doing the things that are necessary to keep themselves and their families alive while functioning well enough to navigate through the world, get so stupid?

Stupid people get stupid for a number of reasons. One of the reasons is the manner in which they are brought up, in other words; the attitude of their parents. Another reason and in my opinion, the largest factor is; the educational system. We are in the undesirable situation today where we are as a country, moving away from personal freedom and moving towards a socialistic type of country that the people in Russia want to get away from. The stupid people that are pushing for this "transformation" need to get into people's heads while they are still malleable and susceptible to stupid ideas. If they wait until the kids are in their 20s then it is too late. The people who come here from Russia cannot believe that we want to be where they are at and have been at since the Bolshevik revolution. They think we are nuts and they are right; at least some of us are nuts because if you recall, stupidity and insanity have the same underpinnings.

One of the defining factors in the socialistic shift in attitudes in most stupid people today is because of brainwashing they have received in the public education system. They are already being brainwashed about the many benefits of socialism in many parts of the country and the adoption of Common Core will not have much of an affect in these liberal places across the country. The only thing that Common Core will add to the educational system in those places is

Chapter 10 - The Future

the systematic data collection from each child that will be kept in some government database forever. The other tenants of Common Core have already been preached in these places for years. I have firsthand experience with this as my daughter grew up and was schooled in Chicago. The Chicago public school system brainwashed my daughter on a number of issues that should not even be a part of the curriculum for any public school.

Here are some of the "educational subjects" I remember her talking about:

- Manmade global warming is a fact and has been proven beyond a reasonable doubt.
- The Second Amendment only guarantees guns to the militia which is the National Guard. Guns are evil instruments of death and the reason so many children are killed every year. Gun control works because everywhere that guns were banned the crime rate went down.
- Fat is bad for you, in fact it will kill you. You can eat all the sugar you want but stay away from evil fat. Fats may just be as evil as guns (I added that part).
- Union manipulation of wages and the administration of a minimum wage is good for the economy. The teacher that put this out probably never even took an elementary course in economics.
- The rich never pay their fair share. Tax increases raise funds for the poor people who have been cheated by their rich bosses.
- Capitalism is evil as it allows the rich to control the poor and is always unfair.
- Social programs are good for the country and they ensure that we are all taken care of.

This is the kind of garbage the inner city schools have been dishing out for years. Cities like Chicago where the illegal population is close to one half of the total, is a petri dish for communism and socialism. Does the illegal population vote? The ones that have gotten social security cards might. How many of them have Social security cards? Probably quite a few have obtained them in nefarious ways. Even if the voting age population can't vote now, in only a few years the crop of young sculls full of mush will graduate and be added to the liberal/socialistic voting rolls to ensure a steady stream of democratic candidates always win office seats and continue the machine politics. By the way, the validity for each topic above is "false".

This is a diabolical situation that will go on forever if something is not done and done soon. Once Common Core is the curriculum of the entire country, it will only take about ten years for the democrats to be in control forever, even if the smart side wins the upcoming election. There are some stupid Republicans who believe in Common Core. These individuals are naïve at best and stupid at worse because they should understand that while this might help progressivism, but there will likely be only one type of progressive following the ten year period; democratic progressives. These RINOs are unconsciously sealing the fate of the Republican Party by backing Common Core, not to mention dooming the entire country to the slavery of socialism.

If the smart people of the United States are able to rid themselves of the plight known as Common Core, they still have a formidable enemy which is called the "main stream media". Nearly every media outlet, with few exceptions such as Fox news, has been drinking communist soft drinks for so long they have bought the grand utopia of communism lock, stock and barrel. I hope I haven't frightened all the liberal democrats reading this with my reference to evil gun

Chapter 10 – The Future

parts. If I were really mean I would chew a pop tart into the shape of a gun and show it to a democrat. They would probably faint from fear.

The stupid media has become a macrocosm for the stupid at large. They display all of the characteristics that I have listed as the things NOT to do if one wants to be smart. They willingly submit themselves as stupid stooges for their stupid allies in the government. They reinforce, back-up and lie, cheat and steal in order to promote the current administration as being right and righteous all the time and about everything. Nothing, absolutely nothing the current administration does is bad in the eyes of the main stream media. Make no mistake, this is simply because of the desire to be deemed intelligent (IRD) and these really stupid media people have convinced themselves that this is the way to prove themselves as being smart.

This is a problem for one reason. The reason is that there are people in this country who believe all the socialistic lies not because they were educated in the Chicago Public School system but because they are simply stupid or they have been raised in an environment that promoted the same types of ideas. People that have depended on the government for many years and people that grew up in households where there were union members who didn't really understand what their unions were doing to them, etc. This is a case where inherent stupidity plays a dominant role. In chapter 6, I talked about how a bell shaped curve was representative of things that could be considered to be "normal". This is where the "normal distribution" is predominant in every respect.

If we were able to accurately measure human intelligence, I suspect that the level of intelligence plotted would have a fair amount of fidelity to the normal distribution. I also previously alluded to the possibility of brain structure being directly proportional to intelligence. In other words, I believe that it is the way individual brains are wired that either promotes or inhibits intelligence. This theory just makes sense because if intelligence is dependent on specific brain architecture then it stands to reason that if an architectural design is adhered to (during natal development) the possibility of *that* brain achieving intelligence is much greater than a brain that did not adhere to the important design criteria features. This is where probability of adherence to design features is the controlling factor for the percentage of the population who can be intelligent and vice versa. The controlling factors may not have anything to do with memory structure but may be more related to the common human emotional traits which we should all be born with but unfortunately in some cases, nature makes mistakes.

Some folks will never be able to achieve high intelligence simply because of personality traits. I previously alluded to the sociopath and how these people will never admit they are wrong. In addition to never admitting error, they also may have the liability of the inability to question their own unwillingness to admit fault of any kind. This may be more of a genetic inherited trait than it is a learned phenomenon and it may be more a primary controller of intelligence level than is the exact wiring memory architecture of the brain. In other words, some people are stupid because they simply love themselves too much and this cannot be circumvented by any known means because these people may be programmed to be this way.

The defining final question and where this is all going is that humanity's freedom which is directly dependent on the majority of people being smart may be totally dependent on some

Chapter 10 - The Future

random biological genetic programming which cannot be easily predicted. What can be done however is attempt to educate the set of people who may have been brainwashed by their parents and the school system but if presented with the truth, may just have a change of heart. In addition to enlightening the older, it is imperative that all forms of things like Common Core are eliminated to prevent the young's indoctrination.

If the reader is confused about the amount of social science rhetoric I am presenting here, this is the reason: humanity's freedom will enable any increase in intelligence and intelligence cannot progress if man is not free. There is very little innovation in countries where there is a lot of repression. The majority of the technological breakthroughs in the last 100 years came from countries in the "free world". Totalitarian countries usually just steal the technology from free countries and claim it was developed independently on their own. This has happened too many times to be ignored. If communism realizes its goal of world domination, the probability of a continuation of the advancement of technology is very low. The world will enter into a new dark age.

RAI - what will it bring?

In the midst of the various battles raging during the stupid/smart war, humanity is plodding along in a feeble attempt at developing a RAI system. An important question which I personally believe many people would very much like an answer to is: How long will it be before we achieve a real intelligent machine? The answer to that question depends to a large degree on the attitudes of the scientists involved in the research. If they have the entrenched belief that humans are some kind of mystical beings instead of a programmed machine, it will be a very long time, indeed. Another question which is a logical progression of the first question, is: When we do have RAI will we even bother giving what it tells us any credence? I may not be able to completely answer the first question but I can give a reasonably accurate projection of how the second question is answered. I don't believe we will listen to what the RAI machine has to say, at least at first. The reason this is so has to do with the types of people who will be asking these really smart machines questions. They won't all be smart people.

Many of the people using this new technology will undoubtedly be government types. This is due to the fact that RAI will require substantial amounts of cash to develop this technology and therefore it just stands to reason that the people who paid for it (actually it will be the common people who paid for it but that never stopped government types from acting like it was theirs) will have first dib's on using it. The biggest obstacle in the use of RAI will be giving it credence after it is up and running.

I now want to play a little fantasy game in which we can pretend that IBM has developed a RAI machine and they turned over the first working version to the Obama administration. Almost immediately, the RAI machine will begin telling the users (the president and his cabinet and advisors) that they are doing everything wrong! It will tell them that government run healthcare will be a disastrous idea and will destroy the best healthcare system in the world. It will tell them that any further attempts at gun control are not needed and will actually harm the security of the country. It will tell them that the southern border needs to be secured and that any form of amnesty will only result in more illegal immigration. It will tell them that the size of government

Chapter 10 – The Future

needs to be reduced as the best way to reduce spending. It will tell them that the military needs to be cleaned up not cleaned out. It will tell them that the amount of socialism applied to the populace is directly proportional to the economic health of the currency. I know there are many more things it would tell them but the ones listed here should give the reader an idea of what it will be like. Do you think the current administration would listen to these revelations? I don't think so. Do you think stupid people would listen? Ditto.

So we can see that the mere acquisition of a RAI device would not guarantee that it would produce instant results. There could be scientific advances but that would be subjected to the same types of usage problems. Many scientists are invested greatly in their own theories and will go to great extremes to prove that they are traveling down the correct avenue. They would have the option of listening to a RAI machine or arguing with it. Many of the scientists that are invested in manmade global warming would fall into this category. No matter what the RAI device told them they would not give up the ship easily. There would be a lot of disagreement with arguments such as "they are only machines" and that sort of thing. This is common stupid behavior and since the stupid do not listen to and constantly attempt to discredit the smart, there should be no paradigm shift instantly with the advent of RAI.

When RAI is accepted as a bona fide intelligent friend, humanity will be on the way to a technological utopia. All of the problems we now face or will face in the future can be potentially solved. We will also be able to achieve anything we can dream of including immortality. If the "singularity" ever comes to fruition, it will most likely happen only after we are firmly in the use of RAI. This far-out concept requires that the human memory be mapped physically and the technological means to access that physiology be completely understood. If and when that happens, we can become immortal, this is high probability. I do not believe this will be possible without RAI as this will require the type of processing that will only be available with a RAI machine. I believe that a more likely scenario is that we become immortal not because we have been transposed into a machine but because we understand everything about the brain and body. This could include making biological copies of ourselves and transferring our memories to our new bodies.

There have been many books and articles written on the dangers of human level intelligent machines. One of the main fears is that the machines will find us unnecessary and decide to eliminate us. I alluded to this in chapter 5 and I will address this concern once more, here. I do not believe that this is a legitimate concern to be fearful of, because when we conjure up these fears we do so; on a purely human basis of emotional origin. We view the world and everything in it from a human perspective and that includes our emotional traits. Recall that RAI will have no emotional traits because if we wanted them to have these purely human functions we would need to program that stuff into them. Programming emotions into machines would not be easily done, in any case. Regardless of the complexity, we wouldn't want to do that anyway because it would make our new RAI machine dumber not smarter.

If we are successful at RAI, the reason we created an intelligent machine in the first place, was to compensate for human inadequacies. One pitfall of the brain is the biological memory mechanisms that produce intelligence are not reliable. Another pitfall is the fact that we have those nasty human emotions which were useful in social environments but are just a hindrance in

Chapter 10 - The Future

the production of intelligence. Why would we go through all the research, design and development of RAI systems that would purposefully include the nasty traits we wanted to eliminate in the first place? We wouldn't do that because it would negate the pure intelligence we are hoping to achieve. The people that espouse concerns about machines taking over the world are committing a cardinal sin of intelligent behavior: They are talking about stuff they have no real knowledge of. Want to be smarter? Don't talk about stuff you know nothing about!

Summary

I do not have a clear prediction for the future events in humanity's advancement in intelligence. I can only guess what will transpire given the current situation in the world and especially in my home country of the USA. Using the current political climate and the clear victories the stupid side has won in recent years I have to arrive at a somewhat gloomy picture for freedom which is directly dependent on the overall level of intelligence of the populace. It seems that the stupid side is winning the war at this particular battle in history. They are fighting to win and they are pulling out all the stops in using every underhanded, dirty dealing historically used tool of the stupid camp. This is a critical time in American history and what happens here will have a profound effect on people all over the world probably for the next one thousand years.

If the stupid side wins the USA, there is very little chance of any further technological advancement but that may be the least of our problems. There are a couple of countries in the world that have wanted to see our destruction for over 60 years. They just may get the chance to do that given the fact that our Armed Forces are being reduced to levels lower than before the start of World War Two. So, if we thought things couldn't get any worse by our own country's stupid taking control of the USA, we may be in for a shock when the stupid of the world attempts to take us over. This is truly a frightening moment is history and I hope that the people who voted for "Hope and Change" in the last two elections will see the light and vote for "freedom" in the next dozen.

Epilog

Intelligence is not what current belief professes it to be. Intelligence is all about survival and in the survival game, if we don't advance, we decline. So, just learning what is already known is not an indicator of intelligence. The true indicator is creating new ideas and concepts out of what is already known. This is known as technological advancement and it is totally necessary for humanity's survival.

Intelligence is the main driving impetus of all human action. This is because we are programmed to value intelligence and this may be due to its value as a survival tool in early human development in groups. I call the main driving force IRD for intelligence Recognition Desire. There is also the characteristic of assessing other's intelligence in an ongoing never-ending trait I call ICP for Intelligence Comparison Phenomenon. This probably has roots in early human groups so individuals could establish some kind of intelligence level pecking order.

Human intelligence is produced with a specific architecture of storage and retrieval of information. Since most people are born with the required architecture, then it stands to reason that intelligence is mostly due to emotionally driven behavior. This is another way of saying that we all have the required hardware and it depends on how that hardware is used as to whether an individual is functionally smart or stupid. We also need to remember that emotions are another built-in hardware aspect and therefore any discrepancy there might also have a dire effect on behavior.

My belief is that the main biological reason for stupidity is the way we inherit emotions from the genetic pool of our ancestors. Some people just get shortchanged when it comes to getting a fully functioning set of emotions at birth. These are the people that get labeled as sociopaths and usually the one emotion that is flawed and is a bastardization of the intended design of the in-born love emotion. Without the ability to outwardly love and care about others, it seems that the love they have for themselves gets multiplied over what it would have been with a "true to specs" love emotion. When people love themselves that much, it becomes impossible for them to admit that they are wrong and that they have other flaws. They want to believe they are perfect and so that gets projected into every action they take in life. If everyone were like this, humanity would have perished thousands of years ago.

What this means is that it could be that there is no cure for true stupidity at this point in time. The level of intelligence could be due to how many people get left out in the emotions game. Being born with a corrupted love emotion is probably very much like being born gay or lesbian. These people will tell us that they were always like that and they were born that way. It is not a matter of choice; in fact they all say they would not have chosen to be that way on purpose mainly because of the misunderstanding and mistrust they receive on a daily basis. It is tough being gay or lesbian mainly because of all the stupid people who stand in judgement of them. They can't

Epilog

help the way they are any more than the sociopath can repair the love emotion they have inherited.

The construction of biological machines such as humans is governed by the laws of mathematics and as such, it is evident that the number of criteria for being labeled a sociopath will vary from zero to infinity. People can just have a propensity for lying to cover up weakness or they can end up being be full blown sociopath serial killers. It is a continuum of characteristics from the slight to the severe. Humanity's freedom will ultimately depend on the average number of truly stupid people there are. We may survive, but our freedom is not guaranteed by any measure.

There is no doubt that many of the comments I have made in this book will anger many people. I also have no doubt that the people who will be angered by my words are probably stupid. This is common sense. The important point is that I don't care how angry stupid people become because what I have said here is the truth and there is no way of being politically correct with stupidity. Don't like what I said here? Tough. You are the people who through your stupidity will eventually cause the slavery and misery of hundreds of millions of people, many of whom will undoubtedly be smart people. Everyone suffers because of your denial about the level of your own intelligence.

RAI machines have the potential to grace humankind with the complete knowledge of everything. This includes cures for biological human intelligence failures. These machines will help humans in the quest for a complete knowledge of everything. The only obstacle in the way of solving any problem is the lack of knowledge and understanding of the problem at hand. The development of RAI will give us the ability to save us from ourselves. We really need to do it and it is not just a nice thing to have, it is necessary. If this book sounds like I am trying to transmit a dire warning, then the reader has grasped the meaning entirely, because I am.

A few years ago, I produced a condensed very terse version of my ideas for the optical memory described here along with the same basic explanation of what produces thought. I presented my paper to what was supposed to be an AI conference group, the members of which were all supposed to be "experts" in this field. Not one of the members came close to understanding the basic concepts of my ideas. All of the comments were negative and they all went far beyond criticizing me for lack of technical expertise. Some of the comments were just plain nasty. This speaks volumes and does the reader care to guess why? I hope by this point this analysis should be easy. When people get nasty, they do so because they feel threatened in some way. In this case, they were projecting their fear of being found out as an incompetent, I think it is pretty obvious. The one comment that will always stick in my mind was, "This paper is mainly philosophical psycho-babble. I was expecting to find new memory modules, but there were none." He went on further with this, "Arguably, memory is only a small aspect of brain function, the largest problem being the mass parallel processing problem."

There is a mass parallel processing problem; really? Wow that's amazing. I didn't know that. After all, how could I know that when it simply isn't true? The ability of the brain to take inputs from a multitude of modules (for thought) is really no big deal and to say it's the biggest problem is just ludicrous. It is bad to be criticized by the competent, but to be criticized by the UHS is

220

really an experience you do not easily forget. It drives home the correctness of the hypothesis that I have presented here.

This is the type of backlash you can expect from people whose only purpose in participating in a conference such as that is to promote their own smarts while simultaneously making others (like me in this case) to appear stupid. This is a classic example of IRD. The interesting thing is the fact that if this individual knew anything about computers or AI, he would have understood what I was talking about and it is very apparent that he did not, which makes the post-mortem of his comment easy. He might have been expecting some "more of the same" memory technologies but why would he expect that? I stated very clearly that it was an entirely new concept. My opinion is that when someone is downright nasty like this guy was; they might as well sign their remarks as, "written by stupid".

I close this by stating that there are no guarantees that humans will remain free. This is because the war between the smart and the stupid continues to this day and will always be until the day comes when humans develop an anti-stupid vaccine. I can only hope that the electorate in the United States rejects the socialism which has taken over the entire Democratic Party and a large portion of the Republican Party in the United States. If these UHS gain control this time, all hope is lost for humankind's freedom for decades to come, perhaps forever. I believe the mechanism I have presented for brain function demonstrates that humans are all pretty much the same, hardware wise. The big factor in the lack of intelligence is the fidelity of inherited emotions to design specification.

The big question mark in all of this is the smart people who have potential high intelligence but have been brainwashed with Democratic Party soda pop. It is they who will decide whether humans remain free.

A scenario that didn't happen but could have

Hillary Clinton becomes president of the United States. Immediately after taking office she appoints the most liberal justice she can find to the Supreme Court. Shortly thereafter justice Ruth Bader Ginsberg becomes too ill or passes away leaving another open seat. Hillary fills that seat with another liberal. She also has stated publicly that she wants to sue firearm manufactures for liability if their guns are used in crimes. This is akin to suing Ford Motor Company because someone used a Ford pickup truck to drive up a sidewalk and mow down a bunch of pedestrians.

This is the type of convoluted logic that people like Hillary Clinton believes in. Her stupid followers have no idea what the second amendment is all about and to them guns are just scary instruments of death which in their feeble minds should be eliminated for the safety of the public.

When the next challenge to the second amendment comes up, the court will rule that it does not guarantee the individual the right to keep and bear arms and that its' main purpose is to maintain the National Guard. Once that happens, cities and states can impose outright bans on all types of guns. The Federal government also can impose any gun ban they want.

Epilog

So it should be apparent, that there is no need to repeal the second amendment in order to get guns out of citizens' hands. The only very simple thing they need to do is change the interpretation of what the second amendment says. The government can shut down gun makers, outlaw ammunition and even impose a nationwide gun ban if they want to. Civil war is a very real possibility if this all comes to pass. Of course, people like Hillary are too stupid to grasp this fact because the only thing on her mind is controlling the people.

I end this dystopian future possibility with the disturbing fact that if Hitler had the same technology we have today, it would be unlikely that even one Jew would have escaped the gas chamber. The United States of America could very well deteriorate into the worst totalitarian country the world has ever seen. The only thing that could stop that is an armed populace and people like Hillary Clinton know this little fact all too well.

Just in time addendum

The presidential election is over and Donald Trump is our next President. The events that have transpired since the votes were counted and Mr. Trump received the proper number of electoral votes to win, serves to bolster the many hypothesizes I have lain out in this book. The actions of the losing side (the Democratic Party) are real time, real world proof that my ideas are 100% correct. What have I said about truly stupid people? One thing I said is that truly stupid people will never, ever admit they are wrong, even when the facts are staring at them one inch from their face. Not only will truly stupid people never admit fault, wrongdoing or bad decision making, they will deny all of it and make excuses, just like a group of people we all are very familiar with; children.

This is what is happening at this very moment with the hard line supporters of Hillary Clinton. They just cannot admit they had a flawed candidate so instead of conceding and congratulating the other side for their victory, they continue to cry foul, attempt to point the blame at a foreign government (Russia), make attempts at changing the votes for the electoral college members (actually threatening some of them with violence), create phony vote recount measures and generally cry like the big babies they are. Recall what I said about immature people and how that condition relates to intelligence. Immature people cannot be as smart as their mature human counterparts because the hardware that supports intelligence is just not there. It's either the hardware or they have learned to be immature but have rejected that notion wholesale which means they are stupid for other reasons in addition to being immature. So we are left with two possibilities. One is that the brains of these people never fully developed. The other is that they are immature because they learned (were brainwashed) into believing that being immature is the correct way to act and they are not smart enough to understand that fact.

From the perspective of mature human beings, the immature people I just described appear stupid and it doesn't matter much what caused the immaturity. It's there and it causes us all kinds of problems. It's not our responsibility to psycho analyze these people, it would serve no purpose if we could. They are the people who will eventually enable enslavement of all of humanity. It's time to put them in perspective and identify who and what they are. It's also time to educate the people who believe some of the garbage immature people generate but could be saved.

References by Chapter

A reference listed in any chapter will also be relevant in later chapters

Chapter 1 - intelligence and stupidity defined

The Oxford Handbook of the Archaeology and Anthropology of Hunter-Gatherers - Cummings, Jordan, Zvelebil (Editors) – ISBN 0199551227

A Hunter-Gatherer Landscape: Southwest Germany in the Late Paleolithic and Mesolithic (Interdisciplinary Contributions to Archaeology) - Jochim , Bettinger (Foreword) –
ISBN 0306457415

Human Intelligence - Hunt – ISBN 0521707811

Biology, Brains, and Behavior: The Evolution of Human Development - Parker, Langer, McKinney – ISBN 0933452640

Beyond IQ: A Triarchic Theory of Human Intelligence – Sternberg – ISBN 0521278910

An Indigenous Peoples' History of the United States – Dunbar-Ortiz – ISBN 0807057835

Chapter 2 – spiritual and intellectual enlightenment

Ancient Ideals: A Study of Intellectual and Spiritual Growth from Early Times to the Establishment of Christianity - Taylor – ISBN 1451002424

ASAP: Ages, Stages, and Phases: From Infancy to Adolescence, Integrating Physical, Social, Moral, Emotional, Intellectual, and Spiritual Development – Fosarelli - ISBN 0764815016

7 Steps to Spiritual Empathy, a Practical Guide: The Spiritual Philosophy of Emotional Intelligence (The Intelligence of Our Emotions) (Volume 1) - Florence - ISBN 0995507902

Chapter 3 – The brain

The Scientific American book of the brain –Damasio - (introduction) –
ISBN 1585742856

Exploring Cognition: Damaged Brains and Neural Networks – Cohen, Johnston, Plunkett –
ISBN 1-84169-217-4

References by Chapter

A Celebration of Neurons, Sylwester – ISBN 0-87120-243-3

Circuit Complexity and Neural Networks - Parberry - ISBN 0-262-16148-6

Neural Network Learning and Expert Systems - Gallant – ISBN 0-262-07145-2

Shadows of the Mind, Rodger Penrose – ISBN 0-19-510646-6

The Mystery of Consciousness - Searle – ISBN 0940322064

Consciousness Explained - Dennett – ISBN 0316180661

Consciousness a user's guide - Zeman – ISBN 0-300-09280-6

Migraine – Dr. Oliver Sacks – ISBN 0-375-70406-X

The Ancient Origins of Consciousness: How the Brain Created Experience - Feinberg, Mallatt – ISBN 0262034336

Animal Minds: Beyond Cognition to Consciousness - Griffin – ISBN 0226308650

Dog Body, Dog Mind: Exploring Canine Consciousness And Total Well-Being - Fox – ISBN 1599210452

Computer Architecture a Quantitative Approach – Hennessy, Patterson – ISBN 1-55860-329-8

Computer Organization and Design - Patterson, Hennessy – ISBN 1-55860-428-6

Operating Systems Principals – Bic, Shaw – ISBN 0-13-026611-6

Distributed Operating Systems – Galli – ISBN 0-13-079843-6

Data Structures - Gilberg, Forouzan – ISBN 0-534-95216-X

Chapter 4 – The mystery of thought

Thoughts on Thought - Hunt - 0805802657

How to Create a Mind - Kurzweil – ISBN 978-0-670-02529-9

Artificial Intelligence – Russell, Norvig – ISBN 0-13-790395-2

Database Systems, Elmasri, Navathe – ISBN 81-297-0228-2

Database Processing - Kroenke – ISBN 0-13-101514-1

Multimedia and Imaging databases - Khoshafian, Baker – ISBN 1-55860-312-3

Introduction to Algorithms - Corman, Leiserson, Rivest – ISBN 0-07-013143-0

Evolutionary Robotics: From Algorithms to Implementations - Wang, Tan, Chew – ISBN 9812568700

Chapter 5 – Computer science and artificial intelligence

Supercomputer Architecture - Schneck – ISBN 0-89838-194-0

Software Engineering - Pressman — ISBN 0-07-118458-9

Computer Networking – Kurose, Ross – ISBN 0-201-97699-4

Computer Vision: Models, Learning, and Inference - Prince – ISBN 1107011795

Software Engineering – Pressman – ISBN 0-07-118458-9

Compilers – Aho, Sethi, Ullman – ISBN 0-201-10088-6

Expert Systems - Giarratano, Riley – ISBN 0-534-38447-1

Fiber Optics & Optical Isolators - Georgopoulos, Price (Editor) – ISBN 0932263216

Photonic Slot Routing in Optical Transport Networks (Broadband Networks and Services) - Wedzinga – ISBN 1402073488

Wavelength Division Multiplexing: A Practical Engineering Guide – Grobe, Eiselt – ISBN 0470623020

Chapter 6 - Social implications of stupidity

The Sociopath Next Door Paperback - Stout – ISBN 0767915828

The Peter Principle: Why Things Always Go Wrong - Peter, Hull - ISBN 0062092065

The Power of Others: Peer Pressure, Groupthink, and How the People around Us Shape Everything We Do - Bond - ISBN 1780746539

Join the Club: How Peer Pressure Can Transform the World - Rosenberg – ISBN 0393341836

Never Trust a Liberal over 3-Especially a Republican - Coulter – ISBN 1621571912

Demonic: How the Liberal Mob Is Endangering America - Coulter – ISBN 0307353486

References by Chapter

The Communist Manifesto - Karl Marx, Friedrich Engels - ISBN0717802418

The Black Book of Communism: Crimes, Terror, Repression - Panné, Paczkowski, Bartosek, Margolin, Werth, Courtois, Kramer (Editor, Translator), Murphy (Translator) – ISBN 0674076087

Das Kapital - Karl Marx, Samuel Moore (Translator) – ISBN 145388632X

Atlas Shrugged – Ayn Rand- ISBN 0452011876

Inferno: The World at War, 1939-1945 - Hastings – ISBN 0307475530

The Devils' Alliance: Hitler's Pact with Stalin, 1939-1941 – Moorhouse – ISBN 0465030750

The Jeffrey Dahmer Story: An American Nightmare - Davis – ISBN 0312928408

Adolf Hitler: The Definitive Biography - Toland – ISBN 0385420536

Climate Change: The Facts – Plimer, Micheals, Lindzen, Soon, Carter, Abbot & Marohasy, Lawson, Moran, Delingpole, Partridge, Nova, Green & Armstrong, Darwal, McKitrick, Laframboise, Steyn, Essex, Lewin, Franks, Watts, bolt – ISBN 0986398306

More Guns, Less Crime: Understanding Crime and Gun Control Laws - Lott – ISBN 0226493660

The Founders' Second Amendment: Origins of the Right to Bear Arms - Halbrook - ISBN 1566639719

Ruby Ridge: The Truth and Tragedy of the Randy Weaver Family - Walter – ISBN 006000794X

Ashes of Waco: An Investigation - Reavis – ISBN 0815605021

Twilight: Los Angeles, 1992 - Smith - 0385473761

Left Turn: How Liberal Media Bias Distorts the American Mind - Groseclose – ISBN 1250002761

Why Are Professors Liberal and Why Do Conservatives Care? - Gross - ISBN 0674059093

The C++ Programming Language - Stroustrup – ISBN 0-201-70073-5

Chapter 7 – The medical profession

Medical Law, Ethics, & Bioethics for the Health Professions - Lewis, Tamparo, Tatro – ISBN 0803627068

References by Chapter

The Paleo Diet: - Cordain - ISBN 0470913029

Wheat Belly - William Davis, MD – ISBN 1609614798

Celiac Disease: a Hidden Epidemic – Peter H.R., M.D., Green, Jones - ISBN 0060766948

Celiac Disease the Hidden Epidemic! - Ridd – ISBN 1532952937

Three Mile Island: A Nuclear Crisis in Historical Perspective - Walker - ISBN 0520246837

Effect of a chemical manufacturing plant on community cancer rates - Mannes, Emmett, Willmore, Churches, Sheppeard, Kaldor - U.S. Library of Medicine, National Institutes of Health PMID 15811184

Cardiovascular Effects of Inhaled Ultrafine and Nano-Sized Particles - Cassee, Mills, Newby (editors) - ISBN 0470433531

Heart Disease: A Top Killer - Shelton - ASIN: B00OIME7HI

The Emperor of All Maladies: A Biography of Cancer – Mukherjee – ISBN 1439170916

The Essential Diabetes Book - Mayo Clinic – ISBN 0848743393

Dr. Atkins' New Diet Revolution - Atkins - ISBN 006001203X

Everything You Always Wanted to Know About Nutrition – David R. Reuben MD – ISBN 0380443708

The Great Cholesterol Myth: Why Lowering Your Cholesterol Won't Prevent Heart Disease-and the Statin-Free Plan That Will - Bowden , Sinatra – ISBN 1592335217

Why Radiologists Make So Many Mistakes: - Macevoy – ASIN B00K4F6QFE

How Doctors Think - Groopman – ISBN 0547053649

Chapter 8 – UFOs

The UFO Experience – Hynek – ISBN 1-56924-782-X

UFO The Government Files, Brookesmith – ISBN 0-7607-0218-7

Abduction: Human Encounters with Aliens - Mack – ISBN 0684195399

UFOs: Generals, Pilots, and Government Officials Go on the Record - Kean, John Podesta (Foreword) – ISBN 0307717089

Twenty Thousand Leagues Under the Sea - Jules Verne - ISBN 1512093599

The 4 Percent Universe: Dark Matter, Dark Energy, and the Race to Discover the Rest of Reality - Panek - ISBN 0547577575

Chapter 9 - How to identify stupid people

How to Drive: Real World Instruction and Advice from Hollywood's Top Driver - Collins ISBN 1452145296

Trust and Betrayal in the Workplace: Building Effective Relationships in Your Organization - Reina & Reina – ISBN 1626562571

It's Always Personal: Navigating Emotion in the New Workplace – Kreamer – ISBN 0812979931

Chapter 10 – The future

Animal Farm: 1984 - Orwell – ISBN 0151010269

The ISIS Apocalypse: The History, Strategy, and Doomsday Vision of the Islamic State - McCants – ISBN 1250080908

Death from the Skies! : These Are the Ways the World Will End - Plait – ISBN 0670019976

The New Terror: Facing the Threat of Biological and Chemical Weapons - Drell, Sofaer, Wilson (Editors) – ISBN 0817997024

How the End Begins: The Road to a Nuclear World War III Paperback – Rosenbaum – ISBN 1416594221

Appendix

(A-1) - Non Conscious Information Processing

Paul (Pawel) Lewicki
Professor of Psychology
Nonconscious Information Processing Laboratory
Psychology Department, University of Tulsa

http://www.mwbp.org/research/lewicki/

The following papers can be viewed and downloaded online at the above URL:

1. Conclusions of the Research on Nonconscious Information Processing (A quick "non-technical" summary)

2. Internal and External Encoding Style and Social Behavior
   Pawel Lewicki, Elizabeth Phillips
   University of Tulsa

3. Nonconscious Acquisition of Information
   Pawel Lewicki University of Tulsa Thomas Hill University of Tulsa
   Maria Czyzewska Southwest Texas State University

(A-2) - Attribute, Object, Relation Model of Human Memory

Dr. Yingxu Wang, University of Calgary, Alberta, Canada.
The International Institute of Cognitive Informatics and Cognitive Computing (ICIC)

http://www.ucalgary.ca/icic

(A-3) - Evolutionary Algorithms and Brain Functioning

Denise Sawicki

The above paper can be viewed and copied at this URL:

https://web.archive.org/web/20040103150539/http://www.cs.rochester.edu/users/faculty/dana/csc240_Fall97/Ass6/Denise_Sawicki.html

Reader's notes

Index

Index

Index

Index

Index

Index

Index

Index

Index

Index

Index

Index

Index

Index